THOUGHTS
In BETWEEN

From Earth Until Then...

CRYSTAL R. TOLSON

Copyright © 2016 by Crystal R. Tolson

Thoughts In Between
From Earth Until Then...
by Crystal R. Tolson

Printed in the United States of America.

Edited by Xulon Press.

ISBN 9781498484817

All rights reserved solely by the author. The author guarantees all contents are original and do not infringe upon the legal rights of any other person or work. No part of this book may be reproduced in any form without the permission of the author. The views expressed in this book are not necessarily those of the publisher.

Unless otherwise indicated, Scripture quotations taken from the King James Version (KJV)–*public domain*.

Scripture quotations taken from the Holy Bible, New International Version (NIV). Copyright © 1973, 1978, 1984, 2011 by Biblica, Inc.™. Used by permission. All rights reserved.

www.xulonpress.com

DEDICATION

This book is dedicated to my parents, Robert and Louvina Miles, who believed in the principles of training a child in the way they should go. These are the ones who made Sunday school a priority for me and my sisters and church activities a part of our lifestyle. I am eternally grateful for their comforting words of love and wisdom. With their adoration and support they have pushed me beyond my expectations.

In loving memory of
Robert Countess Miles
I feel his ever-present spirit with me always.

ACKNOWLEDGMENTS

To Andre,
who has been a grand supporter,
loving husband and confidant.

As I have completed this book, I have found a greater appreciation and genuine love for all people. I understand God's purpose for gifting me with my daughter Diamond. Derived from my name and by definition, she is a hard crystal and a true jewel. She has been my strength throughout the years driving me to persevere while providing an example for her to follow. My bonus daughter Jasmine has also been a blessing in my life as we have become the textbook blended family.

I owe a special debt of gratitude to Dr. Timothy Wood and Dr. Mark Roberson from Calvary Christian College in Waldorf, Maryland. Not only are they unpretentious men of the Most High God and biblical scholars, but they are also the most honest and genuine men I have encountered. It is through my biblical studies and their lecture notes that I have found help with my summations and compilations of thoughts.

Special acknowledgments to the family of God at the New Home Baptist Church in Landover, Maryland, particularly the new members' ministry that welcomed me with open arms to fellowship and commune as one body of believers. To my pastor, Bobby D. Hicks, an authentic servant of God: thank you for exhibiting humility and your endurance to preach Jesus Christ in a world where He is so rejected.

Special thanks are due to my sisters Tama, Sharlene, Tina, Tonika and Areela; best friend Senetria; cousins Baylon and Karen; advisors Donna and Andrea, for always rallying, supporting and giving me reassurance to pursue my call in ministry.

TABLE OF CONTENTS

Preface.. xi
How to Read This Book xv
You Don't Matter 17
Through the Fire 20
Press On 23
Pump It Up 26
The Brain 29
The Way Up Is Down 32
The Free Gift.............................. 35
The Sandpaper 38
Patience — A Virtue 41
Finding God's Will (Part 1)................. 46
Finding God's Will (Part 2)................. 51
Our Walk with God........................ 55
Count It All Joy........................... 60
Safe from the Storm 65
The Pursuit of Happiness 68
The Event 72
The Road to Recovery 76

PREFACE

Maranatha! Christ is coming again. Ready or not, He is coming! What are you doing with your time in between now and then? What are your thoughts? What's on your mind? At times, my mind becomes restless, and I cannot stop thinking of ways to improve my thoughts to be more like Christ. I realize that if we want to be fit for the kingdom we all have to change our thoughts and become more Christocentric (focused on Christ). Each person is at a different level spiritually, but I have learned we must meet people where they are.

A year ago I began to write "thoughts of the week" for my ministry at church. One family member read one of my thoughts and suggested I send it out to the family. I didn't think the family would be interested in it because most of them did not attend church. But I must admit nothing could have been further from the truth. What they seemed to love most was that the thoughts were uncomplicated and easy to read and brought them to a greater understanding of Christ. These simple thoughts with real-life situations have transcending power that reaches across the lines of those who attend church every week to the CMEs (Christmas, Mother's Day and Easter service attendees). It extends to those who understand the high Christology of Jesus Christ to those who are struggling with their faith. People have come to enjoy reading the thoughts because they get it! The stories are not above them or beneath them—but are them.

The family became my motivation to write. The more I learn in theology school as a current doctoral student, the more I want to share. Through my biblical studies and lectures I aspired to impart the knowledge I have gained about the Messiah to my family and friends. I prayed they would begin to change their thoughts. Guess what? It worked!

Over a year of writing thoughts for friends and family to ponder, it has confirmed to me that it is now time to advance the gospel even further. Since I

Preface

began writing a year has now passed, and many things have happened. Life has thrown a few curve balls, but changing my mindset has been the key. I used to dread going to work because it was a place with such low morale, but then I recognized I have no ability to change anyone. The only thing I can change is my own thoughts and how I view things.

Since then I have completed my master's degree in biblical studies, worked diligently in ministry and just delivered my initial sermon, "The Road to Recovery," about becoming a licensed minister. Despite all of this, I am grateful to be a humbled servant of Christ. It's time to step out on faith believing in God's Word—that His Word will not return void. God's Word has transforming power, and I have personally witnessed that. No matter how far you have made it in your Christian journey, sometimes people need help in translating the Word of God while making it relevant to their current life's journey. In this Christian journey I have found that people are always searching for something, and that everything starts with a thought. If people can change their thoughts, they can help change the world.

What I have learned the most through this experience is that no matter how many times you graduate in life, you will never graduate from the gospel. It never goes out of style, and God reveals something new to us in His Word almost every day. Christianity is a lifestyle change, and we have to begin thinking like Christ. Whatever your thoughts and beliefs are in between this life and your next one will determine where you will ultimately end up.

HOW TO READ THIS BOOK

This book is a simplistic read and thought provoking. It is intended for self-examination and personal edification. How often have you heard or read something and thought, If only I could share it with a certain person, or if only that person was here to receive it? Well, these thoughts are not for them, but strictly for you.

This book should not be read like a novel; rather, read it one section or thought at a time. Take time out to meditate, reflect, read Scripture and pray you will have a Christ-like mind. At the end of each section think about how you can apply the thought to your life. Read it again if necessary before moving on to the next thought. It may take you a day, a week or even a month to digest what it means to you. At the end of each section take a moment to reflect and think. Pause and consider: What would Christ do? The key is: At the end of each thought you should always be led back to Jesus Christ.

Take it seriously! Discuss it with others and write down your own thoughts. Let's share God's Word as we continue to advance His kingdom.

YOU DON'T MATTER!

I know this might seem harsh to most. Before you get the wrong idea of the title, though, hear me out. This is my story.

Recently I had a part-time retail job to make some extra money. I was told to vacuum the floor and clean the shelves at the end of my shift. One day I said to myself, Here I have two degrees and a good government job, and yet I am standing here cleaning the floor. I honestly felt some kind of way about it. In my eyes, to make matters worse, the store manager left me there all alone to do it. While I was vacuuming I thought, The nerve of him! And on top of that he doesn't even appreciate it. Luckily this was all in my head; I never complained out loud. I just cleaned.

The next day two of the younger employees came to me. One said, "I'm so glad you started working here." The other said, "I look forward to coming to work every day just to see you. You are so positive and upbeat and have helped us in so many ways."

I cried when I got in the car that night because God showed me it's not about me. It's about the Holy Spirit who lives in me and allows me to touch lives in a positive way every day. While the two young ladies were younger than I was, God sent them to give me exactly what I needed. I needed to know I didn't matter; rather, it was more important that others could see God's light through me. Matthew 5:16 tells us to let our light so shine before men that they may see our good works and glorify our Father who is in heaven. In the end, it didn't matter that I was vacuuming and no one recognized me for doing so. It only mattered that I was walking in God's light and He was glorified through me.

Satan is called the prince of the power of air (Ephesians 2:2) and is a "god" to many of the world. He transmits wrong ideas into the atmosphere and confuses people about their plan and purpose for God. In fact, many people do not realize the effect he has over the world, let alone believing they themselves are caught in his trap. Satan is always on the attack with our minds, deluding us into believing our purpose involves anything other than glorifying God.

When we get caught up in our feelings, insecurities and things that hinder us from our past, we allow Satan to rob us of the opportunity to let God's light shine. Get out of God's way, and let Him use you according to His will. Today I vacuum in boldness, proclaiming God's Word and trying to live by example. Others are watching Christians closely to see how we react to situations. Do we panic instead of pray? Do we have faith enough to lean on God's Word and believe He will never leave us or forsake us? Are we victims or survivors?

THINK: At the end of the day if you truly live for God and study His Word, the more you will realize You Don't Matter! Do you know your purpose on earth is to glorify God and is not about you?

ACTION: Think of some things you dislike, such as a job or even people. Can you think of some ways to let God's light shine through you even in the midst of your circumstances? Put your feelings and emotions to the side and focus solely on God.

Spread the word, post it or tweet it—#itsallaboutGod.

THROUGH THE FIRE

～～～

We see so much construction these days on our roads, avenues and streets. Nearly everywhere we turn is a sign that reads, "Men at Work." We see construction hats, warning signs and flashing signals to derail us from going into the construction area. For Christians, we have the same sign in front of us because we are under construction. Sometimes we do not see God's sign on our lives. But it is always there, and it reads, "God at Work," because He is always working in us. Sometimes it doesn't feel like it. It seems as though we are always in a season of storms. Every time we fix one thing, another one comes.

We sometimes ask the question, "Why me?" We think, My children are ungrateful, I'm not appreciated at my job, and no one understands what I am going through. Even through all of this, God says that, no matter what, He will complete the work He started in us. Therefore, the storms are a divine cleansing.

When Christ comes into your life, you will still have problems and sometimes even more. In fact, Christ told us Himself that we will be hated because of His name (Matthew 10:22). However, He is long-suffering, and He is perfecting us, polishing us and purifying us. He even turns up the heat on us because we are His treasure. It is interesting to note that a diamond must undergo extreme pressure at approximately 725,000 pounds per square inch and heat to about 2200 degrees Fahrenheit before it becomes one of the most beautiful jewels on earth.

The same is true for us. We will go through intense heat, and it may become uncomfortable. But we must endure to the end so we may become glorious like the Father. We must walk through the fire because it is the fire that cleanses us. Fire purifies and brings impurities to the surface. We need the trials in our lives for cleansing as we become more Christ-like. Just imagine that each time we go through the fire God sweeps the ashes from our faces removing all of the debris. He repeats the process over and over again, sweeping the ashes from our faces. God will continue this process until He sees Himself in us. Do you know that one day after all the ashes are swept away we will bear the image of the heavenly Father? When that time comes, oh, what a time it will be! All of the fire (tests, trials and tribulations) will have never mattered in the first place because we will be glorified and fit for the kingdom. So the next time the fire comes, start praising God!

THINK: Instead of complaining today, is anyone grateful for the fire?
ACTION: Think of some tests you have been through. Remember and share how God brought you through. How did you know it was God?
Spread the word, post it or tweet it—#togodbetheglory.

PRESS ON

As we begin to heal as a nation from so many tragic deaths, it is important now more than ever that we continue to press on. In Philippians 3:14 Paul says, "I press toward the mark for the prize of the high calling of God in Christ Jesus." This "pressing" that Paul is referring to is equivalent to a strain. It's the strain of the athlete who runs a marathon with the look of perseverance, frustration and determination. It is the one with the agonizing desire to finish the race no matter how draining, wrenching or laborious it is. Have you ever heard of "no pain, no gain"? It is painful when we go through things, but it deepens our fellowship with God. We know Him in the fellowship of His suffering. We run the path of the cross. We are not motivated by hate, but love. We are not hasty,

Thoughts In Between

but patient. We don't retaliate; we forgive. We are not self-centered; we surrender. We have to go down the road of the cross to be resurrected.

In light of the tragedies in the world we have to run with new vigor and a new energy like the athlete who has gotten his second wind. It is time for us to stay focused and have some sense of forgetfulness—forgetting those things that are behind us and pressing forward to those things ahead. Too many times we allow our past to hold us back. Let's take time to do some self- examination as we continue to press forward. Let's forget or move beyond the 4 Gs that hold us back.

1. Past **GUILT**—God has forgiven you; now forgive yourself and others.
2. Past **GRUDGES**—People will often do you wrong, but you will *never* be able to live or move forward with past hatred and bitterness.
3. Past **GLORY**—You can't keep polishing your same old trophy and talking about the good old days; move on.
4. Past **GRIEF**—There is a time to mourn over losses. Setbacks will come, but some people never get over hurt. There comes a time to heal, though.

Despite the condition of this world, let's continue to press our way toward the mark. Always remember: "If revenge is your motivation, then God is **not** your inspiration." Pray for our nation.

THINK: What is it time for you to move past?
ACTION: Think of some tests you have been through. Remember and share how God brought you through. How did you know it was God? If you are hindered by the past, set an expiration date on your calendar for when you will move on. Pray and place it in God's hand. Do not look back.
Spread the word, post it or tweet it—#movingforward.

PUMP IT UP

Here is a tip for today: Never start games with a two-year-old that you do not intend to finish. I blew up a balloon for my two-year-old niece, and I began to hit it in the air. I'd smack it, slap it and volley it to her until my arms were tired. My goal was not to let it hit the ground. Unfortunately for me, she never got tired. I started thinking I really needed some helium to let this thing stay up.

Each time I reflect on that day it makes me smile. When I remember the balloon going up and down it reminds me of life. Often we pump ourselves up or rely on others to give us a lift. Like the balloon I created with my own air, we depend on ourselves, our significant others and things around us to "pump us up." At church we depend on the pastor to give us a good hit, slap us around and exhort us in order to keep us lifted in the air like that self-inflated balloon. For some, it is the choir that keeps them "pumped up." Unfortunately, sometimes people hear a great word on Sunday and get deflated by Monday. Like the balloon, we are back down on the ground the next day and back to business as usual.

Why is that? Perhaps it's because we depend on our own breath without the in-breathing from God. We depend on our own strength even though our arms get tired. We depend on self-help books even though we have a complete instruction manual for life called the Bible. We try to understand things that are beyond our understanding instead of simply trusting God to "pump us up" and complete the work He started in us knowing He cannot fail. Are you sick and tired of being sick and tired yet? Are you ready to stay inflated? Cast all of your cares upon Him and let Him fight your battles because He will keep you "pumped up."

The older and wiser we become, it should be evident we can no longer rely on our own strength because we will fail every time. Nehemiah 8:10 says, "The joy of the Lord is your strength." Sometimes we don't have strength on our own, but with God all things are possible. Don't inflate your own balloon; He will give you all the helium you need. Just trust in Him.

THINK: Are you tired of holding yourself up? Allow God to hold you up, and cast all of your cares upon Him.
ACTION: Get a prayer box. It can be a simple, homemade box such as a shoebox. Write down your prayers and place them inside the box. Once inside the box with the lid closed, you are no longer allowed to worry about it. Let it go and give it to God.
Spread the word, post it or tweet it—#giveittoGod.

THE BRAIN

The brain is a fascinating part of the body. You may be surprised to know it changes according to your mind, almost like plastic. It is true. With your thoughts you can shape your mind. Between your second month of life and second birthday, 1.8 synapses are created per second, and we end up with more than two hundred billion. The synapses are bridges of nerve impulses that connect the brain. Why is all of this important? It is very important to a Christian because, depending on how you think, you can either strengthen the synapses or destroy them. For instance, if you think negative thoughts the synapses bridge gets stronger. Unfortunately, the positive bridge gets weaker and eventually burns away. This bridge acts just like a bridge we cross over; once it burns down we can never cross it again.

Have you ever heard the mind is a terrible thing to waste? It is the truth. We spend too much time worrying about everything. We fill our heads with negative thoughts, news, music and gossip. We should be anxious for nothing—rather, relax our minds in the peace of God. We are commanded not to worry; in fact, worrying is a sin although we seldom choose to label it that way. *Worry* shares the English root word with *strangle*. In other words, worrying strangles us. It is a thief of joy. We worry because we feel inadequate, have a feeling of failure or feel as if we don't have budget resources readily available.

It is time for us to turn to God who is adequate. He will take care of our needs according to His bank roll and resources. It's time to remold our brains by thinking with certainty that God has everything under control. Imagine if we can make the positive bridge so strong in our brain by reshaping our mind with the Word of God. It is truly time to surrender and cast all of our cares on God.

Strengthen your synapses with happy and positive thoughts today and allow the negative ones to burn away so you may never have to cross it again. Seriously take time to meditate and at least just for today, despite what you are going through, give your mind a rest and have no worries!

THINK: Have you been negative lately?
ACTION: Each time you have a negative thought, replace it with a positive one. Can you think of moments when you have acted negatively? What could you have done differently to change the outcome to a positive one?
Spread the word, post it or tweet it—#thinkpositive.

THE WAY UP IS DOWN

How do you define success? Is it the new house or new car you bought? Maybe you define it by perhaps the status or position of your job. The sad news is that many people define themselves by material things and material gain. It is what gives them joy as they feel a sense of accomplishment. To make matters worse, some people will get to the top even if it means stepping on someone else to get there. But if you ever want to succeed at the expense of others it means your heart is not in the right place. Does this mean you should not have ambition? Absolutely not! Philippians 2:3 says, "*Let nothing be done through selfish ambition* or conceit, but in lowliness of mind let each esteem others as better than himself."

The Way Up Is Down

In other words, humility doesn't mean being a doormat for others to step on because you should have self-respect that leads to self-preservation. But it does mean you esteem others and have proper respect and appreciation for others. It means understanding you are not the only person going through something. Get over yourself and think of others. It also means you are certainly not superior to others.

Recently while sitting at a stop sign I witnessed several homeless people on the sidewalk. My heart went out to them, and whenever I have the opportunity to give I do so. This time I watched a man shoot heroin into his arms, and at that moment tears rolled down my eyes. I empathized with him, but most important I said to myself, That could have been me, but by the grace of God.

The point is: We are all in the same boat. We are all sinners and fall short of His glory (Romans 3:23). No matter how far you think a person is, we can never graduate from the gospel until such time when we are called home to glory even if we have the title Doctor in front of our name. We have such an over-exaggerated opinion of ourselves because we cannot recognize our limitations. We have a lack of love for one another because we are so pre-occupied with our own interests. If you ever truly want to get to the top, live a life of humility. Humility is a life that glorifies God. It is the opposite of pride. In fact, when you start to lose joy in your life, you may want to check the pride and humility in your life. I have found that the number one joy killer is pride. Remain humble and rejoice in the Lord always!

THINK: When was the last time you thought of someone else other than yourself? Be humble, but don't lose your self-respect.

ACTION: Know the difference between pride, humility and false humility. Where do you honestly fit in? Spread the word, post it or tweet it—#stayhumble.

THE FREE GIFT

Most people who know me would say I am an avid student who loves school. For one straight week I studied vigorously for a test. In fact, a person told me years ago that if I placed all my study notes under my pillow it would help me remember. I admit I have slept with many notes under my pillow (lol!). In any event, this day was no different. I did my normal ritual of worrying, writing all night on index cards while trying to commit everything to memory. Needless to say, I put in a lot of effort. The next day I got up and felt as if I was ready to take on the world. Come on, test!! #Igotthis.

I walked into class, and everyone was turning around. Come to find out, the teacher decided we were no longer going to have a test. He decided everyone was going to receive an A. Many people got so excited and walked straight out the door. The others of us (me included) couldn't believe he would just give out an A. Really? Did he not see all the hard work we put in? The few over-achievers lagged behind because we failed to recognize the teacher's intention of demonstrating GRACE. As a matter of fact, we even had the audacity to talk about the teacher. During the next class he told us he wanted us to understand God's grace. We didn't have to do anything to earn the A, and we certainly didn't deserve it. More important, it was free.

How many times have we questioned God's grace toward us? How many times do we question anything that is free? We are typically left wondering, What is the catch? Nothing in life is free. Like the over-achievers in the classroom, we were not satisfied with the free gift of an A. In a way we still wanted to prove we deserved it by taking the test. Some people still act this way toward God. They constantly try to prove their worthiness by doing good deeds. They have not yet realized God has freed us; He has given us an A in life without our ever deserving it. Grace and salvation are a free gift from God. He sent His Son to rescue us from the penalty of past sin while gradually freeing

The Free Gift

us from the power of sin. The truth of the matter is that *"whosoever"* believes in Christ will never perish but have everlasting life (John 3:16). As sinners, we stand before God as the accused, and by having faith in Him we are declared free. I love being an A student always in God's eyes. He has wiped our slate clean! Who wouldn't want to serve a God like that? Thank God for this free gift!

"For by grace you have been saved through faith, and that not of yourselves; it is the gift of God, not of works, lest anyone should boast."
—Ephesians 2:8-9

THINK: Do you truly understand the free gift of salvation and God's grace?

ACTION: Stop boasting about your own works. Understand that everything comes from God. List some things God has done for you and thank Him. Spread the word, post it or tweet it—#begrateful.

THE SANDPAPER

Have you ever taken a drive to North Carolina via route 85? Or perhaps just a long drive when you saw nothing but trees. I remember vividly taking this drive and being so tired from the road. Watching the trees made me so sleepy I must have dozed for a split second and found myself waking up because of the rumble strip on the side of the road. Thank God for the rumble strip because it saved my life. Every now and then God will put a rumble strip or friction in our lives to get us back on course. Some people think it is a bad thing when friction is in our lives; but, like the rumble strip, it is necessary to keep us on course.

Look up an acacia tree. The wood from this tree was used to build the tabernacle (the place where God dwelt) in the Old Testament. When we look at this tree, one may conclude it is twisted, ugly and even deformed. But this was the tree God chose as the material for His house. God chose two highly skilled craftsmen who were also filled with the Spirit to chop down this tree and smooth it out in order to construct the tabernacle. The two used sandpaper to make it smooth so it would fit perfectly together. Sandpaper is a product that goes against the grain. In this case, it was needed and necessary to smooth out the wood. The greatest end to the story of the acacia wood is that once it was smoothed it was covered with gold.

Can you imagine how long it took to smooth out this tree with sandpaper? Imagine the friction of constantly going against the grain. Like the tree that was separated from its roots, we too are rooted in the value system of the world. God wants to separate us and smooth us out while bringing us into His care. We are like the acacia tree: grotesque, ugly and twisted because of our inherent sin nature. In comparison to the tree, God will take sandpaper or friction and put it in our lives to make us smooth. Typically, our sandpaper is a person, and when this person is put in our lives, they persecute, mistreat, misuse or aggravate us. Here is the good news: When we find sandpaper in our lives, we should rejoice because God is preparing us for a special place in His house and our eternal reward.

Do you know what happens when we become so smooth that the sandpaper no longer does its job in our life? He gives us more sandpaper to work on other areas of our lives, but it requires patience. Like the acacia tree that had to be smoothed out to fit together for building, God wants us to fit together in His house, so He shapes and preps us to be ready. Like the acacia wood that was covered with gold, it is a reflection of our own life and the gold that awaits us in heaven. If God could take this ordinary tree, smooth it out and cover it with gold, surely He can do the same thing to us. Thank God for the sandpaper!

THINK: Do you frown when friction comes into your life? Do you know God sometimes tests our faith to stretch our faith?

ACTION: Who or what is the sandpaper in your life? Now praise God for the sandpaper. Praise God for helping you to become more Christ-like. Can you see how God is molding you?

Spread the word, post it or tweet it—#workinprogress.

PATIENCE IS A VIRTUE

I was speaking to my sister yesterday. She works at a popular retail store. She was telling me of a young lady who switched the price tag on a Ralph Lauren (Polo) shirt from $49.99 to $9.99. In fact, she had switched many price tags on her clothing items. Needless to say, she was caught by security. I tell this story because while studying God's Word I realized that early in my Christian walk I too had switched some labels, but not on purpose. I was confused about the difference between the strong vs. the weak.

When I was growing up, I thought the strong were the ones who were the no-nonsense Christians. They were the ones in the Sunday hats, with a Bible in their hands and a long list of rules of what not to do. They frowned upon others who did anything they thought was worldly or ungodly. Now here comes the "but": Thanks be to God that when I was child I thought as a child, but now that I have grown up I know I erroneously switched the labels of the weak and the strong. While I thought having a list of don'ts made you strong, I realize now it can actually make you weak.

I have grown in this journey to understand what Paul was talking about in Romans 14. I understand now that the weak should not judge the strong and the strong should not despise the weak. So who are the weak? One would imagine the weak are the people with little faith or the ones out in the world, but it is quite the contrary. The weak are the same Christians I originally thought were strong. They are over-fastidious with so many taboos, restrictions and rules that they become no earthly good. This may surprise you, but the truth is they are infants in their comprehension of the gospel. They have so many rules piled on to the Bible that they cannot decipher what is doctrine and what is discipline (man-made rules). Their thinking and conscience have not been enlarged through enlightenment so they tend to have a list of don'ts such as "I don't eat this," "I don't sit amongst these types of persons," "I don't drink any wine," "I don't wear make-up"—and the list goes on. The weak Christian cannot stand to think someone in the world is enjoying himself while still being a Christian. I'm so glad Christ did not have that attitude when He came and saved me while I was still a sinner in the world.

Don't get me wrong. The Bible contains moral absolutes, such as lying, stealing and immorality, we should not differ over. These are sin. We should not dispute the deity of Christ, the trinity and other doctrinal certainties. But strong Christians understand holiness and liberty in Christ. Furthermore, they understand the balance between the two. Strong Christians understand salvation has everything to do with grace, confession and belief in the resurrection of Christ—and nothing to do with what you eat or wear or the disciplines man has contrived. The strong know the truth and have been set free (John 8:32). Where the Spirit of the Lord is, there is liberty (2 Corinthians 3:17). Sadly, some do not understand this.

This is where the two come together (the strong and the weak). In Romans 15:5 we are reminded to be patient with one another. It is inevitable that we will disagree on many things, even religion. But I have learned in this walk that every person is not in the same place of spiritual maturity. Some are weak, and some are strong; but we must be willing to meet people where they are in their pilgrimage of faith. Sometimes Christians get so holy that they are no earthly good. As Christians, we should be united so the enemy cannot get through. We should not be so quick to hold on to our authority or position that we are not able to surrender. Let's be patient with one another. When we acquire long-suffering we learn that the problems or problem people do not go away, but God changes our perspective as to how we view or react to the situation. So here is a good question: Are you the problem person or the one who finds everyone else to be the problem? Are you the strong or the weak? Whatever you are, we must be careful not to let it divide us. The problem is that we are so busy judging and despising one another instead of treating each other with love and patience. Even if we are right, we need to learn how to retreat at times. Family and friends, let's stick together.

Let's pray for one another and not judge each other as we continue to advance the kingdom. The truth of the matter is, no matter where you are in the journey (weak or strong), we all fall short of His glory! Just make sure you are at least in the journey.

THINK: How often are we divided between denominations and secondary doctrine? We need to remember we are all God's children.

ACTION: Have you treated someone differently because they are different from you in some way(s)? Try loving everyone despite their differences. Get out of your comfort zone. Introduce yourself to someone new and let them meet the Christ in you.

Spread the word, post it or tweet it—#Godislove.

FINDING GOD'S WILL (PART 1)

Have you ever pondered over what God's will for your life truly is? We walk through life many times not understanding our true purpose on earth. Some discover it very early, some discover it later in life, and sadly some never discover it at all. It is important to discover what God's will is for your life. One may have often heard that you must pray to seek it, but many times people don't even know how to pray. People may pretend they know, but they truly struggle with prayer. In the Bible you will find even the disciples struggled with prayer. In fact, they asked Christ to show them how to pray. We have several ways to pray, but most important pray the Scriptures, pray in response to the Scriptures, pray the promises of God and pray for His will to be done in your life.

Finding God's Will (Part 1)

So how do we find God's will for our life?

1. **Pursue spiritual growth to become a person of wisdom.**

   We are sometimes "right now" Christians. We want everything right now. Many believe answers will appear magically through signs and we will be relieved of making choices. In fact, many of us suffer from the anxiety of decision-making (decidophobia). When pursuing wisdom, you will begin to make right choices because it is in the Scripture. Pursuing the knowledge of God will help you discern right and wrong, as well as positive and negative spirits. God wants us to be excellent choosers as we grow in Him. Wisdom is not how high your IQ is or how advanced your degree is. It is acquiring the knowledge of God and applying it to your life. It is remembering choices ultimately form your character, and sometimes wrong choices can take us off the path of being Christ-like and discovering His will for us.

2. **Be humble, trusting in God and seeking Him.**

   Understand that God will direct your path and do not lean toward your own understanding

(Proverbs 3:5-6). He gives us peace to guide our decisions. If something disturbs your peace, it is a red flag. Take heed.

2. Be passionate and prayerful in your present assignment.

We often spend our time daydreaming about something else or someplace else we would rather be. A wise person once said that if you think the grass is greener on the other side fertilize your own yard. Success is one percent inspiration and ninety-nine percent perspiration. It takes work, but you must accept where you are now. With prayer God will bless you where you are right now. If you are faithful with the little things, God knows you can be faithful with bigger things. When you are devoted and diligent where you are now, God is preparing you for where you are going next.

3. Know what your problem is.

What is your problem? You will be defined by your problem. What do I mean by this? In other words, what burdens you the most? Is it child abuse, at-risk youth, bullies, cancer or something else? When seeking God's will through

Finding God's Will (Part 1)

Scripture, you will find that the call on your life will be for you to become the answer to whatever troubles you the most. For instance, Moses despised slavery, and God used him to free the Israelites. David couldn't understand why everyone was so afraid of this big giant, and he was used to slay Goliath. Paul was upset that the Gentiles didn't hear the gospel, but God made him an apostle to the Gentiles. Whatever ails you the most, God wants you to be the answer. It is what you are most passionate about that is most likely God's will for your life. Instead of complaining about things and being frustrated, get up and do the will of God and give Him the glory.

Saints, as we continue to strive toward the advancement of the kingdom, let's be reminded to pray, "Thy kingdom come, thy will be done on earth as it is in heaven." Let's pray against the things that displease God on this earth and ask Him to send some of "heaven" down upon us. Let us pray against racism and oppression and things God has no delight in. Let us pray we are doing His will so that in the end He will say, "My servant, well done."

THINK: Have you found your purpose yet?
ACTION: What are you passionate about? It could be something that excites you or annoys you.
Spread the word, post it or tweet it—#Godislove.

FINDING GOD'S WILL (PART 2)

Have you come to a point where you hate turning on the news? It's one tragedy after another. We are in a state of emergency, saints. God is calling on us to be vigilant as we become contenders and defenders of our faith. We have no time to sit around and wait. It's time to make choices because choices form our character. Now let's pray for God's will to be done in your life. Here are more points about finding God's will for your life.

5. **Seek godly counsel.**

    Have you ever sought advice from a friend when you were drowning only to find out they can't swim? Be careful whom you ask for advice. This cannot be stressed enough. Even those who may say they are walking in the Spirit may not truly be "walking in the Spirit." Scripture teaches us that some "will honor me with their lips, but their heart is far from me" (Matthew 15:8). In other words, it is important to seek wise counsel from those who will counsel you concerning God's will. In addition, it is a great thing to have a prayer partner to help you with discerning things. At times you will find safety in the multitude. When seeking counsel you must understand that not every criticism is a rejection. If you are a leader you must understand humility comes along with it. Never seek to do it all on your own or be a dictator.

6. Faith and courage.

Often times we get discouraged easily and give up on our purpose or assignment because we feel as if it isn't working. Sometimes we will run into troubles, trials and tribulations, but we must remain steadfast and do God's will. Poor Jeremiah! Why did he weep? Can you imagine talking over and over to people who would not listen to God's message? And then not being able to indulge in the human creature comforts such as marrying and having children because

Finding God's Will (Part 2)

God has sent you on a mission that doesn't seem to be working? He preached for forty years, and it didn't seem to change a thing. *But we cannot judge God's will for our lives by the world's standards.* What seems impossible to us is always possible with God. At times, we may think we are failing, but God is working it out for our good. We must have faith and courage while ministering His Word because He has proven it will not return void.

7. **Rest/Refresh/Pray.**

Before making major decisions in life, make sure you are well rested, refreshed and prayed up. Resting and prayer become of utmost importance when you are making huge, life-changing choices. Make sure you are in a good frame of mind and not tired or exhausted. Remember Elijah, who was going to give up his career choice of being a prophet. He was frustrated and tired. But watch this: What did God prescribe? Forty days of rest and prayer. He was then able to hear the voice of God and continue on his path. Sometimes when I'm at my wit's end and can't think of my next step,

Thoughts In Between

I simply pray and go to sleep to think about it the next day.

Saints, I'm not sure about you, but it certainly hasn't been an easy journey. So many tests, trials and obstacles have been in the way. At times, the adversary will even have you thinking you have chosen the wrong path because sin looks so tasty and tantalizing. It's so easy to get caught up in unforgiveness, gossip and other reckless behavior. It's time for us to fight harder, pray harder and love more than we ever have before to shake off the enemy. We are constantly under attack because Satan does not want us to do God's will. It's our time to fulfill our purpose, follow our dreams and be true disciples of Christ; this requires discipline. Remember: Dreams without discipline can turn into nightmares.

THINK: What is God's will for your life? Whatever it is, the ultimate goal should be to give Him glory.
ACTION: Pray today that God will reveal your purpose. Spread the word, post it or tweet it—#prayingforpurpose.

OUR WALK WITH GOD

In Genesis 5:24 we read, "Enoch walked faithfully with God." It doesn't say much else about Enoch in Genesis. It doesn't tell us what he did, what his line of work was or what made him happy or sad. It simply says he walked with God. For all intents and purposes that is enough. It denotes that here is a man who dedicated his life to being faithful to God. As a reward he did not die but was translated to be with God.

When we look at the benefits of walking, we can conclude it is one of the healthiest things a person can do. In fact, the American Heart Association reports that walking reduces risk of coronary heart disease, enhances mental well being and improves blood pressure and sugar levels. There is also a method to walking. In many modern-day boot camps you will learn that you should walk a certain way in order not to hurt your body, especially your knees. It is also a dependent motion, which means you can never walk faster than your arms move, or the faster you move your arms then the faster you will walk.

In Enoch's case, he did a spiritual walk with God, which proved to have even greater benefits and rewards than physical walking. As physical walking is dependent on the feet for movement, spiritual walking is dependent on Jesus. Walking signifies a habitual and consistent thing. In other words, Enoch's spiritual walk included giving his life over to God each and every day. So we can conclude that true communion with God requires vigorous daily exercise of faith. Interestingly enough, God said He was pleased with only two people: Enoch and Jesus. This lets you know Enoch's faith was strong and he had a reverence for God while walking with Him.

So how do we please God? How can we walk with Him when we have so much evil around us each time we turn on the news? Many may look for a list of rules to do this because they do not understand His sovereign grace. The answer is: We are to have faith in God. "But without faith it is impossible to please

Him, for he who comes to God must believe that He is and that He is a rewarder of those who diligently seek Him" (Hebrews 11:6). To walk faithfully with God we must conform and surrender to His will in an effort to keep His commandments. We must walk in love, joy, peace, patience, kindness, goodness, faithfulness, gentleness and self-control (Galatians 5:22-23). We are all encouraged to walk in the Spirit (Galatians 5:16). So how can we walk with God in times when we have legalized drug use and ordained same-sex marriages and people are being murdered, abused, burned and tortured? The story of Enoch encourages me to come up with ways to walk with Him.

Being out of step with the world

Often times we straddle the fence by having one foot in the world and the other one out of the world. God calls us to come out from among them and separate ourselves from uncleanliness (2 Corinthians 6:17).

Agreeing with God

You must agree with God in order to walk with Him (Amos 3:3). Can you imagine walking along someone you don't agree with? It's hard to walk with them at all.

Enoch must have agreed with God without argument or rebellion to keep a three-hundred-year journey.

Perseverance

Enoch walked for a long time—three hundred years—which means he had endurance and perseverance. Hebrews 12:1-2 reminds us to run with endurance and look to Jesus, the founder and perfecter of our faith. It is important to point out that Enoch stayed on course and walked to the finish line.

Deliberate Steps of Faith

Enoch made a decision to take steps of faith. As a reminder, our walk with God should be deliberate in our actions. We should want to be faithful and obedient in our actions because Christ said if we love Him we will keep His commandments (John 14:15). We should wake up daily and count it all joy (James 1:2). It is not a kicking and screaming thing to come to Christ— rather an effectual call or conviction. Our walk should include walking in the Spirit, love, light and newness of life. We are to walk in the light of the Lord's return, considering the judgment that is coming on the world (2 Peter 3:9-13).

Progressive

Walking is a progressive movement. Each day we walk with God we are progressing through the process of sanctification. Our light will begin to shine more and more each day (Proverbs 4:18).

Saints, sometimes it may not be easy to have faith in God while we are living in such a wicked world. But we are living in the last days, and we can no longer make excuses that the world is so bad it is difficult for us to do the right thing. The world has been bad since the fall of Adam and Eve. But Enoch still walked with God, and so can we. It may require long-suffering, but I'm encouraging each of us to walk with God. He is the only way!

THINK: Are you making excuses when it comes to your walk with God? What can you improve on? (Hint: None of us is perfect.)

ACTION: Take a quiet walk alone and have a conversation with God. Try to make it a daily practice. Memorize and recite Scripture so you can be obedient to God's Word.

Spread the word, post it or tweet it—#walkwithGod.

COUNT IT ALL JOY

~~~~~~

"Joy is the serious business of heaven." —C.S. Lewis

Joy is second on the list of the fruit of the Spirit. Joy is defined as calm delight or cheerfulness; but it has little to do with your emotions. Joy is described in the biblical sense as something that is manifested in the spiritual realm. It is a supernatural joy that gives us spiritual strength (Nehemiah 8:10). The prophet Isaiah refers to it as the joy of salvation (Isaiah 12:3). We find that natural joy is easy. When someone gives us a gift or we give someone else a gift, we may experience natural joy. But true joy goes beyond natural joy. It extends to having joy in the midst of suffering. In the Greek, joy is spoken of as an expression so deep that words cannot express it. It's almost as if you can't even talk at times because people wouldn't understand you. Peter describes it as joy unspeakable (1 Peter 1:6-9).

Luke 10:21 reminds us Jesus lived a life full of joy through the Holy Spirit. For us, however, when our focus is wrong, we lose out on joy. Many times we get caught up in our circumstances not realizing we are above them. Our happiness often depends on what is happening, but joy does not depend on the conditions around us. If we allow circumstances to control our joy, then we won't have joy when things are going bad. Circumstances encircle us but should not control us. In glorifying God, sadness, depression and moping around are not His will for us. The problem is that we sometimes place burdens on ourselves when our position is not affirmed in Christ. Salvation lets us know that we have been forgiven and God loves us unconditionally. We get so consumed with what is going wrong in our lives that we don't rejoice at the fact that our names are written in the Book. When our position is not strong in Christ, we allow the devil to steal our joy. Instead of complaining, we should rejoice without worrying because of who we are in Christ. Worry is from a Latin word *sollicitudo*, which means to strangle, as noted earlier. If we are not careful, the devil will play tricks with our minds and strangle our joy.

Here are some statistics and a sad reality of the things we worry about.

40% of the things we worry about never happen; we make them up.

30% of the things we worry about are in the past and we cannot control them.

12% of the things we worry about involve our health, even when we are not sick.

10% of the things have some basis in reality, but they don't necessarily pertain to us.

8% of the things we worry about actually pertain to us, but prayer can cover them.

Here are two ways to obtain joy (but we're not limited to these).

Joy in salvation—Isaiah 12:3: "Therefore with joy shall ye draw water out of the wells of salvation." Joy is rooted in our salvation. We should have prayers of thanksgiving and not focus on the things we are always complaining about. We tend to be superficial because we do not understand we live in an atmosphere of grace.

Salvation addresses the big problem of guilt and condemnation. We cannot have joy in our lives with guilt because guilt is a destructive force. Through Christ's dying on the cross we are free from the bondage of sin, guilt and shame. This should give us joy.

Joy comes through Scripture—Deep joy comes when we dig deep into the Word of God. It is like finding a treasure, the equivalent to your diving in the deep ocean to find an oyster with a pearl. We will discover riches in the Word, but it may not be on the surface. It requires us to meditate on the Word and to replace negative thoughts with positive thoughts. The joy that comes through the Scripture requires us to be involved in Bible discussions, readings, teaching and preaching. The Word should be etched in our hearts and minds at all times so that when it is time for us to use it we will know what the Scripture says. It is divine joy that results from an experiential knowledge of God's Word.

Again, saints, this is a supernatural joy that comes from the Holy Spirit who dwells in us. Do you know how good it feels when you can say you have joy in the middle of your storm? People are always looking at me strangely when I'm calm through situations. I can't say it has always been the case since the fruit of joy must be cultivated to grow. As we are all a work in progress, let us be reminded that rejoicing is a choice, and it is what God wants us to do. Some people have no strength because they have no joy. What a wonderful feeling. Don't miss out!

THINK: Are you lacking joy in your life? Do you know God wants us to have joy in our lives? What do you need in order to find joy?

ACTION: Write positive quotes on sticky notes and place them where you can see them. As soon as you wake up, decide life is worth living and you are going to make it a joyful day.

Spread the word, post it or tweet it—#joyfulday.

SAFE FROM THE STORM

~~~

Many people have heard the story of Noah. Even those who have never set foot in the church or read the Bible have at least heard the *"Reader's Digest* condensed" version of Noah and the ark. One of the greatest problems with seeing the in-depth meaning behind Noah and the ark is just that. Many think it is a great story with no intention behind it. In fact, many movies have been made in Hollywood with some truths but many historical inaccuracies. The sad truth is that so many have made a mockery of Noah's ark because many have reported it as pure entertainment and a fictional story. Somehow we miss the point of Scripture at times and the lessons we must learn from them. Many great flood stories permeate mythology around the world. But the flood that took place in

Genesis teaches us about human depravity, faith, obedience, judgment, grace and mercy.

Like Noah, we are living in wicked times. Back then, God made the ultimate decision and came to a poignant conclusion that He regretted humans even being on the earth (Genesis 6:6). Thus, He destroyed the earth with the exception of Noah and his family. The ark was a type of Christ as it showed God's mercy. It is with the ark He would give the earth another chance. By sparing Noah and his family, God gives us hope that future generations will carry on the legacy of His love for His people.

Let's take a second and reflect on the ark. The ark was gigantic and made with cypress wood. It was painted with a tar-like substance to sustain it from rotting. Apparently this was some strong paint to withstand the harsh stormy weather. The paint secured the ark in position and sealed the boat from any cracks so no water could get in. In other words, everyone on the inside of the boat was safe and sealed from God's wrath, which was the water on the outside of the boat. To put this in perspective for today, we can compare this to salvation. God dipped His paintbrush in the blood of Jesus and covered us with His blood, thereby, as with the ark, keeping us safe from His wrath. Like the ark sealed by the paint, we are covered by the blood and sealed by the Holy Spirit. The ark represents Christ who went through the storm of God's judgment on the cross, as Noah went through the storm in the ark.

What have we learned from Noah and the flood? The message is that God is the Creator, and sin has consequences. In Noah's time people lived and did whatever they wanted to do. They didn't take the time to seek God or repent of their wicked ways. This same thing is happening today. In Noah's day grace came in the shape of an ark, but today it is in the shape of the cross.

THINK: The question today for believers is, will we be standing in the boat or in the world when Jesus returns? Perhaps people do not understand that God's wrath will come from heaven and the only safety net we will have is in Christ Jesus.

ACTION: If you are repeatedly doing something you know is wrong, stop doing it. You may stop in stages, but be sure you are making progress each day. Keep a chart of your progress.

Spread the word, post it or tweet it—#safetyinGod.

THE PURSUIT OF HAPPINESS

We have heard the phrase "pursuit of happiness" many times, but what does it mean? Thomas Jefferson affirmed in the Declaration of Independence that Americans have the right to the pursuit of happiness. In fact, he even changed the phrase from British political philosopher John Locke's statement that people should have the right to life, liberty and property. Apparently, Jefferson disagreed with property and replaced it with the "pursuit of happiness." Again I ask, what is it? Many people come from miles across the globe in search of happiness and the "American Dream." Will Smith and his son even made a movie titled *The Pursuit of Happiness*. The point is that everyone tries to pursue happiness to varying degrees.

But they often look in the wrong places, which leads them to a less than meaningful life.

Let me explain: If we don't understand the authenticity of God, that He is the true vine, we can get into false relationships. You will go on wild goose chases to find happiness, but you will never find it. People try to find it in cars, houses and other material things. Others try to find it in alcohol, drugs, gambling and get-rich-quick schemes. Some try to find it by being busy in church, school and other places, yet not bearing any fruit. In other words, the pursuit of happiness is a false sense of reality. Happiness is a by-product of having a meaningful and fruitful life with Christ. So what am I saying? If you pursue a meaningful life in the Spirit of Christ, happiness is a bonus.

A meaningful life is a fruitful life—one in which we understand the Vine is the source of light and life is only in the Vine. Do we have a life-link? It's not good enough simply to be associated with the vineyard. Our desire should be to have a fruitful life. As Christians we should bear fruit because it is the evidence of life. Granted, our fruit may be green, red, big, small or even immature, but we should have some fruit. We should have new testimonies, victories and virtues in our lives.

Be careful not to get tangled up in the vineyard and not be connected to the Vine and thus become a withered branch. Remember: Judas was in the vineyard but was never connected to the Vine. Fruit is sweet and delicious, and the beauty in fruit is that seeds in them produce more fruit. In other words, it is the beautiful expressions of God in our lives. God is cultivating maximum fruitfulness in our lives as we continue to grow. Let's compare ourselves to the branches of a tree. What does the tree need to grow?

1) **Sunshine**—A tree needs sunshine (photosynthesis) which turns it ultimately into food.
2) **Darkness**—A tree needs darkness to rest; during the night it assimilates the food that was produced in the sunlight.
3) **Inclement weather**—A tree needs harsh weather to strengthen its roots and structure.

How does this relate to our lives? We are the branches. Christ loves us and is our source of light (*sunshine*). At times we will have *darkness* in our lives so we can be still and rest and thus be rejuvenated. Trials and tribulations will come in the form of *inclement weather*, not to destroy us, but to make us stronger. He doesn't spare us from pain or shield us because we would not be able to develop properly. As Christians, instead of always trying to pursue happiness let us pursue our true purpose, and that is to seek the will of God and always glorify Him. He orders our steps and controls the climate in which our fruit can continue to grow. Don't be fooled by the pursuit of happiness. If you are not walking with Christ, you will never be truly happy because you will always be yearning to fill an empty void. Saints! I can say I am happy. What about you?

THINK: Do you have Christ in your life? Are you really happy?

ACTION: If you don't have a personal relationship with Christ, please read Romans 10:9 -10. Stop what you are doing and confess the Lord Jesus and believe in your heart that God raised Him from the dead. If you have accepted Christ, now pray for the supernatural happiness only He can give.

Spread the word, post it or tweet it—#iwanttobehappy.

THE EVENT

Have you ever hit rock bottom? I mean really hit rock bottom. The term "rock bottom" can be different to many people. For some, it's when they have lost a job or a loved one, or perhaps life just got the best of them. For others, it's when they could no longer look themselves in the mirror after taking their last hit of drugs or the last taste of alcohol. The reason I ask is because people tend to remember what that feels like in hopes of never returning to it. In comparison, once you begin to know God, you should not want to return to your old ways. The moment comes when you absolutely know that if it were not for a true and living God you could not have gotten out of your situation. Sometimes it takes our reaching our lowest point before we begin to look up. When we are going

The Event

through it, we often say, "It's the devil." But I say that God continues to test our faith. At times, He must knock us to our knees to put us in a posture of prayer so we will have no place to look but up.

We can learn many lessons from the Israelites. They endured nearly four centuries of oppression, and then they were delivered out of bondage to freedom. Slavery was their rock bottom, and the exodus became a remembrance that God alone freed them. For them, deliverance out of slavery was their "salvific event." Although they went back and forth, they seemed to turn back to God because they remembered that day of deliverance. Each time they were in trouble, God provided, so this event of deliverance gave them a greater understanding of God. In other words, they knew Him by what He had done. We should rejoice in the fact that our salvation event comes from the cross when Christ died for us. That is the event that should change our lives forever. Despite the event on the cross that was witnessed and documented, it sometimes takes an up-close and personal event in our lives to let us know who God is.

Each time we stumble along the way or get off track, we should always be led back to the cross, our salvation event. Each time we remember the circumstances He brought us out of, we should be reminded of the cross and the day we became free from the condemnation of sin. I can think of many moments in my life when I felt as if I were going to lose my mind (literally). Each time I think about that moment I rejoice in the fact that God brought me through. It is through our personal events in which we have an epiphany of who Christ really is. Many times this revelation comes from remembering when we were in a pit, and somehow we make it out alive. It is then we understand the magnitude of who God is.

Perhaps you can't identify with serious life-changing events. Maybe life hasn't dealt you a bad hand yet, but keep on living. When you have been in the valley you can appreciate the mountain experiences. Saints, when you look back over your life, remember how He spared you, protected you and restored you. What event let you know He is real? When you know what that is, then you can have true worship with Him because you will understand that the only reason you are here today is because of Him! If that doesn't lead you to worship Him, I don't know

The Event

how many more miracles you need. Just make sure it's not too late. I thank God for *all* the events in my life.

THINK: Do you remember the event in your life that brought you closer to Christ? If so, you should praise God each time you remember how far He has brought you.

ACTION: In remembrance, write down some things you know God has brought you through. In addition, write down things you need help with right now. Continue to view your list over time and see how God works miracles in your life.

Spread the word, post it or tweet it—#Godsaves.

THE ROAD TO RECOVERY

Sometimes we drive down the road and take a wrong turn. How do we get back on track? Do we pull over to ask for directions or put the directions into our navigation system? Do we continue down the wrong path without having a clue we are lost? Every now and then God sends us signs that we are off track or out of right relationship with Him. During these times we must yield to the Holy Spirit. We must get out of denial, recognize we need recovery and repent (a changing of the heart). We must remember to practice what we preach and teach. No other steps lead to salvation than what is stated in Romans 10:9-10. Never allow anyone to put you in bondage of believing anything different. Salvation has everything to do with grace.

The Road to Recovery

When we get off track, God asks us to humble ourselves, pray, seek His face and turn from our wicked ways (2 Chronicles 7:14). The great news is that God is like our earthly parent in a way. Imagine having a fall-out with your mom or dad or falling out with your children over something they have done. You may be upset with them at the time, but you will never stop loving them because your love is unconditional. It is the same with God when we get off the road: He **never** stops loving us because He loves us unconditionally. Remember that when we took those two steps—confess with our mouths the Lord Jesus and believe God raised Him from the dead—we are saved! No one or nothing can pluck us from His hands. At the same time, though, we want to make sure we are in right standing with Him and never take Him for granted. Every now and then do a self-checkup to be sure you are on the right road; you may find you need a tune-up. Stay on course!

THINK: Have you ventured off the road lately? Repent of your sins and return to your first love—CHRIST!
ACTION: We are all made in God's image. If you are in bad standing with anyone, take the higher road

and attempt to make it right. Be sure you approach the situation in a Christ-like manner with love. Pray and have no malice in your heart when doing so. It's time to love again and remember God is love.

Spread the word, post it or tweet it—#Godislove.

MY SEA
MY LIFE

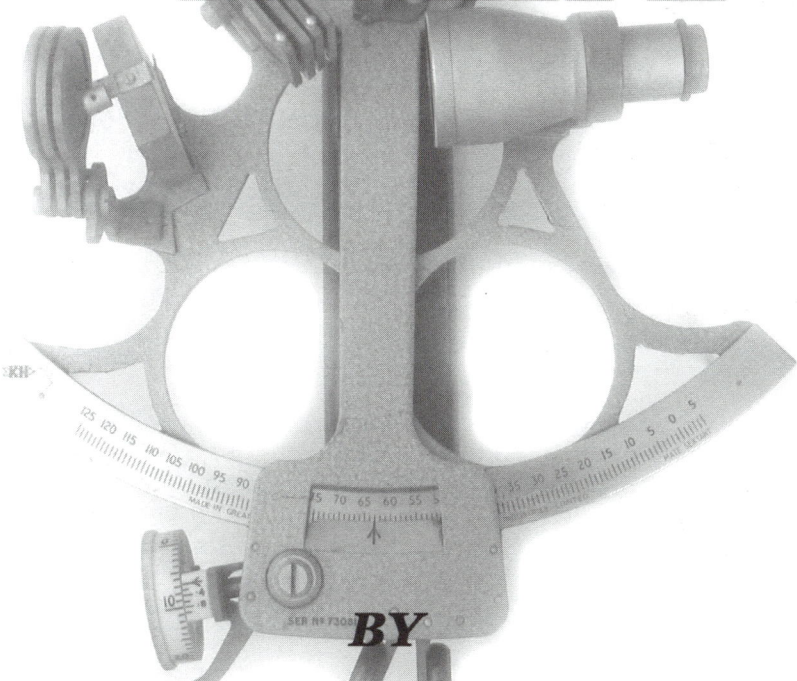

BY

MICHAEL G. RAZOS

Maximilian Press Publishers
920 S. Battlefield Blvd., suite 100
Chesapeake, Virginia 23322
757-482-2273

Copyright © 2005 Michael G. Razos
All rights reserved,
Including the right of reproduction
In whole or in part in any form.

MAXIMILIAN PRESS PUBLISHERS and colophon
are registered trademarks of
Maximilian Press Publishing Company

Author Michael G. Razos

Cover Design by Maria Razos
Formatting by John Walker

Manufactured in the United States of America

10   9   8   7   6   5   4   3   2   1

ISBN: 1-930211-72-4

Paper used in this publication meets the minimum
requirements of ANSI/NISO Z39.48-1992 (1997)
(PERMANENCE OF PAPER)

THE SEQUENCE LIST

DEDICATION v
MY THOUGHTS. vii
ACKNOWLEDGEMENTS ix
THE SHIPS. xi

THE BEGINNING. 1
MY FIRST SHIPS 5
TRITON - AN OFFICER. 43
THE CONNECTION (MEET THE IN-LAWS) 75
THE AIRPORT – DIANA 107
NORFOLK – THE WEDDING. 123
BACK TO MY ROOTS (THE SEA). 131
NEW YORK – HOTELS – LICENSE 143
MMP (APPLICANT YEARS) CITRUS PACKER. 151
THE TANKERS – OVERSEAS VIVIAN – OVERSEAS ALICE . 173
TRANSCOLUMBIA 187
RELIEF TRIPS 199
MEMBERSHIP – THE GOLDEN YEARS 207
DISASTER STRIKES 229
THE LASH SHIPS. 233
DESERT STORM – SCAN 241
MY BACK – DIEGO GARCIA 255

FINAL THOUGHTS 263
MEMORABILIA FROM THE ARCHIVES:
    ARTIFACTS SAVED THROUGH THE YEARS. 265
BIOGRAPHICAL SYNOPSIS 287

DEDICATION

I dedicate this book to my family, especially to my partner, my wife, who tolerated me for all of these years.

MY THOUGHTS

The weatherman is broadcasting. The storm is moving from the Midwest towards the East. Happily the weatherman broadcasted that in a few hours this storm is going to be safely out to sea, like nothing is out there, only fish. Guess what? We are out there, the unknown entity.

They call us seamen. Who am I? I am one of the many seamen, and my story applies to thousands upon thousands who make their living by crossing the high seas. Famous? No! Celebrity? No! Nevertheless, we have an interesting and colorful life, and hopefully interesting for all of you to read.

ACKNOWLEDGEMENTS

I'd like to express my special thanks to Jennifer Call for typing and to Mr. Carey Brown for typing the Triton. I cannot emphasize enough how grateful I am to the dynamic duo Kyki Razos and Nancy Eger for proofreading, correcting and editing the manuscript. Last but not least I'd like to give special thanks to my creative daughter Maria Razos for the design of the cover.

Thank you all, Michael

x

THE SHIPS

1. S/S Kastor
2. S/S Thetis
3. M/V Pythagoreon
4. S/S Triton
5. M/V Diana
6. S/S Phoenix
7. S/S Clarksville Victory
8. S/S Citrus Packer
9. S/S San Juan
10. S/S Overseas Vivian
11. S/S Overseas Alice
12. S/S Transcolumbia
13. S/S Hess Voyager
14. S/S Defiance
15. S/S Edgar M. Queeny
16. S/S Lash Atlantico
17. S/S Lash Italia
18. S/S Boston
19. Sea Land Anchorage
20. S/S Tampa
21. Mount Washington
22. Del Viento
23. Fortaleza
24. Santa Lucia
25. S/S American Lynx
26. S/S American Archer
27. S/S American Legion
28. Export Challenger
29. C/V Lightening
30. Export Freedom
31. S/S Borinquen
32. S/S Resolute
33. S/S Robert E. Lee
34. Sam Houston
35. S/S Scan
36. S/S Thompson Lykes
37. Austral Rainbow
38. S/S Expedition
39. Green Harbor
40. Trixonis
41. Zues
42. Cronos
43. Kavo Grossos
44. Bayamon

THE BEGINNING

The trip to the airport was hot. The small passenger van's air conditioner wasn't working. On top of everything, this was the hot, muggy, rainy season for Singapore. Not that it ever got cold, but with the peak of the rainy season, it was about to rain any minute, and most of the time, it would be down right pouring. We had to be at the airport a few minutes before takeoff to go through security, get tickets, etc. The driver of the small bus was late, as usual, and so we were running a little late. I arrived in Singapore the day before with a C8 passenger plane converted to a cargo plane with room for 34 passengers in the back. I was not sure if it belonged to the military or to a civilian company, but one thing was for sure, that plane had seen better days. Leaving Diego Garcia late, we arrived in Singapore late enough to miss the commercial fight to San Francisco. So, I had to spend a night in Singapore and catch another plane the next day

      Let me tell you little about Diego Garcia. Going by the name of DG it is a small atoll island located in the South Indian Ocean, a part of Chagos, Archipelago, at about 7 1/2 degrees South Latitude, and 72 degrees East Longitude. Actually it is in the middle of nowhere. D.G. is the top of a volcanic mountain where the old crate of the volcano forms a lagoon today. It is surrounded by a small strip of low tropical land with a small entrance to get in and out of the lagoon to the ocean. Just outside of the lagoon the mountain is very steep, and when I say steep, I mean steep. To give you an idea, leaving the port the Fathometer reads 8 or 10 fathoms and as soon as we pass the entrance of the lagoon, it drops to 400 to 500 fathoms, and then more. That is true all around the island. Inside the lagoon it is a safe haven for quite a few ships, all serving the military. The South Indian Ocean has a strange topography. There are a few islands here and there. Actually they are the mountaintops of an underwater ridge that starts all the way in India. Some say that it is the remains of the lost continent Limuria. Inside the lagoon and around the island of DG are all the kinds of fish and sea life: from fish you can eat to the exotic. A combined effort by the British, who control the island, and the U.S. who use the island as a base, has been made to preserve the beautiful environment, and I think they have done a good job

Many times in the past, I was stationed in Diego Garcia. This time I was a third mate on the last vessel the Green Harbor. At the port, I had the four to midnight watch. It was after 11:30 and I was finishing my entries in the logbook, ready to close my day. My relief was coming momentarily. Anyway, he used to come a few minutes before to shoot the breeze, as they say in seaman's language. I went outside of the wing of the bridge to read the temperature for the log, and I pulled the heavy side door of the ship. The doors were old and occasionally got stuck. I forcefully pulled it so it would open. I felt something like a knife stuck in my back. I froze and couldn't move. My back went out. I slowly crawled to the couch at the back of the bridge. That is where the other third mate found me when he came to relieve me. He was sorry and upset because he knew that I would have to fly back home. We were good shipmates, and he was unhappy to see me leave.

The next morning, I went to the hospital, and they kept me outside on shore and tried to stabilize me with medication, to ease the pain, so I could fly home. With that, and trying to schedule me for a flight out from DG, it took about a week, which I didn't mind. It gave me a chance to recover a little so I could tolerate, with the help of medicine, the long flight back. With all the problems in the Persian Gulf ports, and the limited space of the cargo plane, I was lucky to get out that soon. I didn't mind because every day that passed helped my back. At this time, to travel to and return home from Diego Garcia, I had to fly on a cargo plane to Singapore, and then on a commercial flight to the U.S. regardless of the shipping port, East or West Coast. That travel system was done because of the fear of terrorism in the Gulf Ports (Bahrain, Fujaira, and Dubai). This would be a long trip to say the least, from DG to Norfolk, Virginia, my home.

We were on board the little cargo plane at the D. airport. It was ready to take off when they detected some mechanical problem, and the delay started. On top of that, the air conditioner in the passenger section of the plane stopped working, and they had to fix it, or it was associated with another problem. Anyway, we didn't have an air conditioner, and before we knew it, the temperature inside the passenger cabin reached 120 degrees. The stewardess was bringing cold towels from outside to keep us a little cool by washing our heads with the towels.

The delay, which lasted awhile, was long enough for us to loose the connection in Singapore. It was followed by the five-hour flight to Singapore. I was happy because I needed the rest for the long flight home. Now they had to again rearrange the flight from Singapore to San Francisco, and then to Washington, D.C. Why Washington, D.C.? If a seaman was discharged from the ship, unfit for duty, he had to go to the Washington hospital for examination and treatment. The doctors from there would decide whether he should go home for the rest of the treatments or if he was cured.

From Singapore to San Francisco, I flew with the Singapore Airlines. Because I was an officer, I could fly business class. What a treat! It was a beautiful 747, a good comfortable seat to rest my back, which I needed badly, and excellent service. I could not ask for more. I had a good adjustable seat, the stewardess with some kind of treat all the time, and a bunch of late movies to watch. This was just fantastic. The airplane left Singapore on time. With approximately a five-hour flight, the next stop, and only stop, was Seoul, Korea. That stop gave me a chance to get out of the airplane and go to the terminal to stretch a little. The layover was about an hour, more or less.

We boarded the airplane again and took off for the long trip to San Francisco. The first hour was very active with a few snacks and then supper. For a seaman, this was a luxury, and for my back, flying business class was a blessing. By now, things started settling down for the long trip home. The stewardess turned the main lights off and every individual could use the overhead lights. Of course, *there were plenty of things to do to pass the time, like watching a movie, listening to the music, or just going to sleep. All the modern conveniences were in the palm of my hands, with plenty of magazines and newspapers at my disposal, and of course, a comfortable seat to sleep. It was up to me to choose one of those, but not really. My mind was running a thousand miles an hour. I was going home, which was very nice. I was looking forward to being with my family again. Even though I did not want to accept it, something deep in my heart was telling me that this was my last ship. I was getting off, and my career as a seaman seemed to be over.*

This time Michael was going home to stay. I tried to watch a movie, but I wasn't patient enough. I changed to music, and I listened for a while, and then I turned it off. I turned off the overhead light, closed my eyes, settled my head on my pillow, and I tried to get a nap. The nap was not coming. In the back of my mind was a movie, which started back from day one on the small island of Ithaca, June of 1960, when I had finished the Nautical Gymnasium of Ithaca. Like all the young men, I was eager to see and to sail the world

MY FIRST SHIPS

Ithaca traditionally is a seaman's island. The majority of the people on the island made their living off the sea, and I was not an exception. To get a job with a ship, I had to go to the main port in Greece. Piraeus is where the offices of the companies and the agents for the companies were located. Most of the companies favor the seaman from the same places where their owners or their big executives were from. Quite a few seamen from my island stayed in Ithaca waiting for a telegraph from a company that was looking for a crew. Of course, they knew what company they were going to again, and they also knew that they had priority. That was the most common practice. Going instead to Piraeus to look for a job could be expensive, especially if it took a while to get a job. I stayed home for a while, like the others, waiting for the telegram, but I didn't have the patience. I packed my bags and went to Piraeus. I had a benefit because my brother lived in Piraeus, and I had a place to stay.

I started going from one company to another and from one agency to another looking for a job. There was a big agency owned by a native boy of Ithaca, Mr. Matarangas. He happened to be a very good friend of my doctor in Piraeus. He was also the doctor for the seaman. To make sure that they were healthy, all seamen were required to get a physical before they could clear to go to the ship. This doctor liked me very much. He always thought it was a waste for me to go to sea. Instead he wanted me to go to medical school to become a doctor. He would take me into his practice. Only a small detail was missing - the money that was required to become a doctor.

My doctor was more than glad to introduce me to his friend, Mr. Matarangas, who welcomed me. After we went through the paperwork, we looked at his schedule of ships, when they would need crew replacement, and how he could fit me into one of those placements. He estimated that in a month or so, the *S/S Kastor* was coming to the island of Mykonos to load mineral. He would be able to ship me out as a cadet (Apprentice officer). Mr. Miltiadis was his right hand, and he would take care of all of the details like paperwork, physical, etc. He expedited all of the requirements nicely for me, especially because I knew Mr. Maratangas and we came from the same island. I was going as a cadet, which was not a big deal. I was a first timer, just getting my feet wet. It was nice of him to be so helpful.

The *S/S Kastor* was a liberty ship, built during the Second World War. The maximum sea speed was 11 knots, and its capacity was 11,000 tons of cargo. My first day on board was hectic and exciting to say the least. I was facing a new world. Even though I grew up on an island and I was around boats all my life, being a crewmember of a ship was completely different. After I settled into my cabin and changed to working clothes, I wandered around the ship to get familiar with it. Thousands of questions crossed my mind, and a worry about how everything would go. As I said, we were taking from Mykonos to New Orleans the minerals that were used for oil rings and for its qualities to settle quickly. To load the ship, it was fairly quick, no more than 48 hours. The first day was the busiest with the change of crew, and taking on stores. I was at the same category as a deck boy. The difference between us was only the name; otherwise, we would do the same job and get the same pay of $33.00 per month. There was overtime, and if I remember well, it was no more than 14 cents an hour. At the end of the second day, the cargo was done. It was time to secure the ship for sea. We would close the hatches, cover them, secure them, lower the booms, and tie them up. The pilot was on board, the ship lines were away, and we were off the dock and out of the port. Later with the pilot away, we were out at

My Sea My Life

sea, and my first trip at sea had begun.

My heart was pounding. Even though I was happy that my dream to see the world was ahead of me, my loved ones were left behind. But, that's the life of a seaman, to tighten up your heart every time you leave for a trip. The crossing of the Mediterranean Sea was an uneventful one. It took almost seven days. The good old *Kastor* was never in a rush.

The most excitement was sailing through the Straits of Gibraltar. It was special; the first time I went through. Going through the Gibraltar Straights I was lucky. We passed the Straits during the day, and the visibility was good. Leaving the Mediterranean Sea, the first sights were the Europa Point and the famous Rock of Gibraltar, big, tall and impressive standing there as a mythic giant controlling the Straits. It was just as I had read and seen in pictures. I was finally there. On your left side was the coast of Africa. It seemed as if the two continents were closing in on each other. From then until we exited the Straits, the traffic was heavy in both directions. There were also ferryboats, other ships, and small boats crossing from all directions. On the bridge the navigation was intense. They had to be careful, especially with the slow moving *S/S Kastor*. Next was the Gulf of Algeciras. Slowly but steadily we reached the last point on the way out (Punta de Tarifa) Tarifa. From then on it was the *S/S Kastor* and the Atlantic Ocean. From that first crossing, I have always enjoyed the Straits of Gibraltar.

After a few hours away from the Straits, there was nothing but ocean all around. This was a fascinating, and at the same time, peculiar feeling for a young seaman. Very soon the other deck hand, an engine cadet, and I became friends. All three of us were rookies. We were first timers, as they say in seaman's language. We were about to get the taste of the big sea. The three of us had no idea what lay ahead when crossing the Atlantic or any other big ocean.

One day after we left Gibraltar, the first welcome of the

Atlantic were fairly good-size swells. Being loaded with ore (mineral) and being bottom heavy, the ship rolls were bigger. Now with swells of 15 feet or more, and helped by the weight of the cargo, the ship was rolling pretty well. For the rest of the crew this was nothing unusual or new. They were securing things more carefully, walking more carefully, and were a little more uncomfortable. For them it was just another day at sea. The three of us, not knowing any better, had a good breakfast of eggs, bacon, toast, and coffee. We started our day with the rest of the crew.

With the advice of experience, the Bosun said, "Be careful. When moving around, always hold on to something and watch yourself because the ship is rolling."

The Engine Cadet started for the engine room while the other deck hand and I got our chipping hammers and the paint primer and headed for the second deck to continue chipping the rust off the old *Kastor*. Both of us settled down and started chipping. A day as... usual, fat chance! Before too long, a little headache started, and the stomach started feeling funny. Anyway, the two fools that we were had overloaded the poor things with a hefty breakfast. Before long, we started feeling that we had to vomit. We thought if we held on then that feeling would go away, and we would not look like fools by getting seasick. But, the ocean and the swell were not forgiving, and there we went. Both of us, almost at the same time, ran for the rail and exploded the rockets towards the ocean. We were not in shape or in the mood to clean the vomit from the decks. At least we had that much sense.

After that, we felt better and both fools thought, "That is it. We are seamen."

We returned to chipping, but in a few minutes, the same feeling returned, and that continued for a while. Both of us did not want to show the rest of the crew that we were that seasick and had to quit the job, since, we had seen all of the crew going around like nothing was happening. Just another day at sea! Then the Bosun came to check on us. There he saw two young seamen sick as dogs trying to hold on.

He asked, "How long have you guys been sick?"

"Since we came up here," we said.

"Well, it's time to go in and rest before you get hurt out here," he said. We got up trying to pick up our tools.

He said, "Okay go! Leave everything here. I will have someone pick them up. Go rest and don't worry. Most of us have gone through the same thing; you will get used to it. By the way, next time you see that the weather is not good, don't eat that much. Keep your stomachs light. Just eat some toast or crackers or something dry until you get used to it."

At the same time, the engine cadet was going through the same thing down in the engine room, and he was sent back to his room. So all three of us were back in our cabins, with a bucket next to us, just in case. By this time, there was not much left to come out from our stomachs. The rest of the crew naturally was teasing us royally. The Bosun, who was a well-seasoned and well-experienced seaman, and who was well respected by everyone, not just by the deck department for his seamanship and his character, chewed them out to leave us alone. Of course he did a little joking with his dry humor. After all, we had to go through the initiation. Everybody kept telling us that after a few days we would get used to it. In a way they were right, but it took a little longer, at least that's the way we felt. The rest of the trip, as far as seasickness was concerned, was up and down. As the weather got better, we got better. The sad part was that every weekend that we were not working, the weather was bad, and all three of us were seasick.

That was my first big ocean crossing. I made it, but I was sick as a dog pretty much all the way. Things got better when we got to the Florida Straits and the Gulf of Mexico. What a joy! We had nice, warm, good weather! We started to rejuvenate ourselves, after a lousy crossing, at least for us.

Finally, we arrived in New Orleans, my first port outside of Greece. I was looking around like a little kid as we were going up the Mississippi River. This was a long trip, especially with the liberty ship. We docked at a place called Macobar, a short distance away from The City, which was about a 15 to 20 minutes bus ride. They told us that daytime it was okay to go out, but at night we were warned to watch ourselves and not be alone waiting for the bus.

They warned, "Don't be outside the gate of the terminal alone after dark."

These things were very new to me. Working on deck, during the discharge of the cargo was also a very new experience from what I knew in Piraeus.

The *Kastor* had five hatches, three forward of the accommodation and two aft. At the three forward hatches, the longshoremen were white. At the two aft hatches, they were black.

With my little English at the time, I asked one of the foremen, "Why?"

Kind of annoyed, he said, "That's the way it is here."

I stopped asking more. That was 1960 and segregation was still strong, especially in the South.

Learning a language at school was one thing, speaking the language in the native country especially around longshoreman was another. I found that out on my first trip. I thought I knew English from school. The school helped a lot, but I had a long way to go. When I was talking with a more educated person, and they would speak kind of slower, I had no problem. But with the longshoremen, I had no idea what they were talking about.

Instead of having us take the bus and get lost, one of the ship's agents in New Orleans, volunteered to give us a ride, take us shopping, and show us around the city a little bit. This was my first taste of the United States, and it was a fascinating one to say the least. I could not help but be impressed at the time. If I remember well, it was right after Thanksgiving, and the city was decorated for Christmas. What an unbelievable sight for us!

Shopping around, it was as if we were in a movie. Our eyes were popping out; we were so amazed. He took us to Canal Street, close to the French Quarter. The place down there never slept at that time. Today things may have changed, but at the time, there was not that much crime. Stores, business, clubs, restaurants, you name it, were open any time, all the time. Later on that night, some more crew from the ship joined us, and we started going around for a good time. That lasted until the morning hours when we returned to the ship.

From what I learned at that time the U.S. was one of the few countries to do your business. Shopping was reasonable. The ports were efficient in handling the loading and discharging of the ship and rarely were there any delays. Before long, we were done in New Orleans, and we were sailing down the river with a lot of good things to discuss about our first port.

The next port was Galveston, Texas to load grain for Guayaquil, Ecuador. From New Orleans to Galveston we took our time because we had to clean the holds for the next cargo, which was grain. In order to load grain, they had to be very clean. That was hard work. For that kind of work we got paid extra, and usually the money was negotiated with the Captain. That was the job of the deck department, and the money would be divided according to our rank. The Bosun would get a certain amount, the ABs another rate, and as for the cadet and the deck hands, the lowest rate. Regardless, we all worked very hard, and that was the way it was. It took three to four days of intense work to prepare the holds for grain. As they say, you could eat from the floor, because it was that clean.

Finally, we reached Galveston. We docked alongside the grain terminal and not far from the city. Galveston was a much smaller port than New Orleans. The ports were coming to me kind of fast in diversity. New Orleans was an established cosmopolitan city. Galveston, Texas was a city with its own characteristics and flavor. Here it was like the cowboy movies that I'd seen in Greece. There were big hats, jeans, boots, and accents, Texas style. Galveston had many Army and Navy stores loaded with nice stuff. Stuff, that a young guy, would like to have, like jeans, Levis, dungarees, kakis, you name it. The prices were unbelievably good and affordable, even for my cadet's salary. That was the good old days. When the label said, "Made in the U.S.A." the item was the best quality at the best price. On top of everything, Galveston was one of the best places for those products. So with all the savings that I could muster from cleaning all the ship's holds, I hurried for the Army and Navy stores for shopping.

Somehow the word spread around that Galveston had houses of joy (girls). Soon enough, after shopping, we asked one of the store clerks where they were.

He said, "Take this street and go down for a little walk. Don't worry; you will see them. You can't miss them."

So the three of us hurried for the Red Light District. Talking and joking and walking, we kept walking, and we reached the Red Light District. We reached the Red Light District all right, but apparently the wrong one. Out of the blue, a police car pulled up along side of us with the siren on and signaled for us to stop.

The policeman got out of the car and asked, "What are you doing here, and where are you going?"

I'm the one, who spoke some English, and I answered, "Sir, we are looking for the Red Light District, and a clerk in the Army and Navy store told us that it was down here."

He looked at us and said, "All three of you get in the car."

I asked, "We did anything wrong?"

He said, "All three of you get in the car!"

Now all of us start thinking that we were going to jail and we'd done nothing wrong. So we got in the car, and he turned the police car around and started heading the way we came from.

He started by asking, "Where are you from?"

We told him, "We are seaman from the *S/S Kastor*, and we have come out to shop, look for the girls or have a drink some place. That's all."

He started laughing, and that was a good sign for us.

He said, "You passed the Red Light District that you were looking for, and you got to another that you're not supposed to be in. It's only for colored people, and it is dangerous for you to be there. Don't ever go in that direction again! Now, I will show you the place that you were looking for."

I took a look at the faces of my friends, and I knew what they wanted. I said politely to the policeman, "That's okay, Sir. We'd rather go back to the ship."

He said, "Good idea."

He drove us close to the dock and left. By the way, from what I heard, Texas was from the few if not the only state to have legal Red Light Districts. We were happy to be back on the ship. It did not take long to load the ship, and before we knew it, we were at sea heading for Ecuador.

Another place that has stayed in my mind forever was the Panama Canal crossing. I'd read about it, but to see it was a different experience. As a young seaman, I was fascinated. The Panama Canal was an amazing project. It was something that I would never forget.

I said to myself, "That was why I became a seaman, to see all of these places."

We entered Colon (Cristobal), we dropped the anchor, and we were waiting for instructions from the Panama Canal pilots to proceed with the transit. We had, that was the two deck boys, the Engine Cadet and I, the permission of the Bosun and the Chief Mate to interrupt our work and sightsee, as we transited the Canal. The only one who most probably would oppose this would be the Old Groucho (the Captain), but we were careful to not have him see us. Anyway for all of us our salaries were not so spectacular for anyone to worry if we missed a few minutes of work, so we could enjoy the various points of the Canal. To go up on the bridge was off limits for us. We were to not even think about it with the Old Groucho around. That would have been a crime, and it would have been serious enough to justify throwing us over the side according to his beliefs. But don't worry; we were prepared. The Second Mate had given us the most important points of interest from the chart to follow as we were going along.

Shortly after arrival, the Canal pilot boarded the ship, and we started the transit. First was the Triple Gatun Locks with their massive steel gates. Trolleys moved the ship from one lock to another and raised the ship 26 meters above the sea level to Lake Gatun. As we traveled through Lake Gatun we passed lots of small islands covered with wild tropical trees and vegetation. It took a few hours with the slow *Kastor* to reach the Gaillard Cut. From there until the Pedro Miguel Lock, I enjoyed the tropical river, which stretched like a snake. The vegetation on both sides was so thick that it was like going through a jungle. Pedro Miguel was a single lock, and it took us down to 16.5 meters above sea level to Miraflores Lake. Then we went through a double set of locks at Miraflores. By the way, all locks were two-way traffic so the ships could pass in both directions. Then we were at sea level. After we passed Balboa, we were out on the Pacific Ocean.

From the Panama Canal, it was a short distance to Guayaquil, located five to six hours up the river. When we arrived at the entrance of the river, we got the pilot. With the pilot boat, customs also came on board. When we had stopped the ship to get the pilot, various small boats were approaching the ship. One of the custom's officers ran up on the bridge to the Captain and said, "Don't let any of these people come on board! They are contraband buyers. Send them away!"

"Sure," the Captain said, "don't worry. No one is coming on board."

The customs officer said, "Good, Captain. Don't worry and we will pay the same price for the cigarettes and whiskey and whatever else you have to sell."

Those were the words of the customs officials, not the contraband buyers. It was so they could have the priority to buy for themselves. Not bad!

The place we anchored was far from everything, and there was nowhere to go. So, for the whole stay in Guayaquil, no one went ashore. For the deck department, it was hard because we had to be

My Sea My Life

continuously on the alert for rain so that we could quickly cover the hatches to protect the grain from getting wet. After all, we were in the heart of the tropics. Finally, we were done discharging the grain at Ecuador to the pleasure of all of us, especially the deck department.

The next cargo was sugar from Peru. Again, we followed the same procedure to clean the holds for the next cargo. It was not as bad as the first time, but nevertheless, it was hard work, especially in the hot tropical weather. We were off again, with a slow speed on the way to Peru, specifically the port of Chiclayo, which was a small port, without docking facilities for the ship to go alongside. We dropped the anchor as close as we could to the port, and they brought the cargo to the ship with barges. Loading time was estimated to be at least two weeks, maybe more, if the swells became high and the barges could not hold alongside the ship.

Peru was my first encounter with Latin America, the music, the people, the food, and, of course, the girls. Today, of course, we have all the kinds of entertainment on the ships. Poor *Kastor*! She was behind even for those days. If someone had a radio, he was probably an officer. Now here we were, in a place with nightlife that was full of life, plenty of music, plenty of food and beer, and an abundance of girls. Of course, everything was very affordable for our pockets. This was a seaman's paradise, not only for the young, but also for all the crew. We were like kids in the cookie jar. The main place of entertainment looked like two strips, one on each side, like a motel, with different rooms where the girls were. At the end, the cantina was set up in a restaurant style with tables, where there was food, drinks, and a place to stay. Of course, there was plenty of music. That place became the regular gathering spot for the *S/S Kastor*.

Besides the entertainment, when I was visiting different cities, I would like to see as much as I could of that place. So I went around Chiclayo to see how the people lived and learn as much as I could, even the language. I have always liked to speak different languages. We stayed a total of almost two weeks, which, I must say, were enjoyable for all of us.

Now the ship was heading back towards the U.S. with the possible port of discharge being New York. After we passed the Panama Canal, the company confirmed that we were going to New York. I liked it. I had heard so much about the place I couldn't wait to get there. In New Orleans, from the time you got the pilot, it took almost a day going up the river to see some city. In contrast, in New York, after less than an hour, you could see the Brooklyn Shore and Staten Island. Then we passed the Verrazano Narrows Bridge, which was huge and impressive! After that, we saw the Statue of Liberty, then Battery Place. The lower part of Manhattan, with very tall buildings, was awesome. It was unreal, unbelievable, and fascinating for anyone who approached New York from the harbor. This impressive view was something that I would treasure for the rest of my life. We docked on the Brooklyn side, at the Domino Sugar Terminal at Green Point.

In Peru, it took us more than two weeks to load. Here in New York, we would be lucky if we stayed three or at the most four days. But it was enough to do a lot. For the most, especially for the other two deck boys and me, the Bosun was good, and he gave us half a day or a whole day off. A small walking distance from the terminal, there was the subway that would take us in about 15 to 20 minutes to Times Square, in New York City.

Times Square was the heart of the city, and in the 60's, it was a bustling place. Everything I could imagine was there or close by. There were stores, food, movies, music, and theater, all within a small walking distance. We were amazed! For the first time I was initiated to the New York hotdog from the street vendors. I would have a hot dog and coke. These were the best hot dogs in the world, and they still are! Times Square and the surrounding areas were busy

24 hours a day, and at the time thoroughly safe. Of course, like in any big city, I had to be careful.

In New York City at that time, and it may be true today, but not as easy as then, a person could leave the ship and stay outside, find a job quickly, get reasonable housing, and live cheaply enough to get by. I would say it was the land of opportunity. You just had to take advantage of it. That was why quite a few young seamen when they didn't have the sea in their blood would jump ship and stay ashore. New York was the primary place for this. Of course with me, there was no worry about me leaving the ship. I was young, I had just started sailing, and I had to see the world! I couldn't wait to become an officer and to navigate the ships. Settling down in some place outside the ships was not in my plans. Period! At the moment I was enjoying too much of New York, trying to see as much as I could. The company's main office was in Downtown New York at Battery Place. I even had an opportunity to see the main office and the people in the office. Plus I was lucky enough to met one of the owners, who was a very nice gentleman.

The *S/S Kastor* was considered a tramp ship. In other words she did not have a specific run, and she was getting cargo for and from all over the world. She did not know the next cargo or port until the last minute. We were almost done discharging the sugar, and the main office finally informed us that the next cargo was going to be scrap iron from New Jersey to Japan. This was not the most favored cargo, but it was not bad either. It would be a long trip, though, from New York to Japan with a liberty ship, considering that it would be at least a 42 to 45 day trip. After we finished unloading sugar, they moved us to the anchorage to clean the holds from the sugar. That was fairly easy considering that we were loading scrap iron. That cleaning took a day or two, and then, we went alongside to start loading. The ports in Japan, where we were going to discharge the cargo, were Mogi and Yawata.

The Bosun took the three of us, the other two deck hands and me, to the stern of the ship and showed us the two empty drums.

He said, "Now in Japan you can sell brass and copper motors, and make a little extra money to go ashore. Here is the deal. Fill these two drums as we are loading the scrap iron. During the trip, sort them out, and by the time we get to Japan, you will have enough copper, brass and motors to sell and get around without getting a draw from the ship. How does that sound? Are you up to it?"

"Of course we are up to it," we said.

"Just be careful when you go down into the hatches," he said.

The Bosun was the nicest man a young seaman could have. He was extremely knowledgeable, good at his job, and a very decent person. He was like a father to us, and all three of us learned so much from him. We ended up following him around the deck like faithful dogs. I was lucky to have him for my first time at sea. He taught me a great deal. By the end of loading, our little business was thriving. Both drums were full and more. Almost everything was sorted out and ready for sale.

So far, I had tasted the efficient and modern society of the U.S., and the simple, poorer, but enjoyable society of South America. Now it was time for the mystical Far East. This was another world that was new to me. I had read books and watched movies, but nothing was the same as being there and seeing it for myself. First was the port of Mogi where we had to tie up the ship to a buoy with the anchor chain because of the strong current. That procedure took quite a few hours. Thank God we had a good, experienced deck department. For me, it was another learning experience.

Japan at this time was still at the recovering stage from the Second World War, but we could see that the country was destined to succeed. These were defiant, hardworking people, and they were very polite. I was also fascinated by the way the people were dressed and by the topography, the buildings, and the shops. Everything was

My Sea My Life

different from the cities I knew. Mogi, and all of Japan in general, at the time, were very affordable for the seaman's pocket. There were not really many things to buy except for a few souvenirs, kimonos, etc, but the nightlife was fantastic!

In a sense that was the first thing on the seaman's mind, especially after a long trip like the one we had. We were not disappointed with plenty of bars providing everything. By now, the three of us had sold our own cargo, and we had gotten pretty good money, by our standards anyway. The money was good enough for a few days out. We had gotten into the habit when we went ashore, to go as a group. Usually there were the three of us plus the Engine Cadet. Sometimes the Second Cook, who was also young, would join us. For a seaman, I cannot claim that I was a drinker, a gambler, or a smoker. I liked to go out and have a drink and a good meal. The cigarettes that I took with me were mostly for the girls. Of course I enjoyed immensely the company of a girl. Being drunk in any place could be dangerous, but this was especially true in a strange place. I had seen during the years, many people get hurt. On our first day out, and after a few hours of drinking and listening to the music, the Second Cook and I decided to call it quits from the bar and go to the hotel with our girls. The others would come later, since they were still enjoying the music.

Forget Ithaca, my island, where the buildings were built to withstand earthquakes, with stone, cement, iron, and bricks all over. Anyplace that I had been so far, the buildings had been similar. The construction in South America was not that heavy, but at least there were strong walls and thick separations between the rooms. Here in Japan, after you got inside the house there were thin separation between the rooms and light sliding doors. You could sneeze in one room, and everybody would hear you. Everything looked so delicate. As far as being safe, that was not a problem. Actually all over Japan, I didn't have to worry about safety at that time, at least, that was the way I saw it. But, the thin walls were unreal to me.

My girl and I went to the room and changed to our kimonos (robes) and she said, " Let's go to the hot tub."

"Hot tub!" I thought. "Okay."

But, I never envisioned burning. This was all new to me.

She jumped right in, and giggling she said, "Come in. Come in. It's so good!"

Without a second thought or hesitation, I took the kimono off, and I jumped in. I jumped out just as quickly as I could! It felt like I had jumped into a pot of boiling water. It was that hot! She was laughing like crazy, while I ran for the cold shower.

She kept saying, "Come in, and you will get used to it!"

After a long persuasion and very slowly, I got in. The Second Cook heard my noise, and the bitching that I was doing.

He asked, "What's wrong?"

I said, "Nothing is wrong. Just be careful with the hot tub. It's boiling water."

He said, "You didn't know that. You've got to get in slowly, very slowly to get use to it."

I said, "Yes, of course I knew it. I had the same one in Ithaca." We both laughed because we grew up without any modern conveniences.

We had a pleasant week in Mogi, and now we were off for Yawata. This time we did not have to tie up at the buoy, but we used the anchor, which eliminated a lot of hard work, and it made our job much easier.

In every port, the ship had to maintain a 24-hour gangway watch. That job was mostly for the six ABs, but sometimes in safe ports, they would leave the day watch for one of the three of us. Sotis, one of the deck hands, spoke only one language, Greek and nothing else. On one particular day, he was on gangway watch in Yawata. I passed by the gangway, and Sotis was talking with a Japanese longshoreman. A little later, I saw Sotis still talking. The third time I passed by, Sotis was still talking to the same man.

I asked Sotis, "Does the man speak Greek? Do you speak Japanese?"

He said, "No."

I said, "But I see you've been talking for more than an hour? Do you know what he's saying?"

Sotis said, "I don't know what he is saying. He speaks Japanese, and I speak Greek."

"Then what are you talking about?" I asked.

He said, "We are just having a conversation." That was new to me, too. I didn't know that you could have a conversation without understanding each other.

Yawata was similar in a way to Mogi, and we had another pleasant week there. It was time for the next port. This time we were headed to the West Coast of Canada to load lumber for East Coast U.S. ports.

We were leaving Japan for Vancouver, our first port in Canada. The North Pacific was calm. Was that good? Yes and no. On one hand, crossing the Pacific in rough weather with an empty liberty was a killer. The ship could have rolled like a pumpkin. By being calm water, we didn't have that. However, we had fog, and I mean fog. As they say, it was "pea soup!" Almost all the way to Vancouver, only for a few days would it clear a little bit, but even then it was still overcast and drizzly. We made it! We had only the gyrocompass and the help of the radio direction finder. We continuously had a lookout up in the bow, and we were blowing the ship's whistle.

Mostly at sea, after supper we had nothing else to do but go to our rooms and read, or go to the mess hall, where we would play cards or just shoot the breeze; as they say in seaman's language. In the crew's mess, the sitting arrangements were limited. In other words, there were not enough chairs for all the crew. Of course the older guys had priority, like the Bosun, the head of the firemen of the engine department, etc. The three of us fell, as rookies, last on the list. The restricted seating was for the crew mess only. The officer's mess had plenty of space. Of course there were fewer officers. That was in general the entertainment at sea during those days. What a difference from today, where there are DVDs, VHS tapes, plenty of music, books, you name it. And with all these modern things, very rarely were people seen in the crew's mess and the officer's lounge. Of course with automation, the crew had been cut in half. In later years, I would miss those old days. Today, after supper everybody would run for his room, because times had changed. Those old days were the days where the sea stories were thriving.

I didn't remember the sequence of the ports that we loaded in Canada, but we loaded in at least four ports: Vancouver, Victoria, Port West Minister, and Port Alberni. We loaded all kinds of lumber. In contrast with Japan, we were now in lumberjack country. These were big, stocky and of course hardworking men. Even though they were using heavy equipment, it was hard work to load the lumber.

The cities on the West Coast of Canada were nice, clean, and country-like. The way of life was similar to the U.S. The main entertainment here for us was fishing. There were plenty of fish around for fishing. We climbed up the logs, which were at the water's edge lined up to go to the mills, and we fished from there.

The main event for us was visiting the seaman's house mostly on weekends. From the ship they would take us to the seaman's house in a van. They always had some kind of entertainment for us. Don't get the wrong idea, because this was nothing like the bars, not at all. That was where, for the first time, I had learned about the Seaman's House. Mostly run by church organizations, they were very helpful to the seamen of all nations. They created a homier environment for the seamen. So, I took advantage of the hospitality and spent time there to get to know people and in the meantime it was an opportunity for me to practice my English in the proper place. They also took us on some tours of the cities. These nice people tried to make us feel at home while away from home.

There I was also initiated to the baseball game. Growing up, the most important game was soccer and sometimes volleyball. I had no idea about American football, or basketball, which was just coming to Greece as I left for sea, and for course, baseball, which was a completely unknown sport to me. It took them a while to explain this game to me. It seemed kind of boring and slow compared to the games that I knew. Anyway, I tried to understand it, and of course I still try today. Sorry, I don't like baseball that much.

Finally, we were at the last port, and we were fully loaded with lumber and with tremendous loads on deck, as far as the regulations would allow. All that deck cargo, had to be secured. That was an extra expense that the company didn't want to pay the Canadians to do, because of their high rate. So the Captain, a fairly difficult man, went with the economic way, and went with the deck department to do the securing. We did not have any objection, but he wanted to pay us very little. After certain negotiations with the Captain, and his stubbornness, the deck refused to do it. The Old Fool, and I mean the Captain, was trying to force the young crewmembers and some of the officers to do it. It was foolish to expect a big, dangerous job like that to be done by a few inexperienced seamen. The ship was delayed. I think that the Agent called the company and told them what was happening, because a message came from the main office and ordered the Old Fool to pay the crew the right amount and finish with that foolishness. I don't think the company was against paying the employees a fair amount. I believe it was the Captain's idea, but I do not want to speculate more.

I'd like to tell you a little about my first Captain. He came from the same island that I came from. When ashore, he was kind of pleasant, but on the ship a seaman didn't want to have him, because he was a completely different person. I never knew if the responsibilities of captain were too much for him or what, but he was miserable on board. Here was a man over 60 at the time, and he was afraid that a young person in the low twenties, who would eventually become an officer, would take his job when he became a captain. It would take that young officer at least, 10 to 12 years, if everything went all right, to become a captain. By that time, our captain would have been in the upper seventies, but he was still afraid. He thought if he kept all of us from going to the bridge to practice navigation, it would save his job.

I spent a year as a cadet on the *S/S/ Kastor*, and not once was I allowed to visit the bridge and practice navigation. This was true not just for me but also for anyone that was planning to become an officer. In order to learn how to steer, the ship, I was getting up at 2 o'clock in the morning, when the Captain was asleep. I would quietly practice how to steer for an hour or two. I would learn a little about navigation, that was, as much as I could learn at two o'clock in the morning. My main objective was to learn to steer the ship well so I could advance to AB, where the pay was much greater. During one of my two o'clock in the morning practices on the wheel, the gyro alarm went off. So, the Third Mate, who was a friend of mine from the same island, ran to the gyro room to check the gyro. Both of us were familiar with the gyro from school. I guess the Captain heard us talking, and he got up screaming, "What is going on? Who is there?"

The mate said, "Nothing Captain. It's just me checking the gyro."

The Captain replied, "But I hear another voice, too."

"It's one of my main ABs helping me."

In the meantime, I ran quickly out the door, so he would not see me. I did not want to get the Mate in trouble.

We did the round and then discharged the lumber, if I remember, at two or three ports on the East Coast. Then we headed to New Jersey to load scrap iron this time for Italy. In New York I had a chance to advance to AB. We changed two ABs because they went home. They had been on the ship for a long time. The company did not want to ship new crew from Greece to save money, so they advanced the senior deck hand, and me to ABs since we were on the ship more than a year. Both of us were able to do the job well.

The promotion was coming from the office, not from the

Captain. I knew that from the people in the office. The Captain called me to his office, told me to sit down, and with an official and serious attitude, he proceeded to lecture me on how thankful I should be and how he grabbed the first opportunity he had to promote me to AB. He also said how he always had my welfare in his mind, even though I was occasionally rebelling. He also said, I should now, with the promotion, be more cooperative and do as I was told. I allowed him finish so he could get it off his chest. Then, in a very polite way, I told him I was thankful for the company to think of my abilities and of me. I felt very confident that I could do the job as any other AB, and I would accept the job only under the same conditions that apply for all the ABs knowing what responsibilities I have. Again, I thanked the company that they thought of me. They should feel rest assured that I would not let them down. So under the circumstances I would take the job, but if he felt otherwise, that was all right, and I would not take the job.

He looked at me as his face turned red and said, " All right, have it your way, but you know I am demanding."

"You will not be disappointed, Sir," I said.

During the trip from the U.S. to Italy, the Captain was watching to see how I steered the ship. He could not figure out how I was doing so well.

He was telling the Mate, "He does well, doesn't he? How did he learn to steer that well?"

The Mate said, (The same one that I was going to midnight practice with), "I don't know, but for sure, he is a good helmsman. I guess, Captain, that he is a natural."

Genoa was a big busy port. All kinds of ships came in and out of there. You name it. What struck me the most was the passenger terminal, with the famous, beautiful liners at the time like the *Colombo*, the *Leonardo De Vinci*, the *Raphaelo Sandi*, and others. They were very impressive ships. Not that I hadn't seen passenger ships before, but these names were the top of the line.

One place to visit in Genoa was the cemetery. Now, what kind of a good seaman would I be, if the first thing on my mind were to visit the cemetery of Genoa, rather than going out for a good time? Well, if this sounds a little strange, it really was not strange at all. The cemetery that I am talking about was the old cemetery. It serves as a museum today. With big mausoleums, statues, art, tremendous amount of marble, it was something different to see. It looked as if all the big powerful families centuries back, competed to see who would have the best mausoleum. Lifestyle-wise, Genoa reminded me of Piraeus, and it was a nice experience. There were many little restaurants with good seafood and good wine. We spent about ten days there.

The next stop was the place where I started, Mykonos. By this time, I had been on the ship more than a year. I didn't want to get off, but I had to. Sometime during the trip I guess I lifted a heavy load and created a hernia, which started to bother me. I figured it was a good time to get off and do the operation. Then I would get another ship. With that ended my first trip at sea with the *S/S Kastor*.

The hospital where I had the operation was named, Agios Spiridon. It was a small hospital called by Greek standards, a kliniki. My doctor, the one that examined the seamen for shipping out, owned it. For a small hospital, it was well equipped for the time and staffed with good competent doctors. Of course, I knew the hospital from before. That's why I choose to have the operation there where they knew me. It was also close to where my brother was living. The first and maybe the second day after the operation were painful. After that, the week that I stayed there was fun. From the second day, I started walking around visiting the other patients and joking with the nurses. My room had become the gathering place for the evening. We would close the door and stay up late sharing a bunch of sea stories. After a week, they released me and of course I needed a little more time before I could get my full strength to go back to sea. My recovery from the operation was quick, and my doctor said it was okay now to go back to work.

So, I started to look for a ship again. This time, with some good experience, I was looking for an AB job. Mr. Matarangas did not have anything at the time. He had no idea how soon he would have an opening. So I went to another office, the owners of the company were from my island, too. That made it much easier. The Port Captain was not from Ithaca. He was from Chios, which was well known for being a seaman's island, too. Chios was much bigger than Ithaca and with many more ship owners.

The Drakoulis Company was a well-respected and established company for years. Their main offices were in London, England. The sons of the old owners, who had died, ran the company at the time that I visited them for a job. Unfortunately, the company was heading in the wrong direction. I guess the sons were not experienced with the shipping industry, and they had the taste for the high life. They'd rather have a good time than spend time in the office. In the shipping business, the owners could not afford to do that. I visited the personnel office; and I filled out the application with all my qualifications, schools, sea time, etc. They told me to wait, and they gave my application to the Port Captain. Awhile later he called me into his office, where he was polite, and he asked me a few questions more.

He said, "Come back in three to four days to see what I will have."

I thanked him and left.

The three days passed, and I was one of the first ones in the office, anxious to go back to work. The Port Captain called me to come into his office, and he closed the door.

He said, "Mike, sit down. Why didn't you tell me more about yourself, and why didn't you give me any letters of recommendations from Ithaca? You did not tell me that you knew Captain Alimeris."

The Port Captain was kind of upset as to why I was not following the proper procedures of recommendations, followed at that time. I had just walked in since I was coming from Ithaca where so many people knew me and liked me.

As calm as I could be, I answered, "Captain, you are a good experienced captain. I will ask you a question. Even though I am young, please don't think that I am impolite. Let's say that I had come with all the recommendations from all the people I know in Ithaca, and they said all nice things about me. But, in a way they did not know my abilities as a seaman. Would they have helped me when I was on watch on the bridge? Captain, I want you to hire me not only because I come with many letters of recommendations from Ithaca, but rather I want you to hire me for my qualifications."

"Well," he said, "I called Ithaca, and everybody had the best words for you. You know how we operate in Ithaca and on my island. Recommendations are important."

Stubborn me, I answered, "But I still would like you to hire me because you think I am worth it."

He said, "You are a little stubborn, aren't you? But I like you; of course I will hire you! Here's the story. *Istros* is coming from the Black Sea to Piraeus on the way to the next loading port for bunker and stores and of course to change crew. We will need ABs, but also we need a third mate. Mr. Alimeris is going to be the Captain, and he wants you to get the third mate job. From talking with you now, I agree with Captain Alimeris. Captain Alimeris talks about you so much and how he has known you since you were a kid, and how you grew up in the same neighborhood. He's glad to have you on board."

I was trying to remember which one of my neighbors in Ithaca was named Alimeris, and he was a captain. I couldn't find anyone. But, since Mr. Alimeris was real and the Port Captain was saying so much about him, I was going along. Still I couldn't remember anyone by that name. The only one that fit the description was Captain Billy, and that was a different name.

The Port Captain said, "Check with me in a few days so I can give you the details, and tell you when you are going to go to the doctor."

I thanked him very much, and happily I left his office. That was much more than I expected.

Those days it was not uncommon for the third mate to be a qualified seaman, but without a license, and he would stand the 8 to 12 watches supposedly under the supervision of the captain. I felt lucky that day, but still, I was puzzled by who was Captain Alimeris? At the main lobby there was a refreshment and sandwich shop. There was Tassos from my island, who I knew very well. He was going as the steward. I told him that I was going on the same ship that he was going and that I was going as third mate. He was very happy. Then I asked him to solve my puzzle. Who was Captain Alimeris who knew me so well from a young kid? I had no idea. He started laughing so hard I thought that he was going to choke.

When he stopped, he said, "Sure you know him. Of course he's your neighbor."

I said, "Stop joking with me, and tell me who he is!"

With a funny face he said, "Captain Billy, don't' you know him?"

I said, "Of course I know him! Now I know," and I started laughing too.

Billy was his nickname, but it was used so much for all these years that I never knew his real name. This happened a lot on my island with the nicknames. Almost everyone had one, and sometimes the nickname overran your real name.

The next few days were busy. I was going to the doctor and finishing the paperwork. Plus, the company had to get the okay from the Coast Guard to sign me as a third mate. The company had to show that no one was available at the time. This was not completely true, but it worked. So here I was ready for the ship and cleared by the Coast Guard, the doctor, everything. I was so happy. This was something I never expected that soon. A couple of days before the ship arrived; I went to the office just to check things. A few seamen who were going with me were in the lobby, and they were talking. From what I sensed from their faces, something wasn't right.

I asked them, "What's going on?"

They said, "You don't know? You haven't heard the news?"

"No," I said.

"The ship is coming alright, but it is going to be tied up in Salamina, and they don't know for how long. The word is for a long time. The London office could not charter the ship," they answered.

I said, "Oh God! Not now! There goes my luck."

I went upstairs to see the Port Captain, and he confirmed it all.

He said, "Michael, this happens in our business. For now, they don' have another charter, and they don't' know how long it will take to get one. It seems that things are getting kind of slow now for these kinds of ships, and it may take a few months."

I asked, "What do you suggest, Captain? Should I wait or should I go to get something else? I don't want to waste my time waiting. I'd like to have my requirements for second mate before I join the Navy."

He said, "I agree with you. I have an AB job coming in a week on the *Thetis*, and I will send you there. You will have to fly to the West Coast of the U.S. to San Diego to join the ship. How does that sound to you?"

"Of course I will take it! I need the sea time, and the job is not bad," I said.

With that I was on my way to the *Thetis* on a long flight, from Athens to San Diego. By the way that was my first airplane flight. At Kennedy Airport in New York, I had to change planes. I had a three to four hour layover before I would catch the next flight. I had a chance to look around the airport. It was big and impressive. All of a sudden, I saw people running as well as photographers, reporters, and cameramen. I wondered what was going on, and from curiosity, I followed them to see. A tall, slender, beautiful girl was posing for pictures and giving interviews.

I asked, "Who she is?"

"Claudia Cardinale," someone said. She was big Italian movie star at the time.

There were and exciting new experiences wherever I went.

Thetis was another liberty and old by now. She was loading scrap iron for Japan. The loading was almost done by the time I got there, and in not even a day, we sailed. *Thetis* was a nice ship to work. When I say nice ship I mean she had a good crew, and the *Thetis* had a bunch of nice people from the Captain all the way down. The Captain was a man in his early thirties from my island. He was coming from a wealthy family, and I knew his father very well. He was educated in England, and he graduated from the Maritime Academy of South Hampton. There weren't many seamen from Ithaca on this ship, only the Captain, one or two in the engine room, and me.

Besides me, there were two more ABs, who were going for officers. Also, the Third Mate was without a license, and he was also studying for a mate's license like the three of us. All of us used to practice navigation together, like sun lines, stars, you name it. The Captain not only did not mind, but he also insisted on our practicing. With his extensive knowledge he was helping us when we had any questions. What a difference this was from the *S/S Kastor* as far as the bridge was concerned.

I had the eight to twelve watch at sea. In the evening, the Captain used to come to the bridge and talk with me about Ithaca. Being away from Ithaca since I was a young kid, he was enjoying my stories. These visits were going on religiously almost every night.

Tokyo was where we took the scrap iron for discharge. The port was busy, very busy almost all the time. We had to wait at least two weeks for our turn to discharge. So, they anchored us at the outside anchorage, and it was a fairly good ride with the launch to go ashore. It was only weekends when most of us got to go ashore. During the week we didn't have time, because we had to work during the day. It was kind of cold at the time and rainy because there was a frequent light rain. Actually, from the crew except for one or two, no one was going ashore from there. All of us were waiting for when we got close to the shore. As far as I was concerned, I was counting on getting my day off plus the weekend to have a good, three day get-away in Tokyo.

On my weekend off, a liner from *Markesinis Lines* happened to be there. It was a beautiful new ship with a high speed, and it was docked alongside not far from where the launch would drop us off. I heard that on board were two friends of mine from school who were there as cadets and the Chief Mate was a man that I knew very well from Ithaca. I went to visit them. These ships didn't stay long in port, maybe two or three days.

After a few hours on the ship, I said, "What are we doing? Are we going out?"

"Mike is right," the Chief said. "You two take off, and I will meet you later in the evening."

We had a ball going from one place to another for two days. The others were back before their ship sailed, and I spent one extra day on my own before I went back to the *Thetis*.

The next port of loading was the Philippines, specifically at Mindanao Island at the Port of Davao. The cargo was coconut shell for Amsterdam. It was hot, very hot in Davao. The nightlife was fair, and a little dangerous in that part of the Philippines. For us, daring and young, we didn't think much of this when going out for the girls. One of the girls, when we became friendlier, gave me a knife, which I still have today, just in case to protect myself.

We stayed more than a week, and after that we start the long trip to Amsterdam. With the speed the *Thetis* had, it was at least a forty daylong voyage.

The next big event was the Suez Canal. This was another place that I wanted to cross and see. Merchants trying to sell all kinds of souvenirs flooded the ship during the crossing. Also, they were buying everything you could sell, too, like ropes, chains, anything. Being in hot weather, we opened the portholes so that the cabin did not get too hot. We had no air conditioner, only a small fan.

As soon as we got to the Canal, the more experienced seamen told us, "When you're not in the cabin, close the port hole because locals will fish your things out through the port holes and steal them."

What they were saying was that the locals, with small boats, would come alongside the ship and climb the little masts of their boats. With a pole with a hook on the end, they would pull out everything that they could get, like blankets, sheets, whatever. Of course we locked our room even if we were in there and sleeping. In general, crossing the Canal was enjoyable.

A company owned before the *S/S Thetis* from Amsterdam. The Dutchmen had installed a diesel generator and air conditioner for all the cabins. The port captains and port engineers never used it because they thought that the expenses to run the diesel were high. Go Figure! In the meantime, the young owners were spending thousands and thousands of pounds at the nightclubs in England and all over the world. These fools were worrying about a few gallons of diesel.

Traditionally, Amsterdam was considered a seaman's heaven. Many seamen would use the place as a base port to stay for vacation and ship out from there, especially when shipping was slow. It was a port with heavy traffic. Amsterdam at the time was affordable for every pocket. The place for gathering for us was a club, which we used to call The Cow, where inside the club on the wall was hanging the big head of a cow. There was music, drinks, and dancing, and of course girls, too. Now with the last one you had to be careful, because one may think that he was dancing with a girl, and when he got to the room, he would find out it was a boy. The Cow had that problem. What the poor seamen went through! But, that was part of the overall diversity of the seaman's world.

The next port was Gdansk, Poland, to load cement for Cambodia. How lucky! In a short period at sea, I had a chance to go through the Panama Canal, the Suez Canal, and the Kiev Canal, which was another very nice place to see and go through. Here, because it was very narrow and the weather changed quickly, the pilot was coming on board with his own helmsmen, and that made it easier for us. In later years, many times I went through the Panama and Suez Canals, but I never had a chance to go again through the Kiev. I'm glad I had that chance at least once.

Poland was still under strict communist control. There were many formalities in order to go ashore and only for a limited time. I think midnight was the deadline. Prices were unrealistically inflated, and if we had to change our money on the regular exchange, it would not go very far. But, if we changed dollars or pounds in the black market, we would get many times more than at the regular exchange. Then everything became very affordable, actually cheap. That was what we did. So we hid a ten-dollar bill and went outside being very careful when we went through the gate. After that, we were okay, and we had plenty of money to spend. Whatever money was left over, we hid some place outside for the next time off. Although dealing with the authorities was rather difficult, the Polish people were kind of nice, and of course the nightlife was good. That went on for about two weeks. One good thing about the liberty ships was that they would take their time to get to the port, but they were not in a rush to leave either.

After Poland, for the long trip to Cambodia, we were scheduled to stop in Navarino, a small port in Greece to take stores and bunker. By this time, the rumors started coming out and especially from a couple of crewmembers from my island. If I remember well, one of them was a relative of one of the port captains. From a letter he got in Poland the news was not great from the company. In fact, it was bad. The company was in terrible financial shape, and it was expected any minute to go bankrupt. The young owners had blown it. After we left Poland, I asked the Captain about the rumors.

He said, "Michael, unfortunately, it looks like they are true."

I asked him, "What should I do? Should I get off or stay?"

He said, "I really don't know, but if I were you, I would most probably get off in Navarino. I know you want to do your sea time, but on the other hand you may get stuck in Cambodia or another lousy place. I have no choice I am the captain, and I have to stay. Get off and you may be able to get something quickly!"

Deep down, I didn't want to leave the ship. I liked it, but I had no choice. So I decided to get off at Navarino. Luckily, I was one of the few people that got paid, and that took me a few trips to the office and a lot of aggravation to get my last paycheck. Sure enough a few days later the company declared bankruptcy, and no one else got paid. Ships with crew got stuck all over the world, and quite a few of them had no supplies. Many of the crew suffered until they got back home. It was a shame to see a good company in that condition. Unfortunately, when I got off, things were slow, very slow. In situations like that, people chose to stay longer on the ships out of the fear that when they got off they wouldn't be able to find another ship easily. That made it more difficult to get a job.

Instead of staying in Piraeus, and looking for an AB job, I found a cadet job through a friend of mine with a small ship of 1,200 tons, which was sailing around the Eastern Mediterranean and Black Sea. The pay was less than half from what I was making on the *Thetis*, but I needed the sea time for my license. Here I was on the

Motor Vessel Pythagorion that belonged to a small family. It was owned and operated by a family, which came from the island of Samos. The navigation bridge was Spartan to say the least. A radio direction finder and magnetic compass were our modern technology. It was almost like sailing with Columbus. The watches were six hours on and six hours off between the Captain and the Chief Mate with one AB on each watch. The Chief Mate was one of the brothers that owned the company, and he was also a part owner. That made him the most powerful person on board. Most of the crew was from the same village that the owners were coming from. The Captain was a tall, slender, older gentleman from Crete in his middle sixties. He was in good health, but his eyesight was not so good. Of course as Captain, he did not expect to stay on watch again at this age.

As far as I was concerned, being an outsider and cadet, I was designated to do the dirtiest jobs. The Bosun and the other ABs were willing to let me have them. Of course, they were all buddies. I had one good thing going for me, and unfortunately not good for them. I knew how to navigate, and that saved me. I think the one who had the idea was the Chief Mate, who liked me.

He called me into his office and proceeded, "Michael, I have a deal for you. Here's the choice. Stay on as a cadet and do all the dirty jobs, or you will be a cadet, but stay on watch with the Captain to help him. I cannot give you a third mate's salary, but I will increase what you get now by fifty percent. You will not have anything to do with the deck. You will be treated as an officer. How does that sound to you?"

Without hesitation I said, "Yes!"

At that time we created a new position cadet/third mate. That was the end of the deck for me to the disappointment of the Bosun and the ABs who had to do the dirty jobs again.

For a small ship, it was colorful and had an active way of life, much different from the big ships. I kind of liked it, especially now that I was the Third Mate and independent. Both the Captain and the Chief Mate liked me. Of course I was a very big help to the Captain at sea and to the Chief Mate in port. The ports we were going to were

My Sea My Life

interesting, and the stay was not bad. For a small ship, we stayed a lot. *Pythagorion* also was not in a rush to leave the port. We went to some interesting ports, like Alexandria, Latakia, Tripoli, Ravenna, and Constanza.

Very soon I learned how to increase my income on a ship like that. In conversation with the Bosun and the ABs I always asked them how they could make it with these small salaries, and why they didn't look for a big ship.

Their answer was, "We're doing well here. You will see."

There was no further explanation. The trick was the extra trade. They would buy things from one port and sell them at another. After I got to know what the combination was, they were right, and I could do very well. So I started to observe what they were buying and where they were selling them and in general, how the whole operation was done. Of course they would not tell me. I had to discretely watch them to learn for myself. They did not want anyone to disturb their little business with competition. Tripoli, Lebanon was one of the best if not the best place to stock up with different items to sell. One of the biggest ports for selling things was Constanza. Of course, other ports in the Black Sea were big buyers, too.

Lebanon was called the Switzerland of the Middle East, and it was a thriving little country. You could do practically anything like buy things cheap and exchange money very easily (all kinds of money from all parts of the world) with no problems or formalities. A guy was coming onboard with a suitcase full of money and was exchanging anything you wanted. We were in Tripoli loading for Ravenna, Italy. Now I had to find what sold in Ravenna so I could sell, too. The Bronson cigarette lighters were the best ones that gave the biggest profits. How did I find this out? The Bosun, another AB, and I were out in Tripoli having coffee.

The Bosun said, "Michael, wait for us here, and we will be back in a few minutes. We have to do something."

I said, "Okay, I will be here taking my time."

I knew that they were going to buy something, so I let them go ahead. I followed them, and I saw where they went to buy the lighters. I returned to my place and waited for them.

They returned with little shopping bags full, and they said to me, "We're going to the ship, do you want to come back?"

"No, I'm enjoying it here so much, that I'm going to stay a little more," I answered.

So they left for the ship, and a few minutes later, I headed for the store. I played it cool so that the owner didn't think that I was ignorant.

I found out about the lighters, and I asked him, "Is it a good seller?"

He said, "Yes, I sell a lot of them, and Italy is the best place. How many do you want?"

So, I bought quite a few of them. They were desirable in many places, so I had nothing to loose. Just one clarification here, the trade that we were doing was nothing harmful to anyone, just good, nice merchandise that the other places did not have. It was all clean stuff.

Now here we were in Ravenna, where the Bosun and his buddies thought that they had a monopoly, and they were asking a very high price. The locals were kind of hesitant to pay this high price.

I approached one of them on deck, and said, "Are you looking for lighters?"

"Yes," he said, "but the price that the Bosun is asking is very high. I cannot afford it."

I said, "What do you want to pay?"

He said a price that was very good, and I was making a good profit. I asked him how many he wanted.

He said, "If you agree on this price, I'll buy all you have."

I said, "Wait here, and I'll bring them to you."

There went my lighters, and they were the first to be sold. All of them were sold. The Bosun sensed that something wasn't right. He was a smart cookie.

He approached me, and said, "Mike, did you happen to sell any lighters?"

I said, "Some."

"That's why these Italians don't ask us anymore," he said kind of unhappily. "You should have told us that you had lighters, too, and then we could have held the price."

"Bosun, I would have told you, but you did not want to include me. That's why you went alone with the other ABs to buy them. If you had included me, too, you would not have had any problems. Right?" I said.

He started laughing and said, "Alright, next time you're included, too. Now tell me the price you sold them for."

The Eastern Mediterranean for centuries had, and still has, her own flavor of trading. You would never agree to pay the price they first asked you to pay. You had to bargain, and sometime a lot, otherwise, you paid too much. Constanza was an old established port in Romania. Again here, like Poland, the Communist control was strong. Also here midnight was the deadline for going ashore. On arrival, the control would come on board to clear and search the ship. By that time my English was pretty good. Also, I had learned to speak a little Italian and that made me very useful to deal with the control. I was the one assigned to take the control around for checking, especially in the crew's quarters.

The crew would line up in front of their doors, and the control officer would come to check the room (the control had the authority to do a thorough search in the room). I would introduce the crewmember, and would say, "Mister, he also has some present for you."

Regardless of whatever everyone was giving, the control would ask each man if he had anything in his room that he was not supposed to have, and everyone would say, "No sir."

The officer would take the present, and walk off to the next room. We kept our merchandise in our rooms. Hopefully this would be the safest place, and it was. The rest of the ship was searched thoroughly. We got to know the officers that were doing the search, and also they were at the gate when we were going ashore most of the time. By the way, the gifts had to be reasonable to please the officer.

So the rooms were loaded with women's under garments, Chiclets, some cigarettes, nylon stockings, and many other thing, nothing that was considered harmful to anybody. Most of the things were simple everyday stuff for the rest of the world, but in Romania, they were great luxuries at the time. Some of the things we would sell right on the ship and some of them outside. Of course, the officer at the gate had to be from the ones we knew and he had to get a generous gift, too, as we passed without a search.

Wintertime in Constanza weather-wise was brutal. The Black Sea in general could be very, very nasty, and it was most of the time during the winter. There was snow, ice, and cold, you name it. God only knows how many anchors had been lost at the Constanza anchorage. We were not an exception. We lost both of our anchors. So instead of cruising outside, like some other ships were doing, we entered the harbor and forced them in a way to put us along side another ship until it was our turn for discharge. Of course, we had to buy new anchors and a certain length of chain that we had lost.

It took us almost thirty days between the waiting and the discharging time to finish the cargo. They usually worked twenty-four hour day shifts regardless of the weather conditions of cold, rain, and snow. They would come to work even if they couldn't do a thing. If they didn't come, then they didn't get paid. That was the rule, and they needed the money badly. So, they wore extra heavy clothes, and they would stay out on deck. During the discharge, we met quite a few people who presented themselves as stevedores. Also they were willing to buy anything we sold. When we had a question or a problem, they always referred us to the same person, a bright young man in his early thirties that usually took care of what we asked him. I got to know him well. He was a very good guy, and he tried to help us in any way he could. I knew that he was married, so the Chief Mate and I thought to give him a few presents for his wife mostly. He was very happy and appreciative when I told him and showed him the presents.

Then he told me, "I can't have them."

I said, "Why?"

"I have no way to take them home. I cannot get them through

the gate," he said.

I said, "All the other stevedores buy tons of them, and you're telling me you can't get a couple of things for your home?"

"Please, I will tell you something, and don't mention this to anyone because I will be in great trouble. All these supposed stevedores are not really stevedores. They have the extra privilege because they are members of the party. Nobody bothers them going in and out through the gate. They are the power. I get checked just like you do when you are going in and out of the terminal," he said.

"Not me. I go in and out without a problem. I'm going to tell you how we're going to do this. I will meet you outside at whatever place you feel comfortable, and I'll bring these things there," I said.

He said, "I will tell you where I live, and if you want you can bring them to my home and have dinner with us. My wife and I would like that. Are you sure that it is not dangerous for you to take them out of the gate."

I said, "Don't worry. It's not a problem."

The Eastern Mediterranean weather-wise could be just as brutal as a big ocean and certain spots were very dangerous. Many ships got into trouble, and one place was the Andriatica. When the north wind was blowing, there was nowhere to hide. I didn't wish anyone to get caught there with a small ship like the *Pythagorion*. I went through there, and I was happy to be alive. That happened on the way to Ravenna. It was wintertime, and the storm got us right after we passed Bari, the Southern part of Italy. On the Italian coast there were not many places to hide and wait for the weather to pass. In contrast, the Yugoslavian side had many places to go and get behind small ports or small bays to drop the anchor and wait for the storm to pass. That was not an uncommon practice for small ships.

As the night progressed, the weather was getting worse and worse. The catavatic wind was blowing from the North, coming down the big mountains and the Andriatica acted like a funnel. It was a night I could not forget. Many of us thought that it was the end. The poor *Pythagorion* would not make it. Slowly, we started drifting the ship towards the Yugoslavian coast, and we hoped soon to find a place to hide until the storm subsided. With daylight we were close to the coast, and we found a small bay. We went inside as close as we could, to hide from the sea and the wind. Then we dropped the anchor. We stayed here and waited for at least three to four days for the weather to clear. In the meantime, we could not communicate with the main office, and they were seriously worried that we were gone. They were ready to declare us lost. As soon as the weather cleared we took off for Ravenna, which wasn't very far. We also established communication again with the main office. They were happy and relieved to hear from us.

My brother had not heard from me for a while, and on the way home, he stopped by the office to ask where we were.

Captain Dimitris, who I think was the older of the brothers who owned the company, greeted him, and he said, "Everything is all right now John. Everything is all right now. We found them, and they're okay!"

Of course my brother had no idea what he was talking about. He had just stopped to ask where we were.

He asked, "Why? Was there any problem?"

Captain Dimitri said, "They got caught in the storm in Andriatica, and we lost them for three to four days. But, don't worry. They are okay. They are in Ravenna."

That was all that my brother wanted to hear, and he said to himself, "When this ship comes to Piraeus, I will take him off of that vessel before he kills himself."

In the meantime, I started thinking that it wouldn't be a bad idea to join the Navy and finish my military obligation; since the extension that I had was almost at the end. When we got back to Piraeus for stores, I was getting off. My brother was there to take me off, too. He didn't have to because I was signing off anyway. So April 1963, I joined the Navy.

TRITON - AN OFFICER

After 24 of my 30 months time in the Greek Navy as a Petty Officer, I received regular salary for the last six months. At the time, they had plenty of young recruits to relieve us, and things were fairly quiet, so they let me go three months ahead. That way they saved a certain amount of salary and benefits.

I had fantastic news. I would be leaving three months early. I was ready to make some good money, with the promise to finish the house for my sisters' dowries. I would also see the world as an officer. A month before leaving the Navy I started looking for a ship.

Vacation would have to come later. Now was the time to go. The sea was waiting for me. Captain Mike was on the move. I didn't have to look far. Shipping was good. As soon as I told Mr. Matarangas that in about 90 days I would be done with the Navy, he said, "You have a job as soon as you are clear. Come back in two weeks when you know for sure the day you are going to be released so we can start the paper work."

My commander had to sign my release. Then I needed to take the paper to the main office, for signature by the Captain of the division, and I was on my own after that. I got kind of wary when the secretary told me, "Come in. The Captain wants to see you."

When he saw me, he said: "It is you. Even you are not leaving from my command with ratings of excellent, excellent. You are without one day of punishment! This is impossible. No one leaves from me without at least one day of punishment, and you are here for two years. Well, there is nothing I can do now. Good luck. You were an excellent petty officer, and we'll miss you."

I thanked him, saluted him, and left. Free!

Mr. Matarangas was good at his word. Not more than one day after I left the Navy I had a job as a second officer on the *S/S Triton*, which was coming to La Spezia, Italy for dry dock. Ten crewmembers were going this time, and I was in charge of the group. As usual all the preparations were done through Mr. Matarangas's Agency, and that was for all nine members, and for me.

Mr. Alkimos Gratsos, one of the owners, asked to see me. His office was in Athens. So the next day, I was at his office as he requested. He wished me a good trip and said how happy he was that I was back again working for his company as an officer. He gave me some papers for the Captain, and the letter for my salary.

I asked, "Mr. Alkimos, excuse me. What are the salary arrangements?"

He answered, "Don't worry. You will be very happy."

By nature I was worried, but what could I say! Mr. Alkimos was a gentleman, and I took his word. Still I couldn't wait for the time to get off the elevator. I turned down the first street after leaving Mr. Alkimos's office, and I stopped to check the papers about my salary.

My eyes popped wide open! My basic salary was 100 pounds plus overtime. It was almost like a chief officer's salary. After all, the house at Agia Barbara would be built very quickly. That was the dowry for my sisters. People must have thought I was some kind of a nut, laughing, joking, and talking to myself.

The trip to Italy was all right. The group of people that I had with me almost all knew each other. We were all excited to be going to work and, most of all me. My first ship as an officer! It felt strange to be called Captain Mike, but I was, and I had worked very hard for that.

La Spezia at the time was a smaller port, not as busy as Genoa or Livorno or Naples on the West Coast of Italy. At the dry dock, the ship was not far from the town and within easy walking distance.

This was a rare treat. Today's terminals are away from everything and without transportation leaving the seaman; with what little time he had, at the mercy of unreasonable cabdrivers, who often would take advantage of the poor seamen.

Italian and Greek foods have many similarities and after work we enjoyed going out for a meal with wine or for a coffee with wonderful pastries just like home. People at La Spezia were friendly. It had the easygoing feeling of a smaller town.

Besides supervising and checking repairs around the vessel, I was busy with chart work, mostly correcting. There was no reason to worry about modern equipment. Poor *Triton* had the bare minimum: It had a magnetic compass, gyrocompass, RDF, and a course recorder. Most of the time the course recorder would not work. There was a support base for the radar, but it never came. *Triton* was slightly more advanced than Columbus's ship, but not by much.

During the repair, I became friends with the foreman who was supervising the repairs for the yard. We talked about everything from soccer to politics and family. I forgot to mention so far about one of my specialties. After they got to know me, people confessed to me very easily, and I mean very easily, about all their worries, problems, pain, everything. I guessed that instead of a seaman I should have been a psychologist or a priest. This confessor business would follow me the rest of my career while sailing on a ship and especially with extended periods of time at sea. Certainly all of us have the need to talk to someone one way or another for many reasons. This need became even more visible in the confined society of a ship with long trips, small places, plenty of time on our hands, limited entertainment and little communication with the other world: family news, etc.

Today this is a little different. Communications are much more advanced. A telephone call to any part of the world and from any part of the world is easy, a little expensive, but easy. In those days, a letter was the main communication with family and friends.

One of my great pleasures was the delivery of the mail. After the arrival in port and as soon as we cleared the port authorities, I would grab the mail for the crew from the ship's agent, and off I went to the crew's mess for delivery. Everyone was up waiting either in his room or in the crew's mess, especially the married seamen. These were the sweet letters from home, the great companion, and the moral boost until the next port of call where new letters would arrive.

Most of the married seamen would receive more than one letter, actually several at the time. It was as if the family was keeping a detailed log for the loved one so he could be up to date. The details of the letters were unreal. They included every little event about the family and relatives plus what was going on in the island in general. It was like you were getting a well-published newspaper with all the news about the family plus an excellent column of gossip. The seamen did not need any other magazines to read. They were well covered for news. After all, on their return, they should be well prepared on everything that went on while they were at sea. Like they say, well informed. Poor Ulysses, how did he survive! No wonder he was unprepared when he arrived in Ithaca. He did not have a single letter in all those years of being away.

Now don't think that from the ship's side that the letters did not have details. Yes, of course, they were just as detailed: a bad storm, a good or bad port, and all the daily activities. Everything was documented on paper except one subject, the nightlife. There was an unwritten code of honor: don't talk about it. After every individual had read their letters alone for several times, it was time to compare and exchange news in the mess hall or gathered in some person's cabin.

On the island, the activities of exchanging news were just as vigorous. Families visited each other and compared and discussed news from the ship. Sorry, I wasn't much for details. I would write only the basic stuff, but of course I wasn't married at the time. For me, the fact that I was okay and in good health was enough for my family to know. I did not want them to worry about a storm, which we would have passed two months ago. When my family asked me

My Sea My Life

why I didn't write details like the others, my explanation was that I kept the stories to tell on my return. It would not be interesting if they knew everything in advance. They were laughing and telling me that they already knew.

Those moments were dear memories to me, and I remembered them with great feeling and respect for the married seamen and their families. I admired the way they went to devise ways to cope with the long separations and how they tried to fill the big vacuum of their long separation from their loved ones and somehow to smooth and fill the two years or more of not seeing each other. It was not easy, not easy at all. But that was a way of life. That's why during all my years at sea I considered the delivery of the letters as a first priority. I understood their tremendous importance from day one.

As I remember from my two years on the *Triton* there was a lighter side of life at sea. On today's ships, almost everyone has his own little refrigerator to go along with all the other modern conveniences. In the days of the *S/S Triton* we had one refrigerator in the officer's mess and one in the crew's mess. The steward would leave some leftovers and if the seaman was lucky a few cold cuts mostly for the men on watch. This so-called night lunch was a common practice, and it would be placed at the lower section of the refrigerator. The upper shelves were left available for anyone who wanted to save something for later, cake, fruit, part of their supper, etc. Everyone knew what belonged to whom, and we never had a problem with something missing.

All of a sudden, things started disappearing out of the refrigerator, and mostly after nine P.M. until midnight. The crew was getting upset. In discussing the situation with the Chief Mate, we were both trying to find some solution to stop this nonsense. It was in vain, because we could not come up with a solution. In one of our conversations that took place usually in his office, besides all the other stuff missing, the Chief Mate mentioned that someone lost a bar of chocolate.

That gave me an idea. The Chief Mate at the beginning was hesitant, and he thought that it was also unorthodox. He was laughing at the idea, but he was still hesitant. Finally I persuaded him to go along with it. The plan was simple. Exlax unwrapped out of the paper looked like chocolate. So carefully I unwrapped two or three pieces and placed them in Hershey chocolate bar wrappings. After we finished, it looked like a chocolate Hershey Bar. There it went into the refrigerator of the crew's mess. There was the bait. Where was the mouse? Sure enough the mouse showed up in the Chief Mate's room about 11 P.M. after the mouse had gone to the bathroom several times thinking that he was poisoned. (By the way the mouse was a young fireman in his mid twenties and a little naïve. He was big and tall, and he thought he was cute by stealing other people's night lunch.)

The Chief Mate, before he even attended to the young man's needs, ran to my room screaming, "We got him! We got him! It worked."

Needless to say the young man confessed the whole thing, and he promised to never to do it again, and he kept his word. The Exlax made a man out of the boy!

Life on the ships was not jail by far. Nevertheless, we became no part of any society. We were cut off from many little things the average person took for granted in the outside society. At home we'd go have a drink, see a movie, watch TV, see our family and friends, pick up a newspaper, read the news, make a telephone call, etc.

On the ship, we had our watch, which was 4-8, 8-12, or 12-4. When we finished our watch, we ate, went to bed, and maybe enjoyed a book. We might stay in the mess room for a while, socializing with other shipmates, playing cards, or talking.

Here comes good old Mike with my nature, my personality, or whatever. I had the privilege to listen and comfort many fellow seamen and some others through the years. I mean everyone from captains to the ordinary seamen. Without arranging or realizing what was happening, I accepted that privilege and tried always to offer my honest advice and comfort with a good word, which was appropriate to the situation. As an unwritten rule, after we finished talking, whatever had been said was dead with no gossiping. With all the above, nothing was formal. Still today, I try to understand what people see in me and, without knowing me from Adam, open their hearts and trust me with their most private problems. I thank God that I feel happy to comfort people when it is needed the most.

It did feel strange when, one day before we completed repairs and would leave La Spezia, the Italian Foreman asked, "Are you going home?"

I replied, "I am on the ship, and I am going with the ship."

He could have lost his job for what he said next. "Every day that I come to work on this ship I am scared that we'll sink inside the yard! I would be much, much more afraid to go on a trip. That is why I am telling you to go home. This is not a strong ship. I have worked for years in this dry-dock, and I know. Please go home. Find another ship."

I calmed him down as much as I could, and of course, I stayed on the ship. My friend was not far from the truth. I was young, and I had not yet developed a fear of the sea. Respect, yes! Fear, not yet! That was 37 years ago, and I stayed on this ship for almost two years more. I may miss some stories, but there are so many to hopefully satisfy even the most demanding reader.

After La Spezia, we went to Genoa to load for the U.S. We stayed there about 7 to 8 days. That was the beauty of a ship like the *Triton* any time we were going to a port we stayed for a few days. I would like to tell about another aspect of a seaman life at the time in different countries and different ports. People were always trying to take advantage of the poor, hungry animal called a seaman, who was looking for a few moments of love in strange places.

The bars in the Red Light District of Genoa were full of music, girls and fun places, but also a seaman could be taken for an expensive ride if he did not know the procedures. For example, the girls in the bars were in two categories. There were the ones who worked there regularly and maybe would go with us late at night after we spent money on them dearly. The others were there to dance and to use drinks they called, if I remember well, "consummation". These girls only danced and drank. The truth was they drank tea or plain colored water, but we paid for these drinks as liquor without knowing it for the privilege of dancing and having their company, of course. They drank like sponges, and pushed for us to drink, also. They split the money from the drinks they ordered with the bar. We think that we had a beautiful girl for the night, and we tried to please her, only to find out later, and after quite a few drinks, that she was leaving.

The seaman said, "Aren't we going together?"

"No Sir. I am going home. I have a family, and I am only here for drinks."

She was gone. If men got upset or tried to make a scene, the bouncer would throw them out. The seaman was at fault because technically the girls did nothing wrong. It was his mistake that he did not ask what was what from the beginning. But, of course he did not know how they operated in this port. As typical seamen, we thought that we were going to charm the girl so she would come with us. Fat chance!

Try to reason with a seaman confined at sea for quite a few days. By the time the girl left, the seaman was too drunk anyway. That was the idea as far as the bar was concerned.

Speaking a different language was a great advantage. As a seaman, it was a tremendous help in many ways. I was able to speak enough Italian to have a decent conversation when talking to different people, especially the longshoremen. I learned most of the ways to get around in new places without being taken advantage of too much. For example, I learned that if I went to the bar to enjoy myself at a show, I ordered a drink, and when the girl came, I would ask her to stay with me. I would tell her when she orders a drink that I would test it. She most probably would not stay. If she did stay, which I doubt very much, it was because she liked me, and I would have hit the jackpot. This was very rare in these places.

If I wanted a girl, I'd go to the street and I'd pick her up. We'd make the arrangement there and never up in the room. Still I was not completely sure if I was being taken or not. Listen to this story. I was out with my friend, the radio operator, and we were looking for girls. One of us was going with the girl, and the other was staying on the street as a sort of backup if something went wrong. He picked up one girl, and I was keeping watch. A short time later, he came down.

I said, "Already?"

He said: "Yes, no problem," without elaborating.

Later I found a pleasant girl who told me "yes" to death, and off we went. When we went to the room, she lay on the bed, and raised her skirt just enough, (I mean just enough) and said, "Are you ready?"

I was still dressed and asked, "Why? Are you not going to undress?"

She said, "Oh, no. If we do that, it will be a lot of money."

For every piece of clothing she would take off, it was a different price. I did not agree, but I pretended that it was okay, and that we should have as much fun as we could. Money was not an issue so far. I didn't pay anything, and that was her mistake. She should have taken the money as soon as we got to the room. She learned this time.

I told her before we started, "I have to go to the john very badly. Where is it?"

Without suspecting anything she said, "Down the hall."

I got out, closed the door, and ran for the street. When the Radio Operator saw me almost running, he said, "What is going on?"

I said, "Keep moving quickly."

We disappeared down the street, and she is still waiting. I had beaten the system this time. I was not taken. Probably my friend had to pay for real, and he could not complain either. Of course, we never passed this section of town again as long as we stayed in Genoa.

The next cargo load was from New Orleans. It was corn for Ravenna, Italy. We did not stay very long in New Orleans. When we went to the silos to load, it didn't take long. It took anywhere from 24 to 36 hours, and we were out again. But don't worry, for New Orleans, there are plenty of stories later on. New Orleans is a fascinating city to say the least.

Crossing the Atlantic any time of the year, we were bound to go through some stormy weather. In winter, it was unusual to go across without a storm, maybe several storms, especially when we had a vessel that made a maximum speed of 11 knots. The route to Gibraltar, after we passed the Florida Strait and the Bahamas, was to run a line with the idea to keep south as much as we could to avoid the heavy storms north of us. We were about one or two days south of the Azores, and we experienced heavy swells and wind from the port quarter. The ship was rolling moderate to heavy. I had the supper relief for the Chief Mate. The Chief Mate always had the 4 to 8 in the morning and the 4 to 8 in the afternoon. The Second Mate (that was me) had the 12 to 4 in the morning and the 12 to 4 in the afternoon. The Third Mate had the 8 to 12 in mornings and 8 to 12 in the evenings.

The Third Mate and I were taking turns to relieve the Chief Mate from 5 to 5:30 in the evening, so he could eat. That day I had the supper relief. It was a little before 5:00 that I relieved him. It was about 10 to 15 minutes later that the ship experienced a heavy roll. All of a sudden, we heard a heavy metallic sound like a heavy piece of iron falling from a high distance.

A chill went through my body, and I knew at once that something was wrong. I got a heavy-duty flashlight and went outside on the wing of the bridge to start checking around.

In the meantime, the Captain, worried, came on the bridge and asked me, "Do you see anything?"

I said, "Not yet. (I was on the port side at the time), but it did not sound good."

He said, "I know."

As soon as I went on the starboard side and looked on deck in front of the accommodation, I saw a crack that ran through the deck and stopped next to the hatch because it hit a vent. I could see the freshly cracked steel. It was definitely not a good picture. I told the Captain, and we both called the Chief Mate, Chief Engineer, the Bosun and some ABs to come out there to assess the damage. In the meantime, we changed course as much as possible to avoid having the seas run on deck. The Chief Mate and the Chief Engineer came on the bridge after awhile to report the damage to the Captain. There was a crack on deck about nine feet long crossways from the side toward the hatch, and stopped when it reached a vent. The vent was round and stopped the crack.

Naturally, when seas washed over the deck, water ran inside the hold. As far as they could see, that was the only crack, thank God. If the crack was going down the side, we probably would not have been able to tell at that time. Immediately the Captain sent a message to the company informing them of the situation and requesting further instructions.

There was no question. We had to go to the nearest port to assess the damage and do some repairs. The closest place was the Azores. Regardless of what the company said, our course was now for the Azores. In the meantime, we had to try to build a box to cover the crack with fast setting cement. It was to be in vain. Every time we tried to build something, a wave would take it away. This went on all night. I never left the bridge until 4:00 A.M. When I went to my cabin, I laid down to rest, but I could not sleep. The next day the message came from the company. "Proceed as you are going to Ponta Delgada at Sao Miguel in the Azores for evaluation and repairs."

During the night I talked with my ABs, but I was preoccupied with the deck and other people coming and going. When I went for the noon to 4 watch and started talking with my AB, he looked pale and his speech was very strange.

I said: "What is wrong with you?" Why are you talking like that?"

He said, "Mate, I have no teeth. What happened is that my mouthpiece is broken."?

The man got so upset and tense the night before that he broke his mouthpiece in two. By the way, he did not go to his room, and all night he stayed in the mess hall. This didn't work very well. I tried to calm him down. The other AB was in much better shape, but he was still shaken. I reasoned with him a little better. The trip to Ponta Delgada seemed as if it would never end. Without trying to upset the R/O (Radio Operator), I told him that it might not be a bad idea to know what ships were around, and to try to keep in touch with them, just to have an idea that we were not alone.

The arrival in Ponta Delgada was a relief for all of us. Port Engineers, ABS and the local yard engineers came on board to inspect the damage, and had devices to look under the hull. The only thing they found was that crack. The repair was to be a patch of heavy-duty plate welded so that it was about 4 feet from each side of the crack. We stayed 2 days more to do the repairs, and off we went again for Ravenna.

For the North Atlantic, and winter, the weather wasn't too severe. Actually, the rest of the trip until Adriatica was uneventful. That calmed most of us down. I knew both of my ABs were leaving in Ravenna. Of course, one of them had no teeth. He had to go fix a new mouthpiece, and the other AB did not want to stay. Entering The Adriatic Sea was strangely calm and warm for that time of year. When we passed Ancona, there it was... Fog.

We could not see our noses. We had no radar, and we could not see any lighthouses. We tried to use the RDF. There were not many radio beacons either. Therefore, it was Dead Reckoning, and "guess the speed." We were going slowly and blowing the whistle (fog signal). Ravenna had a foghorn and a sea buoy. That was what we were looking for. When we heard the foghorn with the characteristics of Ravenna, we stopped and sent a message to the Port Authority and waited for the Pilot.

The next day we received a message from the Agent, asking

My Sea My Life

where we were. We answered where we were. He said okay, and that he was coming to meet us. Four hours later a boat came alongside with the Pilot and the Agent.

The Captain asked, "What took so long?"

They replied, "Well, you were not at the Ravenna sea buoy, but at Garivaldi!"

"But what about the sea horn?"

"Well, Ravenna was not working and Garivaldi had the same signal 40 miles north of Ravenna."

In later years with all of the modern electronics available for navigation (Global Positioning System, Radars, etc.) seeing the new mates complain on the bridge, I was laughing inside. If they had only experienced the good old days of an ancient bridge, as compared to all the wonders of the modern ships.

The good old liberty ship did all right. We docked close to the turn on the river terminal. I was familiar with the place from being there a few years back with the *M/V Pythagorion*, the small coaster. I was as cadet/third mate, a made-up term under the circumstances, that explained a convenient arrangement between the owners and me at the time.

All sorts of people came on board the *Triton* after we docked: the Agent, the custom inspectors, ABS surveyors, company port engineers, and representatives from cargo. These people were to clear the ship and evaluate cargo damage and the condition and seaworthiness of the *Triton*. At last, the cargo damage report showed only damage on the number three hatches.

For two days the inspections and paper shuffling were vigorous. Inspection of the number three hatches and where the cut was on deck showed that seawater had seeped in. By this time, the corn had started to ferment and smell.

As for the good old *Triton*, there wasn't any need for further repairs. *Triton* miraculously passed the physical with flying colors. She was found to be seaworthy and strong as a bull. The discharge of cargo started, and it was slow, especially on the #3 hold, where the rotten corn was. It was estimated that it would take 20 to 25 days to discharge and clean the holds. Anyway, this was a good break for us, and we could have a good time after the very eventful passage.

Soon I found that Ravenna had not changed at all from the days that I was going there with the *Pythagorion*. There was no Red Light District, no bars with girls. We still had to go the underground way to find a girl. Believe it or not, the most visible were homosexuals, and then the girls. Their easiest prey was the seaman. I guess we were the hungriest ones and did not know the ropes. I reached deep into my memory database again from the days of *Pythagorion*. The Bosun knew of a lady in her 50's. At that time she would connect us with a girl in her apartment for a reasonable fee, of course. As a side benefit one of us would have sex with the old, fat chick. We would consider that as a form of extortion rather than a form of accommodation for both parties.

So Nick, the Radio Officer, and I set off to retrace the route and find her apartment. We hoped she would trust me and accommodate us since I was going to mention the name of the *Pythagorion*'s boss, whom she knew very well.

After a little time we found the building, and I went to visit the apartment with the hope that she would remember. The anticipation was building as we approached the apartment. I rang the bell and waited. The door opened and a lady with a couple of kids behind her opened the door. A bad feeling came over me as I saw her. She wasn't what I wanted. By the way, I was the only one who spoke some Italian – not perfect, but more than enough to get by.

I politely asked, "Is Mrs. Gabriella here?"

She was not surprised at all, but rather annoyed, and she said, " What? Again, another one is looking for Gabriella. I am sorry, but she left here a year ago. She had to go back to her hometown because she was getting sick and needed to be close to her family. Sorry."

We left disappointed, of course. Our best and safest source was gone. It was back to the cappuccino.

My Sea My Life

During the discharge of cargo we would get to know the stevedores and, in my case, speaking a little Italian made it easier. Besides other topics, a seaman always came to the main one: "Where do you go to have a good time in an unknown place?" The more inside information we had the better especially in locations like Ravenna, which was not a big port like Genoa and Naples.

Larger ports were more cosmopolitan, and it was easier to know where we belonged as seamen. Having a car was very important. We picked the girl with the car, and she drove us to a safe place to do what we were going to do. We drove back, left the girl, and we were done. There were no police, no hassles, and no records for the girl. Was this easy? Yes. Nevertheless, we needed a car.

My friend, the stevedore, said that one-hour from here at Forli, it was easier. Truly, it was easier, but we had to have a car. At the square in the town, there were a few nice coffee shops. We sat there, enjoyed our coffee and pastry, and killed some time. Italians and Greeks were talkative, friendly people, and we were no exception. Soon we started socializing with the people. Our instincts told us who was who.

This one man, who was well dressed, polite and friendly, was more than a social talker. We sensed that he was looking for prey. His feminine way indicated to us that he was more interested in men than women. By the way, he had a nice car, and he offered to show us Ravenna. A thought came to my mind: We'd pretend to go along with his plan and had him take us to Forli as well. Then, who knew, since he was so nice to pick us up, we would be nice to him. Nick was excited with the idea. Nick and I talked with our friend, and agreed to no specifics. We let him know that our friendship might improve. He thought he had a sure thing. All three of us set out for Forli on Saturday morning. This way we had a full day.

By nature, and being a little older than Nick, I was more defensive, so I stayed in the back of the car. Being polite and not leaving our friend alone, Nick stayed in front with him. He did not think this was a big deal and enjoyed a better view. After a while of driving and talking with our friend, he was explaining different things as we drove along. We must have been half way to Forli when Nick turned on me and started cursing me in Greek. He was complaining that I had tricked him, and put him in front where that the guy was trying to feel him.

In my calm way, I explained," Nick, you should not get so upset. We are almost there, and you need to be a little diplomatic!"

His answer was, "I will kill you when we get back!"

Poor Nick. He did not realize at the time that I had thought of the plan and would fix it as best as I could. Of course, by the time we got back, everything would be forgotten, and we would laugh and joke about it. By the time we got to Forli, it was a little after noon. Our friend suggested we go to eat pizza in a small place that still cooked the old fashioned way in a brick oven. It really was delicious and different. Since then I have eaten pizza in many different places, actually, some very good ones, but still that place was hard to beat.

After our lunch we were ready for hunting. We decided, before starting to cruise for girls, since we were in Forli, it would be fair to take a little time to look around. We took a tour of Forli. It was a nice place, but now it was time for the main event.

So, we drove to the section of the city where we could meet and greet the girls. The first one that approached was reluctant to come in the car with three men. Basically that was the problem with all the girls that we talked to. What they wanted was one person in the car at the time. Finally, after all this, we gave up. We were so close and yet so far. Of course, our obligation with our friend was null. It was never going to materialize anyway.

We started the trip back in almost complete silence, and the poor guy looking at our faces, he knew not to suggest anything, and this was the end of a good time in Ravenna. It would be the coffee shop from now on.

The whole story might sound a little bizarre to the person not familiar with the seaman's world because it was a different world at sea. That was why one can never judge a seaman the first week after he returned from the ship, until he has re-established himself back into the real world. From the beginning of my seafaring career, I realized that I would be two Mikes, one on the ship and one outside. So, when I got off any ship, I left seaman Mike at the gangway, and took the other Mike with me on shore. I was lucky because not too many seamen could separate the two worlds.

Until now I had experienced life at sea only with fellow seamen from Greece. I knew quite a few from my island. Almost all of them were good family people, and we were working as seamen because the pay far exceeded the salaries paid outside if we could find jobs at all. The primary reasons for going to sea were the benefits and especially the money to better our families and ourselves. It was rewarding, but of course, the price we paid was dear. Later, as we stayed at sea, this life grew on us. It became like alcohol in our bodies and flooded our veins, and it would never leave us. By then, we were seamen for life, even if we were able to stay ashore. Still it stayed with a person. In later years I sailed with seamen from all over the world. In general, we were all in the same bucket, but in a sense, from different directions. Some of us came to work and went home. Most seamen did not have a place they called home. The ship was their escape and the place where they felt most at home. I guess they never learned to separate the two, and going home felt out of place. I will elaborate more in further chapters.

The Ravenna stay was almost over. Replacements for the people who were leaving were on the way, and there were quite a few leaving after the incident in the Atlantic. I really didn't blame them. My two sailors on my watch, who were mature, middle aged seamen, good people, and good family men, begged me to leave. They felt that I was too young to stay with that wreck. In spite of my conservative personality, and history of always calculating everything frugally since I was a young kid, I still made the crazy decision to stay with the ship regardless of their warnings. When it came to danger, I guess I didn't worry much, or it attracted me.

My wife used to say and still says, "When there is a dangerous place like war or something, Michael will manage to be there."

Well, thank God, I finished all right, and I must admit that I sailed some beauties as far as seaworthiness was concerned. Some were "good for razor blades" as they say in the seaman's language when a ship was too old.

The journey with the *S/S Triton* continued, this time for Norfolk, Virginia to load coal for Brazil, Rio de Janeiro to be exact. The trip to Norfolk from Ravenna was a typical winter Atlantic crossing, especially with an empty liberty ship. One word described it, "Miserable."

Most of the clean up was done in Ravenna. We knew that at sea we would not be able to do anything this time of year. Still, some cleaning of the hold was needed, and we took provisions for six months. Therefore, in other ports we only needed to take fresh produce. We spent only 3 days in Norfolk, and mostly at anchor. When we went alongside we finished loading in hours. In no time, we were on our way to Rio.

Rio de Janeiro – what a wonderful place! Like any other Brazilian port at that time, it was a seaman's heaven. It was a place where a sailor could clean all the salt from his body and soul. Like the Calypso Island, he could drift for a while to a different world with good food, good drinks, a lot of music and the companionship of a beautiful lady. That was until the ship was ready to sail, and it was like waking up from a beautiful dream.

Nick, the Radio Operator, had a very busy and difficult task this time, not with ship business because that was cut and dry. He just needed to report the position and get some ship's messages, which were not many. After all, we were carrying a full load of coal. What was the big deal? He was busy finding out from other ships about where we were going and getting as much information as he could about Rio.

I had to give him credit for that. By the time we arrived in Rio, we knew more than enough about the port. Now we had to put the news to good use. The anchor was not even fetched up, and the pilot was still on board. A boat full of girls arrived alongside, and they were ready to board before we were even boarded and cleared by Customs and Immigration.

The Captain almost had a heart attack and was screaming, "Don't let them come on board! Turn them away."

The authorities finally cleared the ship, and the poor girls went away, but not before informing the Captain that he should stay on the ship because he wasn't safe outside.

The Ship Chandler was Greek, and he also had a young assistant, 30 years old or so, an ex-seaman. During coffee the Captain was talking about the girls. The Ship Chandler was laughing hard and informed him that this was normal. There were no implications from the authorities if the girls came on board. The girls were right, because he was now on the black list. The Captain wasn't really worried much about that because it was very rare that he would go out. He was in his middle sixties and by now had become the watchdog of the ship. The nice thing about *Triton* was that the ship was not in a rush to do anything, like go alongside, discharge cargo, or even go fast at sea. It was nice for us. We waited one week at anchor for another ship to finish discharging so we could go alongside. Then it took two to three weeks for us to discharge. We had plenty of time. During the anchor time, we had launch service at 6 P.M., 10 P.M., and midnight.

We only had to request to go ashore at daytime, and the Captain would pay. We liked to do that. Going ashore from the anchor was a luxury. For him, three launches a day were more than enough. In a way, he had some merit in his thoughts. Staying that long in a port like Rio, we had to pace ourselves. Otherwise, we would be broke before we knew it. I don't think this was his reason for limiting the launches. He was probably trying to save the company money.

Throughout my time at sea, I always disliked the launch with a passion for many reasons. Being at anchor and having to use a launch service limited our freedom to come and go anytime we wanted. Altogether, this was never my style. Don't forget the drunks, especially the one on the last launch. It was for good reason that we called the last launch the "animal launch." Seamen tended to do strange things when they drank, more than ordinary (not that they knew exactly what "ordinary" was) and they behaved like pigs.

My buddy, Nick, the Radio Officer, and I decided to take it easy while we were at anchor. There would be plenty of time alongside, so we limited the shore leave to every other day from 6 P.M. to 10 P.M., avoiding the animal launch. Our budgets were low.

Eighty to ninety percent of my salary was going to Greece for finishing the duplex for the dowries for my sisters to marry. My father did his trick a long time ago, and he was now an old man. The burden for these dowries was now on my brother and me. It was time to do our share and pay the price. But, that was the way it was. I had no complaints. The fact was that Mike was almost broke, so I had to create some side business for my floating account, like selling some cartons of cigarettes, some liquor, a few Levis, etc. These activities were nothing bad at all, but they provided some extra money for me. Nick, also being on his first ship, had some school expenses and family obligations to cover. We were in similar situations.

After checking a few places, we ended up as regulars at Subway. I really don't know if that was the real name of the nightclub or if the name came to us because it was in the basement level and, going down, it looked like a New York subway. Regardless, it was a nice place.

Let us talk about Rio of the mid-60s. You could not be in Rio without visiting the Copacabana; one of the most beautiful resort beaches in the world and, west of that, Ipanema was still building up. There was tropical scenery with hills. There was Botafogo, with the casino on top of the hill, and the train between the hills. Another fascinating place was Corcovado with the Statue of Christ at the top. To reach it, we had to take a small train up a steep hill. Besides the Catholic religion, there was something else in common to everyone in Rio. That was Soccer. The largest stadium in the world was the Stadio Maracana, built in 1950 for the Fourth World Cup

Competition. It had a capacity of over 200,000 spectators. We attended a few games there, but more about soccer later.

We had a routine for going ashore. We were close to the main gate, so it was a short walk to Rio Bianco. There were a couple of places where we would eat. The most frequent was further up in Rio Bianco, close to the movie district. That place had rotisserie chicken on one side and shrimp on the other side. The chicken was delicious. We got one whole chicken with fries and a salad with one beer. The reason for one beer was because it was so big you could not finish it alone. With the tip, it ran to about 5000 cruzeros, which was a little bit more than $2.00. This was not a bad deal. The shrimp plate was similar. The place was open from 6 to 10 P.M. Then we would take the bus and visit other sections of the city or go to a movie. By 9 or 10 we would go to the Subway. By then, things had heated up on the dance floor. Seamen from all over the world were there, like North Americans and Northern European; you name it. If they drank too much and started drinking at 6 P.M. it was guaranteed that by 10 they didn't know what they were doing and where they spent their money. More over, they would not have the desire to go anywhere with women.

At the beginning we paid for our drinks (copa libra, by the way), which was rum and Coke. The girls, with whom we were familiar, knew that *Triton* sailors stayed a long time in port. They knew that no money was available so they had arranged for us to get free drinks. With the blessing of the waiter, they would bring us drinks, and some other poor seaman would pay because he was too drunk to know what he was being charged.

Everybody benefited from the arrangement, like the bar, the waiter, and the girls and, of course us. We didn't have to pay for the drinks. Some of the seamen took the girls to the hotel. Others were too drunk, so the girls would call a cab and load them into the cab so they could be taken safely back to the ship.

Most of the time we would end up with one of the girls in our group and go home to her apartment. Sometimes we would stop for a late snack or even go to the Copacabana for a late show and then to her home. There was no payment. We would just pay for the food and drinks and for the show time at the club, which did not amount to much. We paid lower prices, and we knew what to order, and what was inexpensive. Thank God these girls understood that I had two sisters to marry off.

Some people have the ability to pick up languages easier than others. I guess I was one of them because before long I knew basic Brazilian to get by. It helped because I knew a little Italian and Spanish, too. Later my Brazilian improved to the point where I could pass as a local to many people. It helped that my two sailors on my watch were Portuguese and spoke only Portuguese, but later for that. So Nick was with me and needed me to translate what was going on.

I was joking with him, and he got mad when I told him, "I hope you don't want me in the room to translate when you have sex."

He answered, "I will kill you if you don't stop."

Leaving Rio we didn't go too far. That was not far enough to recover from Rio. We went 8 hours west of Rio to Angra dos Reis, a small resort and fishing port. The fishing was mostly for shrimp. The port had a small pier, which was just big enough to accommodate the *Triton* and maybe one other small ship. There was a fishing dock for the fishing boats. There was a nice beach, many restaurants and many hotels. It was mostly a resort port.

The pier was narrow and extended out toward the sea. It was difficult for trucks to turn in the area. *Triton* was a big ship and local longshoreman were not used to big ships, if you consider a liberty a big ship. The loading situation involved the cargo of old railroad tracks. I suppose they replaced railroad tracks and recovered them in the area close to Angra dos Reis. The company owning the tracks had a factory in Luanda, Angola, and that was where we would take them.

Loading them became a big problem. The stevedores had no idea how to handle a cargo of this kind. They were use to general merchandise and maybe a load or two of sugar in bags. When they started to load, all hell broke loose. Rails flew here and there, and it was a miracle that nobody was killed and that the damage to the ship wasn't that bad. We stopped loading and discussed how to load best for the buyer, the ship owner, and the shipper. The days required for loading changed to more days and loading could only be done in the daylight. That wasn't much of a problem because the local stevedores did not want to work late anyway.

We, the officers of the ship, would supervise loading and give instructions on how to handle it. The Chief Mate would see to the cargo plan, and we would be compensated extra for doing stevedore work. The shipper was happy to do it because he realized from the beginning that the local longshoremen were unfamiliar and bringing in labor from a big city to load was far more expensive. So things started to move at a slow pace, but it was safe for the worker and for the ship. Now that we had established safe loading, it was time to concentrate on another important thing, a good time. When you are in Brazil that was a cardinal rule. Since we started getting some extra money for the stevedore work, things turned out very nice.

We had two coffee breaks during the day. One was 10 A.M. to 10:20 A.M. and the other was 3 P.M. to 3:20 P.M. The morning break was the most interesting, with the sea stories flying like firecrackers. The Chief Engineer was a real nice guy, and he was close to 40 years old, in good health and fit. He had a nice, good-looking girl in Rio, who followed him at his request to Angra dos Reis. She was staying at the hotel. Every day he bragged about his sexual performance the night before and his great stamina. We worked him a little. We did not believe all that he was saying, but nothing was impossible. Seamen liked to brag about what good lovers they were, but avoided saying how much their love would cost. I was a realist and the Radio Officer was too, so we did not brag. We just worked them a little and had fun.

The resort did not allow bar girls and working girls in them. We had to take a cab and drive up the mountain outside the city. This place had a great view. It was not bad, about a 20-minute drive. That was where we ended up almost every night. Since we were almost the only big ship in town, our crew was the main event. We were celebrities.

One afternoon, it was a little after 2 P.M. and I was on deck. A person walked up the gangway and asked for the Mate. The Brazilian out at the gangway (we had Brazilians standing watch) called me, and he said someone wanted to see me. It turned out that the man was Greek, living in Angra dos Reis. He asked me if we had any Greek coffee. This was a big deal! Here was a Greek who was way out on the other side of the world, and he wanted Greek coffee. It was the least I could do, so I invited him to have coffee with us. I also gave him coffee, along with some Greek olives and feta. All of us were happy to see him. The steward did everything possible to provide him a good Greek hour with us. We had the traditional coffee at 3 P.M. and he enjoyed our sea stories. We asked him if he wanted to stay for dinner. He said he had to go because he had some work to do. He took the coffee and whatever other original Greek items the steward had. He thanked us and left.

The next day around noon a Brazilian showed up with a basket full of big shrimp and lobsters. The steward asked him where they came from and said that he had not ordered anything. The Brazilian said they came from the guy we had coffee with the day before. We asked what the man did, and we learned that he was a very wealthy man who owned a fleet of shrimp boats. In Rio alone, he sent out 4000 pounds a day. The Brazilian showed us a beautiful villa on the water and told us it was this man's house.

He then said, "Anytime you want, you can come over."

So much for who the mystery guest was. After that, we continued to see him, and he came over to visit us, and we went over to his boats.

It would be just about a week before we finished loading, even less if everything went all right. The Captain came down with a pain in his belly and a fever. Like a stubborn old Greek, he did not want anything the first day. The next day we took him to the doctor at the local hospital. They kept him there, gave him some medicine and told him he would be okay in a couple of days. A few days passed and there was no improvement. It was now two days before we sailed. I went to see the Captain around noon. It was as if something was telling me to go. Usually we visited him after five on the way out. However, this time something told me to go earlier to the hospital. When I got there, the Captain was in real bad condition. He was almost dying. Furious, I left for the ship and got the Chief Mate.

I talked to him, "We must do something. The Captain is dying."

At the beginning, he was skeptical. I took him to see the Captain, and he said in a panic, "You are right. What should we do?"

We had to call the Ship's Chandler in Rio to arrange for the Captain to be taken to the Hospital of Etrangeros, which had good facilities. The representative for the shipper, a nice guy, was with us. We called the Ship's Chandler back, and he said to bring the Captain over. Everything was arranged at the hospital, and there was not to be a worry about expenses. He had taken care of it all. Without question, I would go to Rio with the Captain. The Chief Mate could not leave, and I knew a little of the language. I suppose I was the expert in that area.

So there we were in the car, and the Captain and I had set out for Rio. It turned out to be a long (3 ½ to 4 hour) drive. I knew time was precious. On the way, he started telling me his last wishes. I stopped him and told him everything would be all right, but no matter what I told him, he continued. The Captain was a rugged man, older, but strong and tough. Seeing him that way, I knew he was suffering a lot. Towards the end he had almost passed out. At the door of the hospital we were met with a stretcher. They took him to the emergency room and immediately, they took him to the operating room. There was no paper work and no delay. Gallstones had blocked his urethra and started poisoning him. If I had not gone to visit him at the time that I did, he would have been dead.

After the operation was completed, they asked if they could take me to the hotel until morning. I said I would stay in the room and sleep on the chair. I stayed all night. The next morning, we knew he was out of danger, and I went back to Agra dos Reis. He was in good hands. The Ship's Chandler was a very nice guy and took good care of him.

Back in Angra dos Reis we had another dilemma. The

Captain was gone. Were we going to wait for another captain to come? After a few messages back and forth to the main office, they decided that we had enough mates and experience to take the ship to Luanda. This was true. The Chief Mate became temporary Captain. I, the Second Mate, became Chief Mate, and the Third Mate became Second Mate. We would take the ship across to Angola.

Actually, nothing changed as far as watches were concerned. The only change was in the crew list. So we took off for Luanda.

We were not more than a day and a half at sea when the Chief Engineer went to the Captain and said, "We have a problem. We don't have enough bunkers to go across. We have to turn back."

The poor Chief Mate (acting Captain) almost had a heart attack. When leaving port, the first thing to do along with all the other information, was to send a message about the fuel and water and needed bunker and where to get it. The office and the agent make the necessary arrangements. The message was that we had more than enough to get there.

Apparently, the Chief Engineer trusted the First Assistant to do the calculations, and the guy made a mistake. Usually the Chief made sure that it was correct, and he didn't. This was a big mistake.

In this situation, the first action was to personally go and measure and then double measure, then calculate every drop of fuel available. Afterwards it would be decided what to do. So he came back with the numbers. The Captain would try to figure a way to make it work if we could do so without creating a commotion.

After several calculations, we figured that if we slowed 2 knots we would save enough fuel to get us to Luanda. The problem was how to justify a speed of 9 knots with a loaded liberty and the trade winds. It would not be difficult. We would just make the weather a little stronger, and so we did. When we arrived in Luanda we had just enough fuel to get alongside. By the way, waiting for the pilot outside the port, I saw the biggest shark in my seagoing career. It was calmly circling the ship as if nothing was happening.

My Sea My Life

At the time, Luanda was hot, dusty and nasty. One section, where the elite Portuguese lived was nice, actually very nice. The rest was poor and filthy. We lost a few members of the crew and the Chief Engineer was the first to go. A few sailors, dissatisfied with conditions, left on their own. We all thought that the company would send replacements. In the meantime, the Captain was back. He was a little weak, but in good health, and we had a new Chief Engineer, but not sailors. The rumor was that we were not going to get new seamen.

Angola was a time bomb at the time, ready to explode. The things we saw were not pleasant. The labor coming to work on the ship was all black. They came to work surrounded by well-armed soldiers. The scene reminded us more of a group of prisoners going to work rather than free labor.

On deck, in the shade, it was 95 to 100 degrees. I could only imagine how hot it was inside the holds where these people were working. I was at the #4 hold in front of the accommodation, in the shade, watching the operation. A guy came from the #4 hold and asked me for a little water. I took the bucket, went inside and filled it with cold water. It was no big deal. The man took the water, thanked me and proceeded to go back to work. A soldier ran behind him, hitting the poor guy on his back with the back of his rifle. He grabbed the water and threw it away. I jumped and started running toward the soldier to stop him.

The stevedore, a Portuguese, grabbed me and stopped me, saying, "For God's sake Mate, please stop. You have not seen anything."

I asked, "Why? The man did not do anything."

He said, "I know. Please, you don't want to get involved. You did not see anything."

I have never wondered why so much blood had been shed since then.

We got no more crew replacements. Four were missing. They hired Portuguese, who were supposedly seamen. Two of them were in my watch.

In a couple of days we would be ready to leave this wonderful place with absolutely no regrets. From the first moment, I realized that the two men on my watch were not sailors. In fact, I don't think they had ever been on a ship before. The Chief Mate was handling the bow. I was at the stern of the ship undocking, and I happened to have the new seamen. What beauties! Not only did I have to tell them what to do, but I had to watch out for their safety, too. They didn't know how to protect themselves. It was a sight to see. In the beginning at sea, I had to have an experienced AB to teach them to steer the ship – at least the basics. The liberty ships were all hand steering with no automatic steering. That problem was under control after two or three days.

They were not seamen, but they were not stupid, either. They picked up fairly quickly, but the problem was communication. They spoke only Portuguese. Forget about me teaching them Greek. English would take too long. So what could I do? I decided I would improve my Portuguese. That would be easier, and it would benefit both of us. Four hours a day and four hours at night on our watch, I had an intense course in Portuguese. If I had to transform them from hotel waiters to seamen in a few days, I might as well learn another language in the process. The language would be handy where we were going. We were on our way to Maceio, Brazil, followed by Recife. We were to load sugar for New York, which was not bad. Good old *Triton* may have had problems, but the choice of ports was perfect.

Maceio was a small port that exported mostly sugar. We were going to load about 5,000 tons bulk, and the rest would come from Recife, a well-known port farther north.

Maceio might be a small port, nevertheless it didn't lack in the Brazilian flair for a good time, nor did it fail to be a seaman's heaven. When we entered the port, a very short distance to the right, we dropped anchor and tied the stern to the pier with lines. Barges came alongside loaded with the ship's gear. Getting ashore required a small boat. After landing and only a small distance away, there were two or three story houses. At the street level was a store, the second was a bar with music, and the third floor had rooms to accommodate the girls. I think it was the day after our arrival that my friend, the Radio Officer and I went ashore. It was Saturday and after lunch, about 1 P.M. We headed for shore. It was supposed to be too early for the bars to be open, but we figured to go around town sightseeing. As you will see, we did not go far. Out of curiosity, we went into one of the bars that the local stevedores highly recommended as a nice place.

The door was open, so we helped ourselves by going to the second floor where we found the bar and dancing room. Naturally, nobody was there at 1:30 P.M. We looked around and found a guy behind the bar, who was stocking beers and bottles for the night. I started talking with him. He said that most of the girls were still sleeping, but maybe some of them were awake.

He said, "Just go upstairs and look around. It's no problem."

He was right. Most of the doors were closed, but some were open. We walked up and down the long hallway, looking and saying hello to the girls in one of the rooms. I guess it was luck. I stopped and stared at the girl. She invited me in, and we started talking. She was dressed very lightly, and she was good looking and friendly from the beginning. These were all good ingredients for further quick developments. Meanwhile, Nick was doing the same thing further down the hall. He came and asked me if I would be around, to wait for him. Before long I was engaged in friendly intimate conversation with the girl.

What can I say? The girl was friendly. She went to take a quick shower to refresh herself, and she suggested that I undress. When she came out, I was almost completely undressed, in my underpants and lying in bed. She came near me with this funny look and laughed. She told me to show her my back. She laughed and went out in the hallway. I didn't know at the beginning what the problem was.

I thought, "I'll, just wait and see." In a couple of minutes a bunch of giggling and laughing girls came in the room with her and jumped on the bed. They started playing with the hair of my chest and back. The Mediterranean's were known to be hairy people, and I was one of them. To give you an idea, I started shaving at 13 years old. I do have hair that grows in the wrong places, that is not on top of the head. Today I have lost all my hair, but not on my chest, back, and even in the sides of my ears.

In the meantime, Nick lost the girl that he was with, and hearing all the commotion, he thought that something was wrong. He ran down the hallway to find me. When he found out what was going on, he started laughing and cursing at the same time. He took his girl and left and the others started going away. Finally, we were alone, and I locked the door. That was enough of a show time!

She turned out to be a very nice, and she was very happy to be with me. She thought I was a gentleman. We spent the rest of the day together in Maceio. She was very much taken when I asked her to go to the movie in town, and to go out to eat instead of staying in the bar all of the time.

She took extreme care to dress conservatively so that no one would think that she worked in the bar. She always asked me if she looked right. We went to the movies and to a nice local restaurant. Of course, she knew what to order that would be good and how much we should pay. I had a very pleasant 10 days in Maceio. But, as usual, the seaman must move on to the next port, and another temporary relationship must come to an end.

When I told the girl that tomorrow I would sail, tears came to her eyes. She took my hands and started kissing them.

I was taken back, and I asked, "Why did you do that?"

She said, "I know you have to leave, and I didn't expect more than that. But, all the time together with you, you treated me like a lady, and you made me feel good about myself for the first time in my life. I will never forget it. Thank you."

I consider that one of the best compliments to my character I had ever received until then. I believed that regardless of what any woman was and did in life, she was a very important part of our lives, and I would treat her with respect.

On the way to Recife, I got sick. I had a fever on our arrival. I went to the hospital and stayed two days. As soon as I got better I went back on the ship. I thought it was a cold. Not needing to elaborate much about Recife, it was another wonderful place for a seaman and a well-known port.

Poor old *Triton* needed my attention now. It was about 2 P.M. when a stevedore from the #4 hatch came to me, saying: "Aqua! Aqua! Aqua!" I told him to go inside and drink. "No, no, Mate! Below. Below. Below. Come with me."

I followed him, and I was not so happy to go down into the hold with bulk sugar to become a human lollipop. Water was covering the sugar. We went to the side of the ship. The plate had rusted through, and water from outside the ship was coming inside from at least ten holes. It wasn't a nice picture, and it was not good news for the Captain, who, by the way was taking his afternoon nap.

I stopped the loading at #4 hold and on my way to wake up the Captain with "this good news;" I was thinking I should have the mess boy bring a good cup of coffee to go with "the good news", or he should bring a bottle of Ouzo. You see, my whole time on *Triton* was so, uneventful, and we needed some more excitement.

I knocked on his door, and when he opened it and saw me sweating from the heat and sugar sticking to my knees, he knew that something was wrong.

"What is wrong now?" were his first words.

I nicely proceeded to explain what was wrong. Even though I tried to be nice, it still did not stop him from being upset and throwing around a few curses about all the luck we had with the poor old *Triton*. The loading stopped and messages started going back and forth with the main office. Finally they decided to keep loading but on the inshore side, so the ship could list 15-to 20 degrees. This way we would be able to check and repair the damage. So they patched the holes by welding a plate of steel. Poor *Triton* was as good as new and seaworthy again. I was just as crazy and willing to keep sailing with the *Triton*. With all this commotion, we did not lose any loading time. Here we were with a full load of sugar on our way to New York, to Green Point at the Domino Sugar Terminal. The discharge went quickly, and as usually it did not take more than three days.

We were done and told to shift to the shipyard in Brooklyn for our four-year inspection. So, we were scheduled to be there for three to four weeks. There was much to be done. Hopefully, good old *Triton* would be rejuvenated a little. It would also give us a chance to enjoy New York.

New York is and will always be a fascinating place with much to see and lots to do. It was quite different from Brazil with its different good time spots. In New York, you could take care of personal business: You could send money, buy things, see friends, send your mail and visit places.

The ship's carpenter called my cousin's wife and naturally, we were invited over. If I remember it was on 180th Street. They gave us instructions for how to get there, and off we went on a Saturday morning. We had a very nice weekend, and it also gave me a good chance to meet and become familiar with my cousin (from my father's side), whom I barely knew since he left Ithaca when I was very young. He and his wife were really nice people. We stayed overnight and left on Sunday. We took the subway back to Brooklyn with a very warm feeling about meeting a nice cousin for almost the first time.

The repairs were going well and things were moving smoothly. I went to the doctor in the middle of the week with another crewmember. I had myself checked. After the fevers that I had when I was in Brazil, it seemed that I was getting some not-so- high fever, but regardless some fever at the end of each day. The doctor could not find anything wrong, and to pacify me, he gave me some vitamins.

THE CONNECTION (MEET THE IN-LAWS)

By Friday morning at coffee time, the carpenter and other guys from my island called me and told me, "You are invited by Margetta to come to her house for a big dinner tomorrow, and she insists that you come. She will not take no for an answer, and quite a few other people we all know will be there. Please come."

Now I knew Margetta from Ithaca. She was a nice person, but a little loud, to say the least. As much as I liked her, I was not much for visits. I could not resist the offer since I would meet people I had not seen for years. They were right. I was going. Also, she was a fantastic cook.

When they said we would have a big meal, they meant it, and it was. There was food, wine and people we had not seen for years. There were also local Greeks who had been born in New York. We talked about different things. Someone asked me if I had any relatives in the States.

I have to say that I was at an age, which made me a great candidate for a match with a Greek-American girl who was not married at the time. So, when someone started asking me many questions, and some of them on the private side, I couldn't help but become suspicious that it might lead to something, and that would be the end of my freedom. Well, that was what I believed at the time. Getting married was way, way down on my priority list.

Returning to the conversation about my relatives in the States, I said, "Yes, my cousin is here. I saw him last weekend with Pano."

"So you don't have anybody else?" someone asked.

"There is no one that I know of. But wait: My mother always told me if I went to the States to go to Norfolk and see my Uncle Telly. The last time I was there, I asked, but it seems the Greek I asked had no idea of who he was. When I asked about Vasili, who was the husband of his only daughter, they still had no idea."

A woman joined the conversation, and she said, "I know where he is."

I said, "How?"

"Vasili is here on Long Island," she answered.

I said, "I don't know. I don't think so."

She insisted that it was he and that he was from Norfolk, and his family was still in Norfolk.

She said: "I know him very well and see him all the time. He is a close friend of my brother. We are all from the same family, too. His wife is Tassie, and they have three kids, two girls and a son."

From what I knew, the first part was correct, Vasili and Tassie, but I had no idea of the kids. The only thing I knew about was that there were two adopted kids. There were supposed to be a boy and a girl who probably had their own kids because they were older than I was.

I told her this, but she insisted. By now, it was 10 P.M.

She said, "I will call. I am sure it is him."

So, she did. After greetings, we began exchanging information, and "Bingo." Here they were - the unknown relatives. It was really a small world. Who would expect that the first step that would change my life would occur in Margetta's home?

Vasili said, "Don't leave. I will call you back."

I found out later that he called Tassie, and in his excitement, told her that he had found Mihali Moraiti, my mother's brother, who by age was close to my mother.

Tassie and Mihali grew up together. When Mihali came to the States, he stayed with Uncle Telly for years, and Tassie considered Mihali to be like her older brother. Later on, Mihali went to New York. When he was in a hospital for a simple operation, the hospital gave him the wrong blood, and he died. He was young. I think he was in his middle thirties. In those days doctors did not know about

My Sea My Life

R.H. negative and positive blood. His death devastated both families in the States and at home. From what I was told, he was not only a handsome man, but also a very nice person. When I was born, my mother named me after him in his memory.

When Tassie heard that Vasili found Mihali, she got upset with him, thinking that he was joking. He kept insisting and they almost had a big fight until he realized what he was saying and corrected it to Mihali or Michael Razos, son of Maria. So Tassie, as impulsive as she was and quick to make decisions, said for them to come and pick me up to go to see them. Now the time was almost 11 P.M.

Tassie would not take "No" for an answer. Since it was a weekend, I did not have to be back on the ship until Monday. I agreed to go. Forty-five minutes later, here were Vasili and Tassie. Vasili had been a seaman, and he went "the extra yard' to accommodate and welcome me.

For Tassie, it was a shocking experience. Not only did I have Michael's name, but also I bore a very strong resemblance to him. She was in shock to say the least. My mother, as the only girl in the family, was the little darling of them all, including her Uncle Telly, Tassie's father, and she was always fond of him.

My mother would tell me, "If you are close to Norfolk, you must go see my uncle."

So here we were. Unfortunately, it was too late for me to meet the old people. They were gone by now, so Tassie told me about them. I was very interested to know about them. After all, they were two people who were close to my mother.

By the time we finished with introductions, and they said "Hello" to all the people from Ithaca, of course, they had to eat something. (After all, you could not visit Margetta's home and not be treated right). Tassie was very anxious by now, and the time was close to one in the morning. It was time for us to go. You could see in Tassie's eyes that she wanted to get out of there so we would be able to talk, and there was so much to say. A friend offered to drive the rest of the crew to the ship so they did not have to take the subway so late at night.

Anyway, as the most experienced member of the group, I was going the other way, and they had to go to the Todd Shipyard. To do so at 2 A.M. was not a good idea. Everybody was going home. I went back to Long Island with Vasili and Tassie. Personally, I knew nothing about Long Island.

Well, they put me up in a motel for the rest of the night, and they picked me up later in the morning. This was because Vasili rented a room in a woman's house, and there was no space. His family was in Norfolk, and he was in New York for the good pay, which helped him in raising a family of 5. Employment in Norfolk was difficult, to say the least.

They came back to the motel (which was a Howard Johnson) around 9 A.M. and picked me up. Before leaving we had breakfast, and I had an opportunity to talk a little with Vasili, mostly about ships and people that he knew. I knew most of them, too. He struck me as an easygoing, pleasant man. After that, we changed our talk from business, but it was difficult for Tassie. After all, to Tassie I was the reincarnation of Mihali. There was no question that I had his name and his face. Besides his good looks and his wavy hair, Mihali had a very pleasant personality, and loved music. He played the coronet in the band in Ithaca. When he came to Norfolk, Tassie was the only child in her family, and Mihali became the older brother. There was no end to the stories.

We left the restaurant, and we went to where Vasili worked. The stories continued. We didn't know where to start and where to finish. There was so much about so many people, and a few of them were gone.

Once in a while Vasili came into the back room of the burger place that he ran and asked, "Are you all right? Do you need anything?"

Sometimes he did not even get an answer. Until that time I knew only about George and Mary, the two children that Uncle Telly had adopted. I had no idea about the rest of the family.

Now I learned about Kyki, Matilda, and John. Tassie showed me pictures, and I learned a lot about them from her point of view, as I realized in later years. There were many stories that we were able to exchange.

Vasili was born and raised in Kastos, a very small island next to my island. He had sailed with many of the people I knew. Amazingly, Tassie was born and raised in Norfolk, but she knew a lot, and I mean a great deal. I will say that she knew a lot more stories about our families than I did. Being 25 at the time, I certainly did not spend much time searching the family tree. I was more interested in searching and exploring the world.

Since we had come from Brazil, Tassie asked me what I had seen there. Well, since most of my visits should be censored, I said that I had gone to see a football game in Maracana and told her how big the stadium was. This was not very impressive to Tassie, and here came my savior, Corcovado. I explained in detail about getting to the top of the mountain with a special train, the large statue of Christ, and the panoramic views from there. All of this was very true. It was really a fantastic trip with a breath-taking view. The only thing I skipped was the fact that the girls accompanied us. (Anyway, it was not fun to go alone).

I guess from that story in Tassie's mind, she translated that I was very religious and a good boy who as a seaman went to churches. This misunderstanding probably made me look bad later. Anyway, the day's conversation was worth it to me. It was a part of me that I wanted to learn about. After all, I had Mihali's name, and I got to meet two wonderful people at the same time.

I suppose it probably took Tassie days to separate the older Mihali and me (Mike). It was a shock to her .At the end of the day, after Vasili closed the store; they drove me back to the *Triton*. Tassie and I promised to write, and I promised when I came back to Norfolk I would visit them and meet the rest of the family.

On the way to the ship, Vasili laughing slightly asked me a couple of times if I had a headache. I did not give it much thought. In later years when I remembered this with him, I knew why we would both laugh.

In a few days the ship left for Vera Cruz, Mexico. We were going to take a full load of beans to (guess where) Rio de Janeiro. At that time Vera Cruz was a seaman's port. It was a nice place to relax, and the weather was hot, but nice. There were great beaches for swimming and relaxing. There were parks, rather squares, with pastry shops and outdoor cafes to enjoy. We used to go to one, which became our favorite spot. Mostly we would order "Tres Marias," which was like an ice cream sundae. It had three different ice cream cones with bananas, cherries and syrup. They were very tasty. We would enjoy them and enjoy watching the traffic. This was not car traffic. Rather, the traffic was the evening walks for the locals around the park. This was also very common in the Mediterranean countries that I knew. When I was a kid on the island, we called these strolls "peripatos." It was a nice way to get some exercise and talk with friends and exchange events of the day. It was a relaxing stroll.

After I got sick in Brazil, for a few days a small fever remained and would return, especially in hot places. I had gone to the doctor in New York. He found nothing wrong and gave me vitamins. Go figure! In Vera Cruz I went to the doctor again. This time when I described the symptoms correctly, the doctor knew what to look for. After checking my blood, he sent a message to the ship that I would have to stay two or three days at the hospital to clear the blood. It was like a tropical disease. I don't remember exactly what it was called, but something bit me. It was nothing dangerous. He kept me in the hospital because he had to give me medicine intravenously. He put me in the babies' section since he did not have any other room. Between the good-looking nurses and babies crying, I did not get any sleep until I got back on the ship. I was not really sick. I just had to clear the blood. I guess today it could be done with a few pills. So, it was more of a fun time. I was lucky that the doctor took it from the funny side, enjoying it, too. If not, they would have thrown me out. The crew came to visit. They were supposed to come in the evening. Most of the time, they were there until midnight when the head nurse insisted that they leave. While it was nice to be sick in the hospital, it was time to go back on the ship.

Besides the evening strolls, Vera Cruz had a very good nightlife for the seaman. Don't get confused here. Because our budget was limited, we had to rotate between the strolls and the nightlife. During one of those evening strolls, we met two girls and started a conversation. It was Nick and I, mostly me, since I was the multi-lingual one. Now here we dealt in Spanish, but somehow I was able, with my Brazilian and a little Spanish to communicate.

After a few hours of walking and talking, a couple of "Tres Marias," and a few Cokes, it was time to find some place to be alone since we were, by then, friendly enough. But where? A hotel was out of the question for the girls. They were afraid the police would get them. They would have been in trouble. After all, they were just a couple of girls going out for a good time, nothing else.

Well, going to the ship was impossible. That would have been the best solution. Why couldn't we go to the ship? This goofy Chief Engineer, who was very close to the owner's family, stayed up watching the crew and reading the <u>Bible</u> until very late. I mean very late. He had intimidated the Captain since he was very powerful with the company. To take this chance was out of the question. Where there was a will there is a way. We were close to the ship by then. There was a small railroad track beside the ship, with a short train of four or five cars and a caboose parked on the track. I told Nick to keep the girls with him and wait, and I told him I would be back. He wondered what I was up to, but he decided not to question me. He knew me by now and hoped we would not get into any trouble.

When I returned with two blankets, he freaked and shouted, "What are we doing with the blankets?"

I told the girls and him that the cozy caboose car would be the hotel room for a few hours. He would stay outside and talk with his girl, and my girl and I would be inside the car. Then it would be his turn. I told him if he did not like it, then I was all ears for a new idea. He thought it was a perfect idea and the girls, laughing, agreed! When you were young, a little inconvenience was not important. As the saying went, there was more than one-way to skin a cat.

This was different, but funny, and not bad. We left the blankets in the caboose, planning to pick them up on the way back. We took the girls to the bus so they would be safe. We kissed them goodnight and, honestly, we never saw them again. Like us, they had a story to tell. With that, we returned to the ship. We picked up the blankets, and of course the gangway watchman asked us why we needed blankets. I said we were camping on the beach. There was nothing to it. He thought that was cool, and Nick was laughing like hell and cussing me out, but not in a bad way. Well enough for Vera Cruz. It was time to sail to Rio. This time Rio was "new and improved," as they say, in language and experience.

"Rio, here we come!" Vera Cruz to Rio de Janeiro took 22 days. The good old *Triton* liberty ship was slow, but steady. At this time, Rio de Janeiro was filled with grain ships with more expensive daily fees than the old *Triton*, and naturally they had priority. We stayed anchored for at least one week until it was decided what to do. It was much more economical to pay the *S/S Triton* than to pay these much more expensive new freighters.

From the anchorage, we went ashore maybe twice; since the rumors were that we were going to stay awhile. What was the rush? We decided to save our money for later. Anyway, there wasn't much money left to begin with. For all the ports that we were going to so far, the stay was long. There was not enough time to recover financially. It was the prudent course to save for later, since we were going to stay for a while. The cargo owner decided to bring *Triton* alongside the dock at the far end of the port and to use it as a warehouse. The buyers would buy so many tons of beans, and it was discharged using the ship's gear. The next buyer came, and so on. It seemed that we were going to stay in Rio for a while.

Guess what? Nobody was unhappy over that. There were girls, nights out, Copacabana, Botafogo, soccer games at Stadio Maracana, good food; we had it all. There was only a small problem. All of the above cost money, which, unfortunately was in short supply since 85% of my salary was going to Greece for my sisters's dowries. Of course, such a wonderful opportunity could not go to waste. That would be a shame. To be in Rio and to stay so long did not come every day for a seaman. I had to figure something out. There must be a solution. Where there was a will, there was a way.

The way, in this case, was beans. Yes, beans! We had 10,500 tons of beans in bulk. Technically, they allowed a certain amount for "shrinkage." In other words, a few tons of beans less were justified.

I explained my plan to the Chief Mate. He did not want to know about it, and he said "I am out of it now, and I don't want to know anything."

The Captain, of course, did his business with whisky and cigarettes.

He said, "I assume a small percentage of beans are justified and allowed by the agreement. Anyway, I am going to bed early."

So the stage was set for Operation Beans! Before it started. I had to take care of one important element, the Port Patrol. Of course, the poor hardworking men needed beans for their families, so I took care of their bean needs for a few months, and they were very happy and appreciative of that. With that, the door was open when I was on the night watch. A boat would come alongside. I would open a section of the hatch; load beans in a bag and off they would go in the boat. It was not a big deal – just enough for 3 or 4 of us to have some cruzeros to get around. This continued for the duration of our stay in Rio.

No one would ever complain because the *Triton* crew was the darling of the Port Security. They even allowed taxicabs to come all the way to the ship so we did not have to walk late at night. Beans not only have good nutritional value, but extra benefits if they are used correctly. The gates to Rio were now wide open.

The fuel that we needed to make our engine run was found. Normally I had two nights off and one on duty. If I wanted, I could go out every night, since the Chief Mate was going out once a week and the Captain did not mind, since he rarely went out, especially at night. The body could tolerate only so much, even if it was young. Generally I needed the day; first to make business contacts and second to rest. Even if I was going out, the bean operation went on with one of the other three men. It was good for me to be there since I knew the language and helped to make things run more smoothly. I knew the patrol and the buyers better than the others did.

Rio was a fascinating city at the time, and I think it still is. The people and their mentality were pleasant. The Brazilian people were very nice. At least that was the way I saw them, even those around the port. I never had a single problem not only in Rio, but also in all the ports that I visited in Brazil. Of course, the girls were fantastic.

The ten o'clock and three o'clock coffee time stories were plentiful, fascinating, and sometimes a bit exaggerated, especially when we were in a good port. The Chief Engineer, who was replaced in Luanda, had some unbelievable stories of sexual stamina. He was well built, fairly good looking, and single of course, with good pay. He had a steady girl for Rio and Angra dos Reis. She was a beautiful brunette. We were sort of jealous of him for enjoying that beauty, but I guess he well deserved her. Since, of course, she did cost him a lot of money, she was getting the royal treatment. Good for both of them! Our life was good, so where was the problem? There was none.

One Saturday we left early just to get off the ship and wandered around. We decided to visit this house, which was an upscale place for girls. The main hall also had a bar and nice soft music, air conditioning and comfortable furniture. The girls there were very polite, and if someone wanted, they would be taken upstairs. I think I remember that people paid downstairs for the time that they wanted to stay with the girl.

So, there we were, Nick and I. We had a Copa Libra (rum and Coke). We were killing time when here she came: The ex-Chief Engineer's girl. She was just as pretty as we remembered. In the meantime, Nick had already arranged to go with another girl. I was just about to stay alone.

Nick said "Know what?"

I said, "Go. I will take care of her. If she pretends that she doesn't recognize me, I will take another one anyway. Whoever finishes first will wait here."

Sure enough, she not only recognized me, but she came over. I asked her to sit down. We started talking, and I said, "Let's go upstairs."

She gladly said, "Yes."

I went to pay, even though she did not want me to. We went upstairs, and it was very pleasant and good. Afterwards, we started talking about the good old days, of course. She wanted to know what happened to the Chief. I told her the whole story about the fuel, and told her that he had to leave the ship in Angola. She still seemed to be fond of him, but that was fairly common in Brazil. At the time, her financial arrangement with the Chief had been a necessity. After that, it was mostly friendship. At least that was then.

Suddenly she asked, "Why did the Chief spend all that money on me for nothing."

Something seemed to be troubling her, and she had to say it to someone.

I said, "What do you mean? You are beautiful, and you are mighty good. You two looked like the perfect couple. Of course, the Chief bragged about your wonderful sex practically at every coffee time."

With an angry face, she said, "What sex? All that time, we never had sex once! Why? That is what I want to know."

Very much surprised, I said, "I don't know."

I don't know if her story was true or not. The thing I knew was that they spent at least two months together. He seemed to be so happy, and he treated her like a queen. Of course, they had a few arguments sometimes, and she did have a little temper. However, it was nothing that needed fabricating. I just don't know. With that, we went back downstairs, where Nick was waiting for us.

We stayed a few minutes, and I said, "We have to go because we have to meet someone. We are already late."

She asked, "Are you coming back tomorrow.

I said, "Of course," and we left.

Outside Nick asked me what was going on. He knew something was cooking because we did not have to meet anyone. When I told him the story, he almost flipped. He could not believe what he was hearing.

"Unbelievable," he kept saying. "Unbelievable."

"Nick," I said, "unbelievable or not, that is it. If it is true or not I don't know, but we are finished with this place. That was our last time at that house."

I told the Captain that we planned to go out for a weekend spree, Nick, the Bosun, the Chief Mate, and I.

He said, "Don't worry. I am here. Take him out, and don't bring him back until Monday morning, Thiake (Ithacan)."

Since the difficult time that we had from Anrga dos Reis to Rio de Janeiro, the Captain was very fond of me and treated me like a son. So there we were, the four of us. After a nice meal about 7 or 8 o'clock, we decided to go to Subway for drinks and to kill some time. Then we would go to the Copacabana for the 12 to 1 show.

When we went to this nightclub, we had to know how to ask for a drink or our bill would grow quickly. They brought a bottle of the liquor and we asked for glasses. If we made the mistake of filling the glasses, we might have had in each glass THREE drinks instead of one. So anytime we wanted a drink, we called the waiter, and he filled it so there was not a dispute over how many drinks we should pay for.

In the nightclubs, like the Moulin Rouge, or any other along the Copacabana, there were showgirls who dance and the working girls, and they didn't really get along well. The showgirls did not want to associate with the working girls, and the working girls considered the showgirls to be snobs. Of course, we didn't know at first, who was who, and secondly, both got paid. So, what was the problem?

I was talking with a girl, and getting pretty friendly. She was really good looking. Of course, the others were also getting along well with various girls. Our plan was to see the floor show and then leave with the girls to go to some hotel.

By now, the brunette and I were getting along fantastically. She told me that after the show we would leave. That was our plan anyway, and we would go to her apartment. Of course, I didn't have any objection to that. I would meet the others in the morning.

Nothing was very far away. Of course, she said she had to go for the show. I had no reason to dispute her. I did not think that the showgirls were allowed to go with customers, but who was I to question her disposition, especially with such a nice body.

When she left for the show, Nick came along and said, "Mike, we have a problem. Our girls are all upset with your girl. They don't want her with us, and they have another girl for you if you want to leave her."

Angry, I said, "She is nice." He then proceeded to explain to me the difference between the working girls and the showgirls. I answered, "Nick, let me give you the news for the girls. Tonight I am going with this girl to her apartment because I like her, and she is nice. Tomorrow, we'll see. Tell them so. When the show is over, that is what I am going to do, and tell the girls to cool off."

They didn't like it, but they had to go along. When the show was over, we left the others and went to eat something. The other men and I had agreed to meet in the morning.

We had a very nice night. She wanted to monopolize me though, and I was not in the mood for a steady relationship, not in Rio. So the next day I told her that I had to go back on the ship and stay on watch. I left her and went and met the others to continue our weekend. We returned to the ship late Sunday night.

The Chief Mate had found his mate, and he was often a patron of the Moulin Rouge with the girl. The showgirl kept asking for me, but Nick and I preferred to stay with the subway girls that we knew best. It was not an expensive environment. Actually, it was on our level of economy.

On Christmas and New Year's Eve the Captain asked us not to disappear, but to stay on the ship with all the crew. It was a tradition. We agreed to that, but we felt the Chief Engineer should cool off and let us bring the girls on board. Then, after midnight, they would leave. That was what happened. Anyway it was much nicer to have the presence of a few girls instead of all men. This made it much nicer. We had a good time, and even the Chief Engineer finally agreed that we were not big sinners.

Another favorite spot for the weekend was Stadio Maracana

for football (soccer). This was the biggest stadium in the world. If I'm not wrong, it had a capacity of 220,000 to 240,000 fans. It was huge. The fans were something else. Soccer was a religion in that stadium. One of the matches was between Flamenco and Bancou. Flamenco was favored to win, and almost 80% of the fans were for Flamenco, but they were losing 3 to 0. We left 20 minutes before the end. That was the prudent thing to do. Things there were not looking that smooth in the stands, and we expected fights and who knows what to erupt.

It took over 30 days to finish discharging of the cargo, and if it were not for the night beans, there would not have been a way to enjoy the stay. It was amazing what a few pounds of beans could do. "Thank you, beans!"

Of course, Brazil was not over yet. Believe it or not, our next port was Victoria, sort distance from Rio. Victoria, here we come, and we were definitely broke!

The port of Victoria was up the river a few miles and ships docked from both sides of the river. We were lucky, we docked on the city side and then we were right in the middle of the city, within walking distance of almost everything. It was a nice place with some cafés. There was nothing really expensive, not that we could afford anything more than that.

The estimated stay in Victoria was about 25 days. The cargo was various sizes of metal plates for all kinds of uses. We were bound for Tampa, and if I remember well, for Houston, too. In Victoria, if we were looking for nightlife, we had to take a cab and go almost out of the city to a designated area for bars and girls. After a few days, we decided that it was time to visit that area. To my surprise, I met one of the head stevedores. He was a pleasant fellow. He was also surprised to see us.

I asked, "What are you, a married man with kids, doing here?"

He answered, "Well, I need a change of pace. We get tired of the same food." This was the good old Brazilian attitude. "Now, what do you want here?"

I said, "Where do you want me to go? I am a seaman with no

My Sea My Life

ties to the outside world. It was natural for me to come here."

"But", he answered, "you speak the language, you can get a girlfriend. It is very easy and much more affordable. Your expenses are some pastries, a movie, maybe a present. You don't need to come here. Not you. You know your way around Brazil. Yep, right, it is that easy. Yes, it is that easy. Believe me."

That stuck in my mind and the next time I went out alone I decided to try. Well, guess what? The old Valentino was right about Brazil. I expected with weather to be mostly hot, the general mix of people to be more Brazilian. This girl looked as if she was from some North European country. Well, she was working as a salesperson in a store. We started talking, and I was pretending that I wanted to buy something. By the end of our conversation, we agreed to go see a movie after she finished working. I think it was around 7:00 P.M. It was just as easy as that, and the rest of my stay in Victoria was a nice, pleasant experience for both of us. It was a simple, nice friendship. We both knew that this would last as long as the ship would be there. It was difficult for both of us, but it was a reality that ships and rivers didn't stay still, they always moved. Sometimes I thought it might have been better to go up to the campus. Then we both experienced the reality and made the best of our short time together. By no means I was ready to drop anchor yet!

That was Victoria, which was another memory from the seaman's world. It turned out that this would be my last time to see Brazil, as a bachelor, anyway. On the way back to the U.S. we got the orders for our next cargo. After we finished discharging in Houston, we were to clean the ship and go to Freeport, Texas to load fertilizer for India. By the time we would be in the Mediterranean, and on the way to India, I would have been on the *Triton* over 20 months. For many reasons, it would definitely be time to go home: I missed my family. Going to India in the summertime with monsoons, and everything else wrong with the old *Triton* was not appealing. Also getting through the Suez with the *Triton* was not the best idea.

Tassie had kept her promise to write to me. Of course, I was fairly busy, so I did not write back. As soon as we arrived in Tampa, I called them in Norfolk, and she was delighted to hear from me. Of course, I explained that mail from Brazil took awhile or could get lost, but it was not necessary to worry. I just called and everything was okay. She had a fantastic idea, too. If I could, and since we were not going to be around the States anymore, perhaps I could fly to Norfolk to see the rest of the family. At first I did not give it much consideration, but Tassie was very insistent about it, so I talked with the Captain about it at coffee time. To my surprise, he insisted that I go, and he said it was okay with him. He said to meet the ship at Freeport. He said I could call New York and check if there were any changes, since I knew everyone there. It was absolutely not a problem. I do not think that he would have been so agreeable if he had known what would develop from this trip.

The whole thing at the time was to meet relatives that had not even known existed until a few months ago. It was very touchy. So, after we arrived, I decided to go. I took a flight through Baltimore to Norfolk. With a delay and a transfer, I didn't arrive until midnight. The oldest daughter, Kyki, came to meet me at the airport. Because it was late, she was dressed for bed with rollers on her head, no make-up and an orange coat over her nightgown. This was not exactly the most glamorous dress code, but she was still a college kid. She was pleasant, and as soon as we got home she excused herself and went to bed because she had school the next day.

Tassie and I talked awhile and then called it a night. She had to teach the next day and got up in the morning after only a few hours of sleep. Of course, I was used to that. During coffee and breakfast, I met the rest of the family. Of course, Kyki was now dressed more appropriately, for she had to go to college. This was in the middle of the week. The girls were doing the driving, showing me different places around town.

Kyki had a few friends over, and we talked about different

things – music, travel, etc. I noticed that they knew very little about international music, being mostly in a confined area of the U.S. Later, I realized that this was normal in the smaller U.S. cities.

The most extensive talks were with Tassie, of course. She was the one who knew the history of our families, and of course as always the stories about the older Mihali. Tassie came up with all the good ideas. She suggested that on Friday afternoon we leave and go to New York to visit Vasili, and from there I could fly back to Houston on Sunday afternoon. I could also return to Norfolk. I didn't think that all three girls agreed, but it seems to me that Tassie's good idea would prevail. So the schedule was set and decided.

Kyki was busy with school projects. One of them was that she had to create a farm diorama, which she had to complete while we were in New York. She seemed a little frustrated, and, of course, I volunteered to help her with the project. During the farm operation, we talked about different things and became more relaxed with each other. By then Tassie, at every good opportunity, praised Kyki and insinuated that we might be related, but not that closely. I didn't really need to have a Ph.D. to realize what her objective was. There wasn't any reason to be alarmed about it. Kyki seemed not to have any idea or any participation in that, and I wasn't ready for anything more than a visit. The more we talked, though, the more I saw a different person from the girls I had met so far.

But then, I said to myself, "Mike, go back on the ship. Stop thinking deeper. It is dangerous. Keep Mike free. You're not ready yet."

With the farm diorama finally done, visiting New York was pleasant. By then, Kyki seemed to be a little annoyed with her mother. I wasn't far behind. Nevertheless, I caught her looking at me like she was trying to read inside me. When she sensed that I might have seen her looking my way, she quickly tuned the other way.

Tassie ask me what I planned to do. I said I was going to get off this ship and take a short vacation and then go onto another ship. I needed a few more months at sea to go for a Chief Mate's license, and I wanted to do that as soon as possible.

She said, "You should be able to find a ship that comes close to the United States. Are you interested?"

I said, "Of course."

She insisted that we keep in touch by mail and told me not to forget to write. Vasili was a pleasant person. He was hard working, I thought, and loved his family a lot. We had some nice talks, and we shared a few local seamen's jokes.

When we said goodbye as I was going to the airport, he said, "Mike, decide what you want to do with your life. I know nobody can press you, especially not me. But I would like to see you again."

"Me, too," I said.

When I arrived in Houston, the new Steward was with me. The other Steward was leaving the ship after four years. He could not go back to Greece because he had not fulfilled his military obligations, so he had to get off the ship. When the Steward and I arrived in Houston, we learned that the ship was out at sea cleaning hatches and would not go to Freeport for three or four days. We were told to go to Freeport and wait for the ship. We were to stay in a motel while we waited.

"Not bad," I thought. Next to the motel was a country music club, so that was where we spent the evening, and I enjoyed the country music tunes. The rest of the stay in Freeport was uneventful. I called back to Norfolk to say goodbye.

After six long years in school, I was then sailing ship after ship to meet the three years required for the license. This was followed by two and half years in the Navy plus working on the side and studying for my license. Then I got a ship and stayed for almost two years. At last I was looking forward to a well-deserved vacation. At least that was what was in my mind. We sailed from Freeport, Texas, heading towards the Mediterranean. Most of the crew would get off in Crete, and the ship would continue to India to discharge the fertilizer. Crete was where the ship was scheduled to bunker and change crew. During the passage across the Atlantic Ocean this was the talk of each day. Every time the Radio Operator came for coffee or to dine someone would ask, "Do you have any news?"

The closer we got, the more anxious we were to see family, wife, kids and friends. Also there was the promise to meet during vacation. I was living in Piraeus at that time. I was invited by all the crewmembers that lived in Ithaca to visit them, especially Jerry Razos, a distant cousin of mine.

They were all excited about going home, and they would not take "no" for an answer. I had to visit them, and I looked forward to a terrific time. It was the end of spring, and this was the best time of the year for all of Greece. In my hometown, Ithaca, I'll be for the summer. All the Ithacans, who lived in different parts of Greece and abroad, tried to come back to the island in the summer for a vacation. I was going to have a real vacation for the first time.

Do you remember Murphy's Law? Yes, well it never has failed. We were close to entering the Mediterranean Sea, perhaps half a day from the Straits of Gibraltar, when the Radio Operator, who had been a good friend of mine, came to me late one afternoon and told me that he could not get SVA on the radio. He had tried all day and heard nothing. It was like SVA was dead. SVA was the radio station in Athens and was known to be quite powerful in communicating with the Greek Merchant Marine. SVA was a strong station, and it could easily accommodate the fast growing traffic of the Greek fleet. So, not to be able to get the station from outside Gibraltar meant that something must be wrong, but what? There was no warning, nothing. Everyone was familiar with the political instability of Greece during those years, and everyone began to worry, especially those who planned to leave the ship in Crete.

The next day the word was out: Greece now had a military junta, which had taken over as its government. Thank God, so far there was not a war breaking out, nor was there a bloodbath. Things were supposedly under control. What was going to happen with the crew change? The company had no idea at the moment. From the Captain on down, the mood on the ship changed dramatically. None of us who were almost through with the *Triton* wanted to go to India with fertilizer in the middle of the summer, during monsoon season, or during any other season for that matter. If we were going to Brazil or Mexico or any other place, maybe we would go, but we would not go to India in the middle of the summer.

Messages went back and forth, but there were no significant changes for the next couple of days. Nobody knew what was going to happen. To make things more interesting, the Gulf of Lions had a fiesta. We were north of Tunisia and half a day before the turn at the Strait of Malta. We had a pretty strong storm gale force of 7 to 8, maybe more, with waves right from the side. The poor *Triton* was laboring pretty badly. None of us who knew the strength, or lack of strength, of the ship got much sleep. This was not due to the movement of the ship from the seas, but from waiting to hear another creepy sound like the one we heard before when the #3 hatch cracked. What a pleasure, especially when we thought that in 3 to 4 days we would be out of this rust bucket! The Captain and I went into the usual corner of the bridge, and we talked in low voice. This was nothing to advertise.

Nick, the Radio Operator, watched from his room, and later at supper he said, "Mike, I saw you. What do you think? Will we make it?"

"Nick, just pray that we make the turn, and she will be all right."

It was not far that we had to go. Since I am able to write this, it means we made the turn. During my years at sea, I sailed on more rust buckets like this. I guess I never learned or got immune to danger. I guess I just got addicted to it, or maybe I was just plain DUMB!

Two days from Crete, we received a message that the crew was clear, and that the change would be at Crete or at the Suez Canal, depending on the bunker situation. We were all happy again to be going home, even though for some of us it wasn't the way we imagined our vacation would be.

We were young, and we were at the age where when something happened (say war or something else like the Cyprus situation, for example) we would be the first to be drafted back into military service. All my life and still, I have believed in defending my country and family, and I was proud to serve in the Navy. I am proud to say that I contributed with the U.S. Merchant Marine to my new country any time during any type of crisis. In fact, my wife has always said that any time there was some kind of crisis in the Middle East or any other place in the world, I always managed to be there so she could worry.

As a child growing up during the Civil War of Greece, I knew very well how devastating it could be. I did not want that to happen again. Finally, the last message was that we would change crew at Kali, Limenes, and Crete.

No matter how old and rusty good old *Triton* was it would always be a big part of my life, with mostly very good memories. Of course, we had some difficult experiences, but as seamen we tend to forget those. Later on, *Triton* would prove to be the milestone that changed my life. I didn't know this at the time. *Triton* almost brought me to tears. I knew that her old body didn't have much more to go before the last trip to the scrap yard.

The ferry trip from Crete to Piraeus was about 12 hours overnight. These were the last goodbyes with our shipmates of almost two years. From Piraeus everyone went in different directions with many promises to keep in touch, and of course by now it was a must to visit Ithaca. All the crew from Ithaca invited me, and they promised me a good time. Even though I now lived in Piraeus, most of the crew from Ithaca were now good friends. I didn't know them very well when I was there before. They were much older than I. They were established seamen coming and going, and I was a school kid, working hard to get through. Now after almost two years together as a second officer and being together in quite a few difficult situations, I had gained their respect as an officer and as a person.

Now has come the tricky part. Letters were going back and forth from the *Triton* seamen to home during the trip describing the many situations in detail. The wives and relatives knew as much as we knew. In other words, the word about me had spread and being over 25, finished with my military obligations, having my license, and almost ready for my Chief Mate's license, I became a prime marriage target. I had the absolute approval of the elders, who had observed me for almost two years in a close, confined space. My fate was sealed!

"Get him here. We have the brides. He is going nowhere. As soon as he sets his foot in Ithaca, we have him. Just get him here."

Jerry was a distant cousin of mine, although I hardly knew the man. In Ithaca our routes were different. Also he was much older than I. He was almost old enough to be my father. We became very close on the ship. He was a nice person and a good family man. I had the opportunity to help him a few times in difficult situations. Of course he really appreciated my help. By nature, if I could help anyone, I would help him or her. So, I made myself clear to Jerry on the way to Piraeus, and I told him, "I would love to come, but no matchmaking! Not yet. Maybe in two or three more years, but not now."

"Don't worry," Jerry kept saying. "I will take care of that."

Like he had any control over his wife! Fat Chance! So, with that, I was even more concerned.

But deep down, I was pleased. It was recognition, and I considered it an honor to be invited into their families, especially when I knew most of them. They were good, decent people devoted to family and to raising their kids properly.

Ithaca, like most islands, was a small society, and everyone got to know almost everyone. Matchmaking was still very common at the time. I had other ideas in that department. I would be the one to decide my own destiny and not some matchmaker. It was different to be introduced to someone and to get to know him or her. I did not believe in the idea that if the girl had a good dowry, then I should marry her. That was not in my character, maybe was it the way that I grew up. Maybe that was the way I was born.

As I said to an older friend of our family, "I would need to be in great need to be concerned about a dowry, which had better be big, because I believe in love, not in a dowry."

I did not come from a wealthy family by far, and I was born

just before the Italians and Germans invaded Greece, and then came the Civil War. From 1939 to 1950, I lived constantly in some kind of war. In 1952 I almost died from appendicitis complications when finally they had to operate on me on the kitchen table. Because my appendix burst they did not have time to take me to the hospital, which by the way, was on the next island. Traveling by boat and then by car it would have taken about 12 to 14 hours. I would have been dead by then. As it was, my family had to sign a paper that the doctor was not responsible for the outcome of the operation. I survived, sacrificing two years of school because of the complications. Good stuff!

That was not the end. In August 1953 we had the earthquakes in Ithaca, which destroyed the entire island including our home, store, and almost everything that we owned. We had to start from square one, and we became refugees in Piraeus. That was the place where my brother stayed. I didn't blame him at all for not wanting to relocate to Ithaca. He stayed there, and we all ended up there in later years.

From the early years, I learned to be my own guidance counselor, advisor, tutor and all the other modern assistances that the younger generations enjoy today. I created my own allowance and earned my own tuition to go to school. I was born hyperactive so a simple 8 hours a day shift did not exist for me. As far back as I remember, I began earning my own money from at least the age of nine, and I helped in the store, too. I did not have the luxury of doing one thing at a time at my own pace. I learned to hate deadlines because I had to live with them all my life. One important thing about me was that I could not tolerate anyone to tell me that I cannot do something; it just didn't' work, period. I would always decide for myself if I could do something or not. I knew myself better than anyone else.

In spite of all this, I must say that I remember my youth with good memories. There wasn't much money, sometimes none at all. But life was what I did with it, not what circumstances created, and I learned from a very young age to separate them. Sometimes I didn't need many material things to be happy. I had a good family and most of the people I knew were all in the same boat. We created very nice experiences from simple things. For instance, we didn't need 15 soccer balls to play, only one and a few friends. Today I laugh inside when the soccer coach comes with a bag full of balls, and every player brings his, too. This is a little too much, to say the least. But that is the way things are today.

Just because I didn't have it as a child, it didn't mean that I would deprive my children, not at all. In fact, I might even spoil them sometimes or, rather I would leave it to my wife to do so, and I would not ask the price.

They say that the oldest profession is sex. Maybe it is, but for sure the oldest wrong in society is discrimination, to the point that sometimes it makes me think that it is like a virus, which is planted in society with no definite cure. There are enough ways to control it, but not to cure it. Discrimination does not know color, ethnic group, nor language, and it applies whether we like it or not, to all segments of societies, from religion to crime and all things in between. I paint a very gloomy picture, don't I? Well as I say, there is control, not a cure, and control works fairly well. Different methods apply to different situation. There is no such thing as "One size fits all."

In my case I developed my own system of defense against discrimination from the beginning. First, I didn't let myself be overwhelmed. I learned to respect myself and to recognize from the beginning the need to assess my abilities and myself and to develop them. I believed in never giving up and not starting from the negative corner, but starting from the positive.

I always thought, "How do you know that you cannot do it if you haven't even tried? Don't give up so easily. It is a defeat."

I always felt it was important to learn my strengths and weaknesses. We all have them. The one who ignores them and looks the other way is in trouble. I never was an "A" student in everything, as very few people are. I was an "A" student in everything related to

My Sea My Life

numbers, but spelling and Ancient Greek were "zip, nothing." Today it is no better. I would barely pass those subjects. In school, I had to spend the most time studying Ancient Greek instead of math for the exam the next day. Math was "in the bag," but Greek was not. Most other students were afraid of math. Well, I worried about Ancient Greek grammar; go figure.

I have learned to see people for what they are. I don't force them to change; rather I try to improve myself. When I gain the respect of others, their attitude changes. From my experience, I found this to be true, if not all the time, 99% of the time, to say the least. Why all of the above? Because in the small island where I grew up, if someone had two more olive trees than I did, he was rich. The island mentality was that the poor should stay poor so that they could serve. If the poor guy should look at rich man's daughter, it was a crime. At 25 years old coming back to visit Ithaca, I was hunted to get married to one of their daughters. It told me that I had changed the tide. Who me, who was from a poor family? I appreciated that I was welcomed to marry into the family, honored actually, but Mike wasn't ready to marry, at least not yet.

How did I know that I wasn't ready yet to get married? I really didn't know. Love was a whole new mystery to me, because a year later Mike was married 7500 miles away from Ithaca. So much for not being ready! I tended to think that true love and destiny were the biggest matchmakers. I guess it worked for me, and I would not change it for anything.

The plans for a long vacation quickly disappeared after a few days in Piraeus. I loved being home with my family, and I wanted very much to go to Ithaca. I couldn't say that I didn't enjoy being chased after to get married. I felt sort of like a celebrity signing autographs, as long as I didn't meet the girls. It was a cat and mouse game. They tried to catch me, and I would slip away. The first wrong move, and I would be married for the rest of my life. There was nothing wrong with this. I think I probably did the same thing when my sister was married, especially since my father was too old and my brother was a "yes and no" conversationalist. I had to carry the slack as the family matchmaker.

The situation in Greece with the military junta was not stable then. Tanks and armed vehicles were all over. Rumors of resistance came. If something happened, I could be among the first to be called back into the Navy, since I was trained in fast deployment. It was time to go again. There went my vacation. I was very disappointed, and of course the hunters were disappointed, too.

In later years, when I met Jerry again, he laughed and said, "Mike, you disappeared. My wife had designated a nice young chicken for your dinner when you came. The poor chicken waited for nothing."

I went by Mr. Matarangas's office to say hello. Laughing, he said that the Captain was looking for me. Ithacans like to play jokes, and Mr. Matarangas was no exception. He teased me about the hunters at the time. Another shipping company from Ithaca, Vlassopoulos, was growing quickly. I knew the company and the family, especially the mother, since I was a little boy. Before the earthquakes in 1953 we had a green grocer's store. In summertime, quite a few wealthy Ithacans came for vacation. Two big families that we supplied were the Dracoulis and the Vlassopoulos families. Dracoulis had a son who was slow and was under my protective umbrella. That alone secured the account for the summer for our small business. The little neighborhood rascals had no mercy, and I was able to control them, so they didn't bother him. On the Vlassapoulos side, I was the favorite of the Old Lady, and I really took care of her order. She wanted the tomatoes to be round, the peppers to be a certain size, the zucchini a certain way and so on. I would look around and find what she wanted. I was her darling, and she gave me lemonade and pastries plus tips every time I made deliveries.

During those lemonade times she told me, "When you finish school, you come to me, and you will be on a good ship."

So here I was now, going back to the Vlassopoulos family.

The Port Captain in Piraeus was from island of Chios on the other side of Greece. As I said, Vlassapoulos was married to one of the big shipping families of Chios. By the way, without being written in the book, seamen from the owner's island had priority over others unless they commanded a bad reputation.

The Port Captain, not knowing me, got my name and all my information and said, "I will call you."

I left kind of disappointed, because even though I asked, I could not get any further, so I left. A couple of days later, I was having coffee and one of the seamen from my coffee shop came running to me and said, "Thank God, I found you!"

Laughing, I said "Why, I was lost, and I didn't know it."

"No, no. The Port Captain is looking for you, and he said to go to his office as soon as possible."

"Well, what do you know!"

So I went there. This time there was a 180-degree turn.

He said, "Sit down and have a cup of coffee."

I was given the VIP treatment, and I asked, "What is going on?"

"Well, I talked to so and so from Ithaca and found out all about you."

"You didn't have to call Ithaca. I told you."

"Well, if you had given me some details, we would not have had any misunderstanding. Anyway, you have a choice. When do you want to leave?"

"When is the first one?" I asked.

He said, "It leaves in ten days for Amsterdam, if you want it. We have the reefers in two to three months, too."

"Ten days will do. I am going to bring my papers, and *Cavo Grossos* here I come."

In the meantime, Tassie would not give up. In fact, not only would she not give up, but also letters were arriving almost every other day. She had pulled almost every wheel to find some ship that would be sailing above Hatteras. This became like a famous saying between everyone. I told my mother and family about all of them in America, and I told her what had happened to old Mihali, her brother. I thought she should know the whole story.

My mother new what all the letters were about. You could not fool Maria easily.

When she saw all the letters, she asked, "How old is her daughter?"

I said, "Twenty-one."

She said, "They are looking at you for her. You know it! We have some relation, but it is nothing close enough to not allow you to get married. This is just so you know."

"I know, Mom, I know. Many people are looking for me here, too." I said. "They are nice people, but I don't have any commitment to anyone."

I didn't think my mother ever had any objection or disagreement about whom I would marry. Somehow she knew that I would make the right choice. I think what scared my family was the distance to the U.S. and not seeing me again. I wrote back to Norfolk, explaining that I had to leave again soon. It was a good opportunity, and I would write in 10 days from the ship with details. I was on my way to Amsterdam.

Cavo Grossos was an old Ellerman Lines general cargo freighter. It was heavy duty in every way and built to fight winter and the North Atlantic storms. There were steel and heavy gears, but the ship was outdated by the new standards of today's ships with quick light modern facilities on loading and discharging. That is the way the new Ellerman cargo liners were. So the company was selling the old ones for scrap iron and replacing them with new ones. Vlassapoulos bought the old freighters to use as bulk carriers carrying different cargos mostly to underdeveloped countries. The ship had old type gears, but they were useful in places where port facilities were poor. He worked them for a couple of years, and then he scrapped them. Actually, it was a good idea. Qualified seamen were plentiful at the time and not very expensive.

I met the ship at the dry dock in Amsterdam, and it was going through a change of ownership and repairs for certification. It was estimated to stay in port about 2 weeks to complete repairs and to find freight. At the dry dock, life was easy and routine for me. I corrected charts, checked equipment to get familiar with it, and did other navigation duties. I spent some time on deck, to get to know the gears, just routine stuff.

The Chief Engineer was in his late 40's, and he had his wife with him. After supper, they would play chess with a couple of officers, have coffee and talk about different things from politics to family life.

Naturally the woman asked me the question, "When do you plan to get married?"

25 years old was the magic age. The Radio Operator and I knew how well we fit this Magic Age, and we jokingly described the attempts to catch us during our last stay. We laughed that we seemed to have escaped this time. I didn't remember exactly how the conversation came to be about Norfolk, where they used to go with another carrier. I guess we all needed to talk sometimes and without realizing it, I told them about my story there. Both the Chief and his wife were fantastic people. In the conversation I expressed my feeling about Kyki, the older daughter and I guess even though I didn't know it at the time, I was sure something was telling me to see her again. The lady was a mother and a woman, and I think by then she had a good impression of me. She was saying, "Mike, go find her."

That was easier said than done. I was on a ship that was going to Alexandria, Egypt to load cement for Cambodia. We were going from one good place to another. Good old North and South America, I will miss you.

As soon as I received the schedule, I sent a letter from Amsterdam to Tassie in Norfolk explaining the details of the trip. I gave her the ship's name and radio call sign, in case they had to send a telegram. In about 16 days all the details were done in Amsterdam, and we sailed for Alexandria at a moderate speed. We did not have to be there for 2 weeks.

To make life even easier, after two days at sea, war started between Egypt and Israel. The war didn't last too long, only a few days, but Egypt was in a mess. The Canal was closed, and we had no idea if our charter was still good. We kept going slowly for Alexandria. Don't worry; it got better. In the middle of all the worry with the *Triton*, Greece had a junta. Now, going to Egypt there was war. What else?

At about 9:30 or 10:00 at night, the radio operator woke me. I had the 12-4 watch, so after 8:30, I went to bed to rest for the midnight watch.

He said, "Mike, I got a telegram for you. I can't explain. I'll give it to you tomorrow, but I want you to see it now before the Captain sees the traffic."

Yes, you guessed it right. Tassie was working hard and through a friend of the family who was a Captain, she had found a small ship owner who had a small freighter chartered to United Fruit from the port of New York, to Jamaica, Honduras, Guatemala, and back to New York. They needed a mate, and they had arranged to get me there. Tassie could work miracles when she wanted to. Talk about hunters! She was the best. She had beaten all the Ithacans to the punch.

"Let me see it," I said.

I don't remember the telegram exactly, but it went like this: "We have arranged your engagement with Diana. Advise acceptance to arrange transportation from Alexandria."

Get this. Everybody including the Captain interpreted the telegram that I was going to the States to get engaged to Diana, and who in the world was Diana when I was talking about Kyki? The Chief's wife went bananas. She could not believe it, and she had me figured for such a nice young man. Awful!

Of course, the Radio Operator knew the truth, but he would never say anything. He enjoyed it rather immensely. It didn't happen everyday. He was flying and excited to be a part of the plot.

The Captain was upset at the beginning, but he started laughing and said, "What the hell! You are young. Go."

He was thinking that I was going to marry Diana, of course. He told me, "Answer them that you are going."

So the message with my acceptance left 2 or 3 days later. I received a telegram to go to the Olympic Airways in Alexandria. The money had been paid, and the ticket to New York had been arranged. Olympic Airways made all of the other arrangements for the rest of the trip.

I had to deal with the Chief's wife. To her I was a criminal, a low life. I was no good to have betrayed the poor girl, Kyki. Again, the Radio Operator had a fiesta. I never saw a person enjoy the rumors that were flying behind my back as much as he did.

We arrived in Alexandria. It took a couple of days to arrange everything, and I had to leave my pay with the Captain just in case it was necessary for the company to pay the ticket for my replacement, since I left the ship prematurely. It was within their rights.

I said, "Take care of the arrangements, and if there is any money left, send it to my family in Piraeus."

I could not bear to see the Chief's wife in torment, so before I left I explained everything to her, and she promised not to say anything. Actually, it was a great relief for her. She took it hard to think that she was so wrong in thinking that I was such a bad person. She wished me good luck with a hug of relief.

So *Cavo Grossos* became history. The plan as we discussed with Olympic Airways in Alexandria was to fly from there to Cairo, and then to Athens. I was to be a seaman going home to Athens, and not to the U.S. Because of the Israeli-Egyptian War, stating that I was going to the United States was dangerous.

They said, "As for a visa, don't even think about it. Just go."

So here I was on my way to New York. What was I thinking? What was I doing? Changing ships? Okay. What was to be a trip to Cambodia around the Cape, I understood. I was seriously going to meet and get to know a girl, which would lead to getting married!

I thought, "Mike, you must be losing your mind." How come you didn't become so crazy that fast in Piraeus when the hunters were chasing you? You avoided meeting all of them to avoid marriage. You didn't go to Ithaca for the same reason. Now you are traveling 7,000 miles to meet that reason. Are you out of your mind?"

"Don't you know that you are playing with fire?" one Mike was saying to the other.

The other Mike would say, "It is okay. I know what I am doing."

This debate in my mind was going on all the way to the New York Airport. Now I had other things to worry about, like a visa and where my new ship was.

Saturday evening I arrived at JFK Airport in New York.

THE AIRPORT – DIANA

Here I was, at New York JFK Airport, without a passport (the seaman's book at the time was used as a passport) without a Visa and wearing light clothing. Through the customs I moved very easily and quickly, but I approached the Immigration booth very skeptically. I began to explain to the Immigration Officer where I was coming from and why I was entering the country without a Visa. The lady behind the counter wasn't upset, but rather confused. Not knowing how to handle the situation, she referred me to her supervisor, who took me to his office. He told me to sit down, and asked me what was the problem. I explained to him that I was coming from Alexandria, Egypt, that I gotten off from a ship to transfer to another one, but that it was with a different company. The ship was coming to New York, if it wasn't there already.

I said, "Here are the ticket arrangements that were paid for by the company. But, under the circumstances in Egypt, there wasn't any way for me to get a Visa. It was a few days after the Six-Day War between Egypt and Israel. I would not dare tell them that I was going to the United States. They probably would have killed me. So I took the airplane from Alexandria to Cairo with all the papers showing that I was going to Athens, but I was really going to New York. In Athens I stayed a short time just to transfer to a bigger airplane with the Olympic Airways to go to New York. Here were my seaman's papers and my discharge from the *Cavo Grossos*. Many details for *Diana* (the other ship that I am going to) I don't have due to the circumstances. The company's office is in downtown New York. The ship is coming to the United Fruit Docks. I am joining the ship as an officer, that's all I know."

He thought for a few minutes and said, "I can see it's not a big problem, and we can work it out." The Olympic Airways should provide accommodations until Monday, when your company will take care of you."

I said, "If it is all right with you, I can stay with relatives here. I have their address and telephone number, and actually they know that I am coming."

He said, "Okay, but still Olympic will be responsible until you go on the ship."

"That will not be a problem," I said, and with that he sent me to the Olympic Airway's office for the rest of the arrangements. We explained to the lady at the Olympic office, and it was okay with her.

"Just a phone call and the relatives will come to pick me up, and that's the end of the problem," I said to her.

So we started calling, but there was no answer. They must have gone some place; we gave them a little time. We called again, but there was still no answer. We waited, called again with no answer. That was going on for a few hours. The lady behind the counter started getting restless. This went on almost until 11:30 P.M.

By that time she said, "I will have to put you into a motel. This office will be closed in thirty minutes."

I said, "Let's try one more time." Sure enough, we got through to them. By the way, the connection had to be done through the operator.

"Here is the phone talk to them," she said.

In the meantime, some other people were making calls also through the operator. I picked up the phone, excited and happy, and I said, "Vasili, this is Michael. How are you doing? I am here at the airport."

The voice on the other line said, "I don't know any Michael. Who are you?"

I said, "What do you mean you don't know any Michael? I am Mike Razos, who is going to meet you here and go to the *Diana*."

"Nope, I have no idea what you are talking about," he said.

Oh My God! I thought, here I came to meet his daughter and possibly become his son-in-law, and he doesn't know me.

But, something seemed strange to me, and I asked, "You're sure you don't know me?"

"Yes, I'm sure," he said.

"Can I ask you a question? What is your name?" I said.

"Why you want to know my name?" he said.

"Please tell me your name, Sir. It is very important," I said.

He finally gave his last name, which was different from Vasili's last name. My God I thought I am talking to the wrong person.

I said, "Lady, the operator connected me with the wrong person."

In the meantime, Kyki was talking to the wrong person, too. It seemed that the operator made the wrong connections. That was a relief. At least the right people will know me. This time we dialed the right number, and Kyki answered the phone.

I said, "Where have you guys been? I've been here since five o'clock."

She said, "Oh, we had gone to see the Greek movie. My dad likes the Greek movie, and it only plays on Saturday evening. So, we all went to see the movie. We thought that the plane was coming later."

"I am here at the Olympic office at the airport, and they are ready to put me into a hotel. The office is closing in a few minutes," I said.

Kyki said, "No! We are coming to pick you up, tell her to wait, and tell her we will be there in thirty minutes." The Olympic worker had no choice but to wait, and she was happy to get rid of me. Otherwise, she had to worry about me over the weekend. About thirty to thirty-five minutes later, they were there to pick me up. That was my airport journey. It was exciting enough, I think.

It was an interesting weekend to say the least. Vasili, was a hardworking man, and we were full of stories about the sea and the island. Johnny, Kyki's brother, was there from Norfolk, too, working with his father. Of course, Tassie was going through the family tree. Although decades past, but with precise memories of all the events, as if she was born in Ithaca, which she had not seen yet. She had stories to tell me also about my uncle Michael, who I never knew at all, and this went on throughout the whole weekend.

In the meantime, I was looking at Kyki trying to figure out what was going on. She was looking and examining me like I was coming from another planet. We were polite to each other, but nevertheless there was tension, as if we were trying to discover what we were doing there. On the other hand for me, one Michael was fighting with the other.

One Michael said, "What are you doing here? What are you doing, Michael? Just explain it to me. Are you going to get involved deeply? Are you going to get married? Do you want to get married? Are you ready to get married? Remember not long ago, you were telling me you wanted to have your freedom and see the world. You wanted to become a captain as quickly as possible and maybe stay outside later and manage ships. You even thought to maybe go back home and get involved with the movies. Where are all these plans?"

The other Mike said, "Relax. Don't jump the gun. Let's see what is going on. I'm not getting married tomorrow. I just want to get to know the girl. She looks like a nice girl."

But, the other Michael, stubborn, and in disbelief said, "Watch yourself, you're getting into trouble, Michael!"

That internal battle was going on the whole weekend. I have no doubt in my mind that all kinds of thoughts were in poor Kyki's mind, too.

I don't remember well, but I think it was that time that Kyki and I went to see a movie, *The Sound Of Music*. I watched the whole movie, and I don't really remember much after it finished. During the conversation that we had, I probably became too philosophical, and I was thoroughly misunderstood. I was trying to explain my thoughts, and I guess they came out all wrong. I thought at the time that I was explaining myself, but I was wrong. As I found out in later years, after the movie she went home, and she had a big argument with her mom and dad. She thought that I called her ugly.

Actually that never went through my mind. What I was trying to say at the time was that you don't get married only because a person is beautiful. You get married because of the many other qualities that come with a person. To me, beauty was important, but more important was the quality of the person. When I married I wanted a friend, a lover, a spouse, and someone that could understand me. That went for both people. Poor Kyki!

At that time, she had no idea about my background. Realistically speaking, I had no idea about hers, either. I could not realize at that time that here was a girl almost twenty-two years of age, so beautiful and so pure, and so innocent. As for me, from fourteen years old and even younger, I was working all over Piraeus, and I had seen almost everything, bars and girls, all of it. With that background, I was trying to tell her if I settled down with her, it was because we were made for each other. Well, she grossly misunderstood me, and from what I learned later, she had a fit.

The weekend passed, and on Monday at the office, they told me that the ship would arrive the next morning. Of course, they would take care of everything as far as Immigration was concerned. The next day I joined the ship as the Chief Mate. That was a pleasant surprise to me. I thought I was going as the Second Mate. Joining the ship as Chief Mate was of course new to me. Plus, this would be a lot more work and responsibility since the ship was a general cargo ship.

I explained my fears to the owner, and he said, "Michael, from what I see, you will not have any problem! You are a hard worker and a determined, young man. As far as the cargo plans are concerned, don't worry, because United Fruit does those. Even if you want, you can't do the cargo plans, because they bring cargo at the last moment. Sometimes they even delay the sailing while waiting for cargo, they have complete control over the cargo. Your main concern is to know exactly what is going to each port and to make sure that it is secured and delivered right. This way we don't have any over carriages and mixed up cargo."

I said, "That's not bad."

"See. You are already starting to feel easier," the owner said.

That was the truth. Actually the United Fruit did all the plans, and my job was to make sure that it was secure and separated for each port. Of course, United Fruit was very good and in every port they had their own people to come on board to handle the cargo and to secure it for the next port. There were places where the longshoremen were not always cooperative, and I had to be on top of things. That meant running up and down the hatches continuously for long hours.

The U.S. was normally an eight to five stay and very efficient. In other ports like Cortez and Kingston, Jamaica from the time we arrived, usually seven or eight o'clock in the morning, they worked continually until the work was done, sometimes until the next morning. I had to be working or on standby all the time. Barrios was the main port in Central America for the ship. We usually stayed there the most time. They operated like New York eight to five which made it easy. The round trip was about twenty-four to twenty-eight days, depending on the weather and sometimes waiting for cargo.

Diana was a nice midsize ship for that time, about 5,000 tons dead weight with two hatches in the front and two hatches in the back. The accommodations were nicely done and were fairly luxurious. Next to the Captain's cabin was a beautifully furnished and decorated lounge with a bar. It was being used to entertain company employees and other important visitors. The crew was from all over the Caribbean, with most from Guatemala and Honduras. Naturally, as a Chief Mate I had to speak Spanish, otherwise I was in trouble. That wasn't a problem for me with my Portuguese, a little Italian, and my Spanish. I was getting by fairly well. Slowly, I zeroed in on Spanish only. Soon I was doing everything in Spanish without any problem. When I met Kyki, my Brazilian, Italian, and Spanish were almost better than my English. Sometime I would start in English and mix it with the Spanish or Brazilian.

Kyki would say, "Oh wait! Now you're talking another language."

I don't know, but maybe that was one of the things that started the misunderstanding at the movie.

Coming back to New York from my first trip with *Motor Vessel Diana*, it was summer, and we were scheduled to stay in New York at least four days. Even though the trip was very busy for me, especially being my first trip as Chief Mate, I wanted everything to run smoothly, and it did. Still I had time to think about Kyki and her family. Any conclusions? Not yet. Confused? Yes.

When I saw them, they told me that this time it was Kyki, Vasili, and of course her little brother, Johnny. Tassie was back in school. She was up in Cornell University for a short summer course. From what I realized later, this was the best thing that happened for Kyki and me. Besides the traditions and all the paraphernalia that precedes marriage in those days, my mind was made up. When I decide to marry, it would be my own decision and not one that was influenced by someone else. Growing up with little, and even though I had been frugal, I did not value the idea of dowry at all. I just wanted a person with whom I could spend the rest of my life, with love, trust, and respect for each other.

At the time, I didn't realize what pressure Kyki was under. Tassie's intentions were good. But, from what I found out later, she was pressing things a little too hard. Of course, she had no idea who I was. She knew my uncle was a nice person, and she knew from her father that my mother was a nice girl. But about me, I don't think that she had any idea who I was. I was nice and polite, but that was all. She had no details. In her conversations, or arguments, with Kyki, she described me the way she wanted me to be in her mind, which was the way my uncle was, whom she loved very much. He was, in a way, her older brother. Her view was not intentional and nothing bad, but it wasn't reality. I never met my uncle. Having died in a New York hospital where apparently they mixed up the blood, whatever I knew about him was from my mother, and she was telling me that he was a very nice person. I sort of looked like the older Michael from what everyone was telling me.

During my conversation with Tassie, I was telling her about the places that I visited. Of course I skipped the stories around the port, I told her about the sports, the big stadium Maracana in Rio de Janeiro, about the Corcovado with the statue of Christ, and Genoa with the famous cemetery, and mostly conservative places. Tassie was telling Kyki what a good boy I was and I visited only churches in foreign counties. Yea right! Poor Kyki, freaked out, she thought I was some kind of a weird guy. What a GOOF BALL he must be!

This time it was Kyki and Mike alone! Vasili and Johnny spent an enormous number of hours working, usually from 10 A.M. to almost 11:30 P.M. We visited them, but now it was mostly Kyki, and I. It gave us the freedom to sit down and talk and explore each other's beliefs and thinking. In a way, we were evaluating each other, since in the back of our minds (at least mine for the time) we were thinking something permanent might lie ahead for us later down the road. The more time I spent with Kyki, the more I realized that the number one Michael was right about her honesty, innocence, sensible way of thinking, and besides what she thought I said at the movie, her unspoiled beauty. Day by day we were getting more and more at ease with each other.

It was, I think, the third day in New York and the company was giving a party on the ship for the office employees and other friends. Of course as Chief Mate, I had to attend the party. The Second Mate, the playboy of the ship, had arranged to introduce me to a bunch of girls from the office without my knowledge. That man lived to party, and of course, we had to attend the party wearing some type of uniform, at least khakis. I explained to the Captain that I would try to be there as soon as I could, but Kyki was coming to visit me. He understood me very well. Although he was a little older than me, he was going through the same trying period of important decisions with a girl in Greece. In fact, he was rather upset that he was so far away on this ship. He understood very well the trials and tribulations we were both going through. The playboy was the one, who did not understanding the situation. His way of thinking was here was the party, here was the good stuff, don't mess it up, and send her home early.

My Sea My Life

Around five o'clock Kyki arrived. A few minutes later the longshoreman left, so she stayed in my room waiting for me. A little later I was done for the day, and she and I started again talking in my room. Dirty from working on deck the whole day, I had to take a shower. So I took Kyki to the bridge where she enjoyed the view. She could see lower Manhattan, part of the port, and the ships coming and going. She stayed there waiting for me. A short time later, I was back, and she didn't mind it at all. She was enjoying the view, so we stayed in the bridge area. Because it was hot inside the bridge, we went outside at the wings, and we continued our conversation. We were talking and talking. By now it was getting dark, and with that came the famous New York mosquitoes, which have no mercy when they bite.

"Kyki, it's time to go downstairs," I said, and by the way she didn't want to go to the party.

She said, "It's okay, they don't bother me. Really it's okay. We'll stay here."

I said, "It's okay with me, but they bite."

We kept on with our conversation, but from what I found out later, she was afraid to come to my room alone. In the meantime, the Second Mate was going nuts, popping up from different places and signaling me to go to the party. We both ended up with quite a few mosquito bites. By that time it was close to nine o'clock, and I didn't want her to drive home late and alone. I took her to the car and off she went to Long Island.

I went to the party, stayed a little, had a couple of drinks, and excused myself with the word that I had a big day tomorrow and had to go. I disappointed the girls, too bad. I couldn't help it. I wasn't about to get into trouble from the beginning of my new relationship. The next day, Kyki was supposed to meet me around five o'clock. It was our last day since we sailed for the Caribbean the next day. I was waiting and waiting, and Kyki was nowhere. It was almost seven o'clock, and she still wasn't there. Worried, I called her father.

He said. "She left a long time ago. She should have been there by now, maybe she got caught in the traffic."

To my relief a little later, Kyki showed up.

I said, "Kyki, where have you been? I've been worrying."

She said, "You wouldn't believe it, but I had an emergency with Moutro."

Moutro was a little puppy that she had. The poor thing fell from the back seat of the car onto the floor and twisted his leg. The dog was screaming from pain. Kyki naturally took it to a veterinary clinic to check it, and with all of that she was late. We didn't have a lot of time left, and we went to a restaurant close by for a meal and a little talk. We said good-bye until the next trip. That was the second trip to New York with the *Diana*.

Thank God we had that time together alone, because the next trip would not be to New York. It would be from the ports in the Gulf to Central America. I was disappointed, but there was nothing I could do. The new run was New Orleans as a main port in the U.S., Jamaica, Honduras, Guatemala, with Barrios as a main port, Belize, and back to the U.S., to Freeport Texas, Houston, Port Arthur, and finally New Orleans. In twenty-four to twenty-five days this was a busy run. The only time we stayed in port a little bit was in New Orleans and Barrios. At the other ports it was in and out, mostly during the same day. These were long hours for me. We almost doubled the ports in the same amount of days for the round trip. I had to put in more hours, but of course I was getting more overtime. I was young, and I didn't mind.

Now began a new facet in my relationship with Kyki, by the telephone. In those days there were no cell phones and no calling cards, just the good old coin phone. I hoped that I would find one that was not broken, some place on the dock. I would change a ten-dollar bill to quarters, and every three minutes I would put more coins in until they were used up. There was no question that the telephone company received lots of quarters from me. Sometimes, although not very often, the phone company was merciful to me. Once in New Orleans, the operator forgot us. I was calling from a payphone and Kyki was on a pay phone in New York. We must have talked to our hearts content. When we didn't have anything else to say at the time, we said good-bye. That was great, and I thank the operator for that. I could not have afforded the call otherwise. Another great time was in the longshoreman shack in Houston. The payphone turned into a slot machine, and it pumped out coins, more than mine! That extended the phone call quite a bit. Every little thing helped, so thanks again! However, most of the time, I paid dearly.

The run was nice, but very busy, especially for the Captain in the Central American ports, where they had no pilot and no tugs. It made it very painful to dock and undock the ship. In the five months that I stayed there, I changed a total of three captains. The mentality of the crew on these ships was different from the big ships. I had to become accustomed to their mentality to tolerate the run. That's why we had a big turnover of captains.

After a while I started feeling the same dissatisfaction. The whole operation was awkward compared to what I was accustomed to. There were ideas of free love, a good time in each port, and neglecting your job. When these were the ideas of key personnel, like the chief engineer, and electrician, it made working on the ship very difficult. If I wanted them, I had to look for them in the bars, even during the working hours. It wasn't going well with me. My deck crew was excellent. I was good to them and they would do anything for me. My deck crew was mostly from Barrios and Cortez, and I would give them plenty of time to go home.

The last Captain made things more chaotic on the ship especially because he patronized the lovers. I guess he was doing that to be on their good side. Later, I found that he had a nephew already scheduled to take my place. He could not say anything to the company because they liked me, and I was well respected. He was hoping that I would leave on my own. He knew that I was becoming more and more fed up with the politics that were going on.

By now, Kyki and I were moving towards a serious commitment, although Kyki was more skeptical than me. It was not as if I wasn't worried. Even though things between Kyki and me were moving fast, both of us really needed time to digest what was going on between us, and if we were really ready for a commitment. On the other hand, time was not on our side. With all my heart, I did not want to loose Kyki. Did I know her well enough? I probably did not, but because I was a little older and a little more experienced, I felt confident about her. As for Kyki, she probably, was more hesitant, even though you could see that she did not want to loose me.

Imagine! A short time ago, if you had told me that I would propose marriage soon, I would have said to lock the man up because he was totally crazy. Now, I was asking poor Kyki to marry me. God Help Me! From Freeport, Texas, I explained to Kyki what was going on with the *Diana*, and that most probably I would leave the *Diana* and continue from Greece or another ship, hopefully sailing close to the East Coast.

"I will call you from New Orleans. You tell me what you decided, and I will go along," I said. "I do not want to pressure you more."

Three days later I called her from New Orleans, we talked a little and then Kyki said. "Mike, I will do it! I will marry you!"

"Thank God!" I said, "I love you. I do!"

Now, this was how we did it. Since nothing was ever easy for me, this was how we got married. The best way was for her to come to New Orleans to meet me on the next trip. We would get married in a civil ceremony. Then I could get off on the next trip with twenty-nine day permission to stay in the States according to the U.S. Immigration rules. I could then go to Norfolk, and from there continue with the rest of the necessary papers.

The trip went by quickly, and being busy I did not have enough time to really think that in New Orleans I was getting married. In New Orleans there was a Ship Chandler who I met with the *Diana*, even though there weren't many supplies that I could buy from him. Practically everything was supplied through the United Fruit. Still we became friends. He was much older than I. Religiously he would come to the ship every time I was there and spend time talking. When he heard that I was getting married, and that the girl was coming to meet me at my next trip to New Orleans, he was happy for me.

He said, "Don't worry. My wife and I will arrange everything. We will pick them up from the airport and do all the arrangements. We will do everything. You are like a son to me."

By the way, he did not have any children of his own. He was a big, tall man and his wife was petite. Both of them were very nice. The ship was scheduled to stay in New Orleans three maybe four days, and it usually sailed the fourth day in the evening.

When the head stevedore heard that I was getting married, he said. "You are off, and I mean off the ship. I will take care of everything. I will even secure the ship for sea."

This was a thing that was unheard of from longshoreman. We had become good friends by this time.

"What I want from you, are the keys to the office and your room," he said. He and his friend would like to have a drink, and my door was open all the time for them to help themselves. My friend picked up Kyki and her mother from the airport, and there they were at the ship, dressed fit to kill with Kyki in her mini skirt. Normally this was nothing so unusual, because mini skirts were in style at the time. But, for the *Diana* and her diverse crew, it was a little different. We stayed a little at the ship to make sure that everything was in order, and off we went.

Kyki, her mother, my friend, and I picked up his wife, and we were off for the civil ceremony across the river at the Algiers Courthouse. Everything went smoothly, but by that time we were all hungry. We went to a nice seafood restaurant by the lake, and we had a big feast. My friend was a talker. Tassie was also a talker, and they started talking and talking to the point that they had arranged without consulting Kyki or me for the Ship Chandler to be the best man in our church wedding in Norfolk. Now that wasn't a crime, and he was a nice man, but it was our wedding, Kyki's and mine. We should have decided who would be our best man.

I asked to her later at the hotel, "Why did you commit for him to be the best man?"

She said, "He seemed like a nice man."

That was done, and I couldn't change it. Here we were with the Ship Chandler as the best man.

The Port Captain, who was the head stevedore to United Fruit, wanted me to move to New Orleans and work with him. This was a very nice offer and a good opportunity. The Ship Chandler was also insisting on my moving to New Orleans and working with him, which was another good deal. Tassie wanted me to stay in Norfolk, the reason being for Kyki to be close to home; and that saga continued later.

In New Orleans, Kyki and I had a chance to go to a nightclub together alone. We had a memorable night, which we both still remember. Now, Kyki and her mother were at the airport on the way home, and my friend had taken me to the ship, which was ready to sail. The stevedores and my deck crew had really made the ship ready in all respects. They were all happy for me, especially my crew. They out did themselves, to please me. They thought that I was getting married to a very nice girl.

Now traveling down the river and then going out in the ocean, I was exhausted from the last three and a half days, and so I went to bed. That was when it hit me, like a ton of bricks. That was when I realized that I was married. What had I done! Me? Married? I was exhausted, but I couldn't sleep. Is that what they call cold feet? Thank God it was after the wedding. Now I was married, and I still couldn't believe it. I got very little sleep the first night. Very slowly it started sinking in, and I was accepting that I was married.

That was to be my last round trip with the *Diana*, because on the way back to New Orleans, I was getting off. I had to go to the U.S. Immigration office to get permission to stay twenty-nine days in the U.S. From past experiences with other seamen, sometimes the Immigration could be difficult, and so, the Captain came with me just in case. Kyki was terrified for me to go back to Greece and expedited my papers from Norfolk. She had a very good reason for her fears. The political situation at the time in Greece was unstable with the military junta in power. Plus Greece was having problems with Turkey, and Kyki was afraid that I would get stuck there and possibly even be brought back into the Navy.

Here we were now, the Captain and I at the Immigration Office. When I met with the Immigration Officer, I said, "I am Mike

Razos from *M/V Diana*."

Before I could finish, he said, " Oh, yes, Mr. Razos come in." He treated me like I was a VIP. "So you want to stay twenty-nine days?"

I said "Yes, I think that is the limit that you can give me."

"Yes, but if you want I can give you more, it will not be a problem," he said.

I couldn't believe what I was hearing. The Captain also was very surprised. So we proceeded, and I got my extension for as long as I wanted, to my surprise and happiness. I couldn't explain how I got this treatment.

So the first chance I had, I asked the Immigration Officer, "Sir, don't get me wrong. By now I have been around the States a lot, and this is the first time that I have seen a person get an extension to stay that easily. How is that?"

He said, "Don't you know?"

I said, "No."

"Well, we have here a very nice recommendation letter from the Vice President of United Fruit. He guarantees your character, and they will be responsible for you throughout your stay," he said. "With a letter like that, especially from the United Fruit, you don't have a problem getting the extension you want."

I knew the gentleman that wrote the letter. He used to visit the ship a lot. I had gone to his office with different business issues quite a few times. He was the boss there. I am thankful with all my heart for everything he did, wherever he is today.

NORFOLK – THE WEDDING

With that the last goodbye to the *Diana*, I was off to Norfolk, Virginia, and a new chapter in my life would start. At the time I thought that it was a good possibility that the *Diana* would be the last ship that I ever sailed. My first bosun proved to be right when he said that if you stayed long enough at sea, it was like alcohol that got into your veins and never got out. He would be proven right, but this is for later.

It was a busy time for all of us, especially for Kyki. She had to finish the last semester of school and also to get ready to get married. For me, I could not work; I didn't have a permanent Visa yet. I was busy though preparing the papers for the Immigration for my permanent entry into the U.S. After a lot of thought, I decided to file for the entrance Visa with the Kingston, Jamaica Consulate. This was an unusual place, but, nevertheless, it was the most familiar to me at the time. With the *Diana*, I would carry a lot of things and sometimes I would carry special mail for the Kingston U.S. Consulate. I even kept the mail deliveries in special lockers in my room for safety. Almost all of the mail required hand delivery. This way I got to know quite a few of the U.S. personnel in Kingston. With today's communication it's a completely different game, but it was 1968. In Jamaica, the U.S. Consul, besides taking the time to prepare the papers, had to get all the information from Greece. This way it took a little longer to notify me of the Visa. Tassie was very efficient on the procedures and experienced in dealing with Immigration, because when she was young, she worked for them. She was familiar with the procedures, plus she knew quite a few of the personnel in Norfolk.

Norfolk was a good place for me to stay and wait until it was time to go to Jamaica. With the extension that I had from New Orleans, and being on friendly terms with Immigration in Norfolk, I had no problems.

Many would ask why are we waiting to get married. You are already married. You got married in New Orleans. Well, yes and no! The religious ceremony for us was the most important. Until that day, we considered ourselves being more or less "engaged" rather than married. For Michael, until recently, marriage was not in his vocabulary, much more for him to know the details of a wedding. From the little experience that I had in Ithaca, I knew that most of the people that you invite come to the church, and then they leave. With the immediate family, and a few close friends, you go home or to a restaurant and have a little celebration. From there the couple leaves for their honeymoon, and that's it! I had no idea about weddings in the States, with bridesmaids, grooms, showers, and the rest of the paraphernalia. For example, everyone was talking about the showers, but we were talking about different showers. A shower to me was to get washed. I didn't want to sound ignorant, but I was wondering why she had to take so many showers! This was a strange custom to say the least.

Finally, I broke down, and privately I asked Kyki, "What is with the showers? Why do you have to take showers? What is the meaning?"

"That is a custom, and I get a lot of gifts like that," she said.

"You have to take a shower to get presents. Weird custom!" I said.

That is when she realized what I meant when I said "Shower" and she started laughing hysterically.

"No Mike, not that kind of shower, she said, and she explained what a shower was.

The wedding ceremony was at the Annunciation Greek Orthodox Church in Norfolk. Then we went to the Phythian Hall for the celebration and dancing. The house was literally flooded with relatives, lots of relatives. They were mostly from my father-in law's side, and they came from the West Coast, Pennsylvania, New York, and other places. According to my father-in-law, they all could stay at his home. Catering the wedding was kind of expensive, as it always was, especially with all the people that were invited. My father-in-law, his cousins, and his brother, who were all experienced with restaurants, decided to prepare the food themselves. It was not only a lot more economical, but also it was nice home cooking and plentiful, giving the wedding a homier atmosphere.

My father-in-law and I were working at the reception hall until one hour before the church ceremony. The food was delicious, but to anyone who saw the drinking and joking and the celebrating that was going on in the kitchen, they would think, "My God! We're heading for a disaster!" There was not a problem at all. We managed to have a fantastic buffet style dinner with plenty for everyone.

Vasili went to his house to change, and I went to a friend's house to shave, take a shower, and change for the church with very little time to spare, but I made it on time to the church. I opened the door, and who was there to greet me? Why it was Kyki!

When she saw me, she said, "You're not supposed to see me!"

She ran for the dressing room. There were so many people in the house, and there was such a commotion going on, she could not take it and left for the church to find a quiet moment.

Here comes the Thriller in Manila, as they said in the Mohammed Ali-Fraser fight. This time the thriller was in Norfolk, and it was between my mother-in-law and the best man, the same one she chose in New Orleans to be the best man. They both liked to talk and during the wedding reception, my best man proceeded to boast how he would take Kyki and me to New Orleans to work with him and how Norfolk was not the place for us. Although he might have been right about Norfolk, this wasn't the time or place for that discussion. Meanwhile this wasn't what my mother-in-law needed to hear since she thought she was loosing her daughter. That triggered the battle. The sweet talking time between them was over forever, period. Kyki and I tried to calm them down, but I don't think we achieved much. The Capo de Monte was broken. They were purely in their own world, and it was as if Kyki and I didn't have anything to say, especially since no one had asked us anything. As if the pressures of the wedding were not enough, poor Kyki and I had to deal with that nonsense, too!

Otherwise, the evening was delightful, with good music, good food, plenty to drink, and lots of dancing. By midnight, we cut the cake and Kyki and I were ready to take off. There was so much food and drinks, even the photographer got drunk. Most of the wedding pictures, turned us as red as lobsters. I don't know how, but he did it. The studio tried their best to preserve some decent ones.

However that was the last time, I saw my poor best man. We talked on the phone many times. By the time I was able to visit New Orleans, he had passed away. He was fairly old when I met him anyway. Our honeymoon was kind of short, we went through the Virginia Mountains, to New York to sightsee, and back to Norfolk. To my ignorance, and thinking the old country ways, I decided to take the offer of my mother-in-law to stay with them until we settled down, even though Kyki was against it.

Kyki was saying, "Let's go find a place and live on our own."

I said, "Why? There is plenty of room in the house. This way it will give us time so I can get my Visa, and I can work."

It sounded logical to be thinking with the old country standards.

Kyki said, "I will go along Michael, but I have my reasons to believe that this is not the best move."

I could not see that at the time, but she was right.

The waiting period to get my Visa was kind of easy. Kyki was done with college, and she had a job as a teacher for the fall. Finally it was time for me to get my Visa. The Immigration informed me that my papers were ready, and I could go to Jamaica to get my Visa. I was happy because finally, I would be able to start working.

For me, not working wasn't going well. I did a few jobs in the house like painting, repairs, etc., but I wanted to work. I did not consider what I was doing as work.

As I arrived on the island I thought, "Here I am in Jamaica. I will have to stay at least two days, since the Consulate here is a very busy place."

I went to the Consulate very early the next morning; and I couldn't believe what I saw. Even though it was very early, the lines were long. When I say long, I mean long!

I said to myself, "It will take more than two days with these kinds of lines."

Feeling kind of down, I stayed in line waiting. Sometimes one gets lucky, and I got lucky. A lady from the Consulate passed by, and I knew her from the *Diana*. She was one of the officers in the Consulate.

She saw me standing in line, and she said, "What are you doing here?"

After the hellos, I explained to her the reason I was there.

She enjoyed a love story, and she laughed and said, "You will never finish with these lines. I'll tell you what to do. Go to the back of the building. There is a gate there with a guard, tell him that you are waiting for me, and I will come and get you."

So I got inside, but if it weren't for her, I would be still waiting. Quite a few people inside knew me from the *Diana,* and they laughed at me for waiting in line. They thought getting the Visa from Jamaica was kind of strange, but it was also funny to them. They processed the papers quickly, the Consul signed my Visa, and they all wished me good luck. I thanked them a lot, and I was off for the hotel. I called the airlines, and I changed my flight back home for the same day. There wasn't a reason for me to stay longer in Jamaica. I called home, my brother in law, John, answered the phone. I told him that I finished quickly and that I would be home that day. I also told him to tell Kyki so she could pick me up from the airport. I made sure to tell him not to forget it. He also assured me that he wouldn't forget to tell Kyki. It was no problem at all.

Now I'm happily back in Norfolk, with the Visa. I couldn't wait to tell Kyki my story. I did not carry many bags, just one, since it was just to be an overnight stay. So I went through the airport and outside with the idea that Kyki was waiting for me. Kyki was nowhere to be found.

I said to myself, "Maybe she got stuck in some traffic. I'll wait a few minutes."

But knowing Kyki, I knew she would be there. I called home, but there was no answer. After a few hours of waiting, I saw Kyki coming, happy to see me, but a little upset.

I said, "What's going on?"

She said, "My brother forgot to tell me that you were coming. Accidentally, he just told me when I said I wonder how Michael is doing? Then John told me that you called, but he forgot to tell me that you said that you were coming tonight."

Kyki was livid. John was a great guy, but he forgot messages easily, even today, but still he is a good guy.

The waiting finally was over, and the papers were completed. I had my green card, and it was time to unleash myself back to the work force. All the time that I could not work because I was waiting for my Visa, Tassie was trying to keep my spirits up, and she was telling me that she knew lots of people, and I should not worry. When I got my green card, I would find a job.

Vasili vouched for this, and he would say, "Yes, she knows quite a few people, since she used to work for many maritime lawyers as a translator."

Feeling that all of this was true, I felt I didn't have to go anywhere else to look for a job. I was sure I would be able to find a job in Norfolk. Now was the time to use all this wealth of knowledge. I still can't explain it today, but all the connections vanished. All the people that Tassie knew were simply not helping her. Michael had to look for a job himself, but there was no use to cry over spilled milk. Leaving and going to New Orleans or Houston with United Fruit or with the ship's chandler was an alternative, but I didn't know if things would have been better. One thing I did know was that Kyki was right.

Finally, after a lot of aggravation, I found a job at Norshipco. I aimed for a rigger, a dock master, or something that fit my expertise, but nothing like that was open at the time. They told me to start as an assistant ship fitter and when something opened up, they would transfer me.

I said, "That'll be alright. Anyway it will be temporary."

I started working as an assistant ship fitter, a job unknown to me; and it was hard, and nasty, with long hours. With such a small salary, this was quite a difference from being a chief mate. However, I had to do what I had to do, and I hoped that the transfer would come soon. This was not really going to happen. The dry dock company at that time needed labor, and I found out that they had no intention of transferring me.

When I was working as a ship fitter, there were some young men in their early twenties that were called apprentices. Norshipco had a four-year apprentice program with two years of school and two years of actual work, and after finishing a person was a first class mechanic. This was not a bad deal. Working with them was the best part of the whole Norshipco ordeal. After the guys got to know me, they told me about the school, and they asked if I was interested, which I was. With my experience as a mate, and if I had a first class mechanic certificate, I thought that I would be able to work for shipping companies for good money. I went to the main office to apply. Here was another disappointment. They had an age limit of twenty-six years of age, and I was twenty-seven. They were sorry, but there were no exceptions. Often I checked with the office personnel if anything was opening for a transfer, and the answer was always no. More and more, I began to realize that I was stuck there.

BACK TO MY ROOTS (THE SEA)

I stretched it out as much as I could at the shipyard. In the meantime, Kyki was getting very upset, because she saw me beating up on myself, and I was getting nowhere. We decided that I had to do something.

I said, "Kyki, I know my roots, where I come from, and what I can do best, and that's the ships. I am going back to the sea. It will give me the opportunity to make some money quickly."

The question was where? Do I go to the foreign flagged ships or to the U.S. ships? With the little research that I had done, I knew that I could get an AB ticket, any waters unlimited from the U.S. Coast Guard. Then I could go on the U.S. ships as an AB, which would pay me at least three times more than what I was getting at the shipyard with all the extra overtime.

Kyki said, "Michael, I will go along with what you decide. It is no problem with me. I just don't want you to suffer like this."

I have always said, and I will always say, even today, that Kyki has always believed in me and stood by me and trusted whatever I did. We always backed up and supported each other. More and more I was realizing how lucky I was to be married to someone like Kyki.

I went downtown to the Coast Guard office with all of my papers.

"Well, you are more than qualified for an AB ticket. Before we send you to Portsmouth, Virginia for the test, you have to take a small preliminary test here," they said. By the way, they were all civilians at that office, but Coast Guard personnel ran the Portsmouth office. So, I was scheduled for the preliminary test, and I thought that I had done well. I don't know how, but the person, that gave me the test, managed to fail me. Disappointed to say the least, I turned around and headed out.

Another person approached me as I was heading out, and said, "Can I talk to you?"

I said "Okay, now what?"

He took me on the side, and he said. "Look, you have to wait a month now, there's nothing that I can do about it. When you come back, you come to me, don't go to that person again, and you will be all right."

I thanked him, and I left. I didn't consider myself to be naïve. But at that time, I didn't think that a person would fail me because they didn't like my face or my accent. On the other had, the second person seemed to be such a nice, decent person. A month later, I went straight to the right person, and in a few minutes I was done with the tests.

"Now, you need to go to Portsmouth for the big test. Good Luck!" he said.

I thanked him, and I was off to Portsmouth for the next test. AB any waters unlimited was the maximum ticket that I could get without being a citizen. Portsmouth was all business, if you knew the test you passed, and by the way, they were all nice people. With what I knew from my background and experience, the test was a breeze for me, and the practical part with the lifeboats and ropes was fun.

The commander who signed my paper said, "I hope to see you soon, for your mate's license. From what I can see, you are qualified almost for a chief mate's license."

Now with my Z Card, which is the U.S. seaman's card, I started looking for a job. The two main sources, S.I.U. and N.M.U, were the two biggest unlicensed maritime unions in the U.S. S.I.U. had more jobs without subsidy from the government, but I had to pay back dues, actually from the day the union started. Every time the ship was back from a trip, S.I.U. would collect a hefty amount of money from its members. N.M.U. did not have that, but it was a little harder to find jobs with them. It was not that there were not many jobs, but I would say that eighty percent of the N.M.U. ships were subsidized ships and therefore, would only take a limited number of resident aliens. These few slots were almost permanently filled. There were always rules, rules, and rules.

One seaman, I think it was at the S.I.U. Hall, suggested that I try a towing company for a job. The pay wasn't as good as that on the big ships, but it was a very good job, if you can take the seas in the smaller ships. There was a company operating with a schedule of one round trip on and a half trip off. Usually, the run was from Morehead City, North Carolina to Baton Rouge, Louisiana. So, I thought I'd give it a try. The company hired me to join the ship, and I had to go to Baton Rouge.

Kyki took me to the airport, thinking that I was getting on a regular plane. Here was a small four-seat plane for us to board. Poor thing, the plane was a shock for her, and to be honest it was a little bit of a shock for me, too. But, a man had to do what a man had to do, so I took it. Kyki was scared to death. I called her as soon as I got there to calm her down.

I stayed with the tug for a couple of trips, and I decided that it wasn't for me, even though they promised that in a few trips I would become a mate. The seaman at the hall was right, when he said that you had to be cut out for that type of ship. My guts were almost ready to pop out of my mouth, plus Kyki was upset. She saw in the news that at the same time I was on the tug, another tug went down and they never found a single one of the crew.

I figured the best place to stay and wait for a ship was with the N.M.U. While waiting for a job at the N.M.U. Hall each day, I got to know a few seamen plus the local patrolman (the N.M.U. representative). He liked me, and he was rather upset to see a well-qualified seaman not be able to get a job because I didn't have my citizenship, especially with so many jobs desperately needing to be filled.

So one day, he said, "Michael, come with me. We'll try something that might work."

He took me to the Coast Guard at the ship commissioner's office. There was a ship belonging to the American Export Lines, and it was delaying to sail because it was short an AB. He proceeded to explain my situation, while presenting my papers and my qualifications and asked for a waiver for me to sail as an AB even for one round trip.

Unbending, he would not agree, and he gruffly said, "The slots for resident aliens on this ship are full, I cannot do anything. Sorry."

Both of us were upset, and we left for the hall. "Don't worry. I think a job in Sunny Point, North Carolina will be up in a few days, and I guarantee it will be yours."

He was right, and I was so happy. I got my first reasonable sea-going job with the U.S. Merchant Marine. The name of the ship was the *Clarksville Victory*, and a company owned it down in Louisiana that had mostly barges. I think that they had only two victory ships, and since there was no subsidy here, I had no problems. The ship, which was docked at Sunny Point, was loading B-52 bombs for Vietnam.

For the regular N.M.U. members, it wasn't the most appetizing job, especially when they could get jobs on newer ships and closer to home. To me, it was a gift. Now, I only had to persuade Kyki that it was all right for me to go to Vietnam on a ship with a full load of B-52 bombs, just a small detail. She finally accepted it, or at least she tried.

So Kyki, with her mother, who was kind enough to come along, so she didn't have to drive back home alone, drove me to Sunny Point to join the ship. We had a nice seafood meal at South Port. After the meal, we said goodbye, and they headed back for Norfolk. I knew that Kyki wasn't very happy, even though she tried hard not to show it. She understood that I needed something that paid decent money for many reasons. The number one reason was for us to have enough money to move into our own place.

    I signed on as deck maintenance. The salary was higher than an AB's because I got the non-watch standing allowance. Because the ship was short of ABs, I stayed on watch. With that and plenty of overtime, I was going to do very well financially. When I met the ship, the loading was done, but we delayed sailing for a few days in order to complete staffing the required crew for sailing. We were short a third mate. Somehow the Bosun found out about my background and that I had sailed on foreign ships all the way up to chief mate.

    So he went to the Captain without my knowledge, and said, "Mike is more than qualified to be your third mate, we only need the Coast Guard to give us a waiver, and we can sail."

    The Captain agreed with the Bosun, so they called me to talk to them and asked if I wanted to change to third mate. I said I would be happy to, but I didn't think the Coast Guard would agree. I'd been through that before in Norfolk. They both insisted on trying. The Captain took me to Wilmington, and regardless of the Captain's plea, the Coast Guard denied his request.

    By now, we were down to needing only a third mate so we could sail. They finally found one on the West Coast and flew him down to Sunny Point. The man had a third mate's license, but he did not have any deep-sea experience, as well as being well up in age. He sailed mostly inland waters. Although the Captain wasn't happy, he had no choice because the ship had to sail. The Third Mate had the eight to twelve watch, and the Old Man (the Captain) had to keep an eye on him constantly.

    It felt kind of unusual, after so many years as an officer to sail again as an AB. Also, I missed the extras that go with the rank. At least the money was good, and I needed it. Another thing that I had to become familiar with was not the job as a seaman, but the union agreements and the new procedures. They were quite different from those on foreign flagged ships. It looked like almost every department had their own agreements. There was the steward department, the engine department, the deck department, the radio operators, and the mates. It seemed that they were all independent, but they were still working together as a unit. Welcome, Mike, to organized labor. It was not that foreign flagged ships did not have agreements, because they did. But the U.S. ships were much more organized. Also there was a more distinct separation between the licensed and unlicensed personnel. The AB quarters were rather crowded since it was a fairly small room for the two ABs or ordinary seamen, so there was very little privacy. The watch consisted of the mate, the two ABs, and the ordinary seaman. The ships that I had sailed so far had the mate and the two ABs only.

The victory ship was an upgrade from the liberty ship. It was faster and more stylish, and it had better gears, even though there were still hatch cover boards and tarps. For me, there was nothing that I wasn't familiar with.

I had the 12 to 4 watch with the Second Mate who was a sharp young fellow from the King's Point U.S. Merchant Marine Academy. He was sort of a sixty's generation person. He soon learned about my background, and during the trip we had some good conversations on the bridge. We became kind of friends. I used to see him often in later years with the MMP. The Chief Mate was much older than I, and later we became friends and shipmates with the MMP.

Both characters in their own way were alike, but from a different generation and style. The young man represented the sixties wave of the young spirited seamen. The other man was the example of the older class of seamen who did not hesitate to have a good time when the opportunity came. There were a few opportunities during the trip, especially during the Vietnam era.

The ship was technically a tramp. Her main purpose now was to serve the military, as they needed from the East Coast or West Coast to the Far East. The *Clarksville Victory*, for this type of run and being an older ship, would not get the best personnel. I don't mean from ability but rather from behavior. The men knew that the rules would be a little slack; so drinking was constant. If I was unlucky enough to have the first watch on arrival in port, I had a good chance to be on watch for some time, especially at the seamen's ports. We were two day-men on the ship and technically we were supposed to split the twelve to four watch. But the other day man wasn't in shape to steer the ship, you guessed it right: booze. So, I stayed permanently on the twelve to four watch. With the day-man's duties, it resulted in very good overtime for me, not that the other man was behind me, because somehow he managed to receive good overtime, also. Only God knows how! Maybe it was because his room was open to everyone to have a drink, especially for the Chief Mate and the Bosun.

In one incident at Sunny Point, he almost got in trouble because he could not sign his traveler's checks. He couldn't hold a steady hand. Poor Man! He always managed to be broke; otherwise he was a very good seaman. Most of the time, he did not have a problem doing his job, but the man could drink like a fish. I am not much of a drinker or a smoker. I usually have one or two drinks, and only in the right atmosphere and maybe a cigarette once in a while. That was a plus for me on the ship, but it also had its disadvantages, because I was not considered one of the buddies. However, that was only true for some of the men, and it was not in a malicious way. They just wanted someone to drink with them.

They use to say, "Mike, you are a nice guy. Why don't you have a drink with us? Join the party."

I heard that many times during the trip, like there was something seriously wrong with me. However, I never saw the Bosun so drunk that he could not do his job. He was an average size, skinny man, but he could drink like a fish. He was a very experienced bosun, and he knew how to handle the crew and the job. How long could he last going like that? I didn't know. From the beginning the Bosun and I became good friends. We both knew the situation and the condition of the crew. When we had to set the stages for paint, or the bosun chair, or any other dangerous job, most of the time both of us would make sure that they were properly set. We did this double-checking so that we didn't have any accidents. I was young, and in a way, I was enjoying the heights.

We left the States with a destination of Vietnam, or any other base close by there for discharge. From curiosity, I wanted to go there (of course, Kyki did not know about my curiosity). Two days before we arrived, we received a message that the port of discharge was Shatahip, Thailand. There went my curiosity; we stayed for discharge a few days. After a long sea trip like that, a time for rest and relaxation was important. Mostly the military and local longshoremen did the handling of the cargo. For me, going ashore was not my first priority. Of course I would like to go out, do some shopping, look around, have a meal, a drink, and come back, if only for a few hours. For the new and improved Michael, the good old days of finding a girl in every port were gone.

The Bosun, the Chief Mate, and the Steward were going out, and all three were party boys. By now, I had gotten to know them well, and all three of them trusted me. So, I ended up with the keys for the steward department, the deck, and the chief mate's office. For four days, I was all of the above. They came back broke and exhausted, but ready for another trip. Seamen, seamen, seamen! They are like little boys.

The Mate and the Bosun told me, "Go! You are off."

I took a day off to do my shopping and look around, and get this, to visit the beach. This was conservative stuff now.

On the return trip, the routine was to go from different ports, and pick up various cargos, which were mostly the effects of military personnel or sometimes equipment, and then we were to bring them back to the States. There was no commercial cargo, and with that there was no rush. We stopped in Taiwan for the two ports then Sasabo and Subic Bay, and then Okinawa. Practically all of them were party ports for the boys, who had a ball. The miserable one was the man that was unlucky to have the first watch on arrival. Most of the time, he was stuck. I proved to be very useful since I was not partying and not drinking, and I was on the ship all of the time. Not drinking, I guess, redeemed me, for the few men, at the beginning they thought that I was unsociable and that I should drink more. They were happy now.

My watch partner was much older than me; and he was from the Tidewater area, too. We became friends. Actually he had an interesting past. He was well established ashore, and if I remember well, he had a couple of tugboats. But, he made the cardinal mistake to fall in love and marry younger, much younger wives, not once, but twice. This was a sure way to go broke. So single now, he ended up as an AB on the Clarksville Victory. It was as simple as that. Otherwise, he was a delightful person, and he was not a drinker, either, (He was taking a few medicines at the time which, I guess, were the side effects of the younger wives.) So he and I, in the evening, would leave the ship for a walk, maybe even have a beer somewhere or get something to eat. Kao-Hsiung, Taiwan was known for good seafood. We were both hoping to find a good seafood place while walking into town, which wasn't very far away. There were these people called pilots who supposedly would guide guests to find a good place and a good time. Actually they were salesmen hired by the bars to attract us there. On the way to town, the pilots would drive us crazy. My friend was cursing them out, but in vain. They wouldn't leave us alone.

In his desperation, he told me, "Talk to them in Greek, then maybe they will leave us alone."

So just for the fun of it, I started joking with them and talking to them in Greek.

To my buddies' surprise, they answered in English, "You're Greeks?"

I said, "Yes."

They said, "Okay, don't go to these bars that we told you about before. You will pay too much. They're for the Americans, and we charge them more. You go to this other place, and you will pay this price. Tell them you're Greek so that they don't charge you too much."

My buddy got really upset, and he chased them away. There was never one price for every seaman, and I don't think it is today either. I was laughing like crazy, and we were both joking with each other.

I said, "I will teach you Greek, so from now on you can have a fifty percent discount."

The ordinary seamen on our watch, was another man with a colorful history. His real job was a writer and a diver around the

Caribbean. The poor guy got caught in a storm on the Colombian coast and lost his boat. He was lucky to have survived. Here he was an ordinary seaman on the *Clarksville Victory* trying to save some money to buy another boat.

The three of us had a nice watch, and with the Second Mate we ended up having a good trip. The lookout and the way it was done on the U.S. ships were fairly new to me. From dusk to dawn we had a lookout, and the lookout was posted on the bow. Only when the weather was really bad, were we moved from the bow to the flying bridge. Until now I was accustomed to having a lookout only in an emergency, like fog.

So, we were on our way from Subic Bay to Taiwan, and the weather was very nasty, with gale force winds. The lookout was still up on the bow. Spray was coming over the bow. It was lousy. I called the Second Mate, and I described the conditions.

He said, "Come up on the bridge at the wings. There is no need to be there. I don't know if the Captain will like it, but come up here anyway."

The Captain, as nice of a fellow as he was, was kind of fixated with the lookout watch. I moved to the wing of the bridge. The Captain happened to come on the bridge to check on the weather and see how things were going. He saw me outside and asked the mate, "Who is that man out there?"

The mate said, "That is the Lookout. We started taking spray over the bow, and I moved him up here."

"Then why he is at the wing?" the Captain said.

"Where do you want me to put him?" he said.

"On the flying bridge," the Captain said.

I heard the conversation, and before the Mate said anything, I went on the flying bridge, which was wide open to the elements. The Old Man was nice, but he was from the old school. Technically, under these conditions, the lookout is not much help. I believe very strongly in a lookout, but I also believe that the purpose of the lookout is to be posted in a place so he can be useful and protected. That's what I did all my time as an officer. When the weather was really bad, I would bring the lookout into the wheelhouse, which was more protected, and he would be more help. This was to the dismay of some captains, but very few. The vast majority of them liked what I was doing.

Another thing that impressed me on the return trip was the union meeting, which was to discuss the trip, address problems, and make suggestions for the next trip. We felt as if we had a voice, and our voices would be heard. My shipmates touched me. Even though I was a rookie in the union, they asked my opinion in various matters. I appreciated that very much.

Naka, Okinawa was the last port on the way back. That was where I first saw the Toyota Corolla. Actually it was the cab that took me back to the ship.

I asked the cab driver, "What car is this?"

He said, "It's a Toyota. The Toyota Corolla. Very good, very good car."

How right he was! If this car could take the punishment that the cab drivers inflicted on them, it must be an excellent car. I thought that if they brought it to the U.S. it would be a big seller. It was, and it still is.

This was the last port before the long trip home, and the boys were getting the best of the bars, as they were gearing up for the long trip home. The next stop would be San Juan, Puerto Rico, so you can imagine that they all came back smashed. It ended up that another AB and I were the only ones able to steer. It was not that he was not drinking, but he was able to steer. The Captain had threatened them that if we did not have a good helmsman he would have to log them all. It took two days before things went back to normal. In the meantime, for these two days the other AB and I rotated on the wheel.

We all thought that the ship would continue for at least a few more trips. So, on the way back the maintenance was going strong; with painting in and out as the weather permitted. There was plenty of overtime. Actually there was as much as we were be able to do. For me, it was work, a little sleep, and before I knew it, we were in San Juan, Puerto Rico. From San Juan the next port was Bayonne, New Jersey.

One day after we left Puerto Rico, we were hit hard by a

storm. The ship was bouncing around like a pumpkin, and to make it worse, the ship was very light, almost empty. The next two and a half days to get to New Jersey were awful. When we arrived in Bayonne, there was almost two feet of snow on the ground. We didn't stay long, I think it was only a couple of days, when we sailed for Norfolk, Virginia, and docked at Lambert's Point Piers.

Until now, all of us thought that we were making another trip. For me I didn't know if I would be able to make a second trip. Usually when a man was new with the Union, he was allowed to have only one round trip. Of course, I had to talk with Kyki, too. In any case the main purpose was fulfilled and with all the adventures, the trip was fruitful. I had accumulated enough money now to be able to do what I would like to do. I would like to have had another trip, if I could, because that would have helped a lot.

Then the message came out, when the Chief Mate came down to the crew mess at coffee time, and he said, "Guys, I am sorry but this ship is going back into moth balls, and it looks like it's for good."

That took the worry off Kyki and me regarding what decision we should make about a second trip. But that was the way it was. We finished the little cargo that we had for Norfolk, we stripped the ship out, got paid off, and the *Clarksville Victory* was history.

Reaching the end of Vietnam Era, and with the independent ships like the *Clarksville Victory* doing their last trips, it was time for me to think of something else. That was also my last trip with the NMU, and my last trip as an unlicensed crewmember. But, I have to say that my short time with NMU was good, and very helpful.

After a few days back in Norfolk, the first thing was to buy a car. It was mostly for Kyki. There was only one car in the family, and it was rather difficult for everyone. We planned to move out on our own, and we needed the car. We bought a red Volkswagen Beetle, a brand new one! We paid for it in full. It was ours, and we had no payments. We were left with still enough money in our pockets to move on.

NEW YORK – HOTELS – LICENSE

Springtime was coming. Somehow, although I don't remember exactly how, I learned about the Hotel Motel School in New York. Motels were being built all over at the time, and the idea of working in one of them, or in a big hotel was attractive. In general, the hotel industry was very active at the time. I liked the idea of becoming involved in the management. On the other hand, Kyki and I were not fond of the restaurant business because of the long and unreasonable hours that were required there. Having a bad experience when I was looking for a job made it worse.

I learned to dislike the restaurants when I was searching for a job. A friend of the family was telling my father-in-law for me to go and visit the manager of a big steak house in New York; supposedly they knew him very well. He was supposed to give me a job to start as a busboy in this fancy place. They went on and on about how lucky I would be if I were able to get a job there. At the time, I didn't know what a busboy was and what he was doing.

When alone, I asked Kyki, "What is this busboy business so I know before I go there?"

I couldn't figure what busses had to do with restaurants. Laughing and also pissed with them, she explained to me the busboy's job. Of course, I wasn't thrilled with the idea, but I thought if I saw the man and supposedly, with him being in charge, I would explain to him my qualifications. By meeting with me, I hoped that maybe we would be able to work something out. So I visited the place, and I asked for him. They told me that he was doing something right now and that he would be with me soon. He passed by me, and he went back out again. He then stayed and talked with girls, but it didn't seem to me that he was doing anything important, and that went on for more than one hour. By that time, it was all I could take, and I got up and left. That was the end of the busboy business, and that fantastic career choice.

This time I was going to New York on my own. Anyway, on my own did fit my personality better because no referrals were needed. New York, I always believed, was the place to start, and she did not fail me. I rented a room and started school, called the New York Hotel Motel School. After four months of intense training, I would be able to work as a front office clerk with no problem, plus I would have an overall knowledge of the hotel and motel operation. This was to the dismay of the establishment that thought that I had to start from a dishwasher or a busboy. I started as a room clerk at the Sheraton Motor Inn, a four hundred and fifty room motel in New York City. Actually, the twenty story high structure was located on 42nd Street and 12th Avenue at the waterfront, and it was the biggest motor inn in the New York area, right at the waterfront. It was tremendously busy at the time. The cruise ships close by generated a tremendous turnover each week, plus there were many guests that liked the idea of driving their cars to New York.

Kyki finished the school year in Norfolk, packed her bags, and moved to New York with me. Through a friend of ours, we found a two and a half room apartment under rent control in Flushing, Queens. It was very reasonable apartment rent in a very good area. Even though it was a fourth floor walk up, we didn't mind it at all. We were on our own, and we could afford it. In the mean time, Kyki got a job as an elementary school teacher on Long Island. Now we were really kicking. New York, New York!

Kyki was teaching on Long Island, and I was working at the Sheraton Motor Inn in New York. Our nice little apartment was right in the middle of our jobs. We started enjoying life. The hotel business was very interesting, and I liked it. In a big city like New York, I was able to meet and see a lot of people. There was never a dull moment. Being new at the front office, I had the four to midnight shift. I combined it with the weekend shift of eight to four so I could

My Sea My Life

have more time with Kyki when I was off. I remember, that many times we were out until early in the morning. Kyki would drop me off at the subway, and I would go to work while Kyki went to sleep. We were young and energetic, and we had no kids at the time.

Although we certainly enjoyed life, packing my bag for sea was not totally out of my mind. By now it was just about time to get my citizenship. I figured that if I had worked hard enough at sea to get to become an officer, why not get my American Merchant Marine license just to have it?

I went down to the Coast Guard for them to evaluate my papers and ask me what license I was qualified for. I submitted all my papers for review. A few days later, they sent me a letter to go to the Coast Guard. The chief in charge of the procedures told me that I was qualified to take the exam for the third's mate license. The reason that I couldn't go higher than that, was that the last three years I wasn't active enough at sea, and that overran my previous experience. If I was continually active, I would probably have been able to sit for a second mate's or a chief mate's license.

I had to wait for my citizenship appointment, which was coming shortly. At that time, with the end of Vietnam, the last thing that the Coast Guard wanted was another officer looking for a job. In a way it was 'love it or leave it.' It didn't matter much to them because plenty of people were looking for jobs.

Even when I went to enroll at the Bowen Navigation School, Captain Bowen said, "I have to warn you before I get your money, that things are tough now to get a job."

I said, "I have a job. I just wanted to have the license for insurance. I invested too long and too much at sea to let it go to waste."

With that I started school. The good thing was that Captain Bowen would give us the materials and we could study on our own. We didn't have to go to class every day. If we had a question, we could go to him and he would be glad to answer our questions. We could even write to him from the ships with any questions that we had. His materials were excellent. I believe they were the best at the time. It was very rare that I had a question.

As soon as I had my U.S. citizenship I went to the Coast Guard to take the exam. I could take the exam in a two-week span, so I took a two-week leave from the hotel. When Captain Bowen heard that I was going to take the exam, he hit the ceiling.

"Absolutely not! You're not ready! You just started to study, and you want to take the exam! Impossible! There are people here with more experience, and it takes them at least six to eight months of study, and they still have problems. I cannot be responsible. You are on your own," he said.

I said, "That's fine, the only thing that I want from you is during the exam to be able to ask you questions if I have any."

"That is not a problem, but you are not ready, and I don't think that you are going to go far," Bowen said.

Now, you don't say that to Michael. I do not believe in the word, "No," nor in the words, "you can't do it," especially when I have not yet tried. I put my head down, and studied and then studied harder. In order to stay alert and awake, I was drinking black Greek coffee in regular size coffee cups. Kyki was laughing when I told her that I would finish studying the rest of the chapter during my naptime, which was only a few hours a night.

I had to start with the most difficult subjects first. The first test was "the Rules of the Road," and it required ninety percent accuracy to pass. So far so good, I made a ninety-two. I went by the school, and Captain Bowen was happy, but still skeptical. I split the next test into two days. It was "Navigation" with another ninety percent requirement. On the second of the two navigation days, when Captain Bowen saw that I was doing well, he was a changed man. It was as if he had just woken up. To him it was like a small team was winning and upsetting a big team, and he was sensing a big upset. He got all hyped up.

"You cannot fail now. You passed the most difficult tests. You have to watch out! You have to watch out!" he said.

I said, "Don't worry, I have my plan."

He couldn't believe it. I had beaten the odds. Captain Bowen was very helpful during the rest of the exam. He was kind of embarrassed that he hadn't believed in me. I finished the exam with a score well over ninety-five percent. Believe it or not, the test that I had to take twice because it gave me a little bit of a hard time was "Blinking Light." What a pain! I did not like it then, and I do not like it now. But that was considered a minor test, and no one ever failed the entire examination from that test. I could take it as many times as I wanted until I passed. The Coast Guard Chief that was giving the blinking test was laughing.

"Here you are, and you made over ninety percent on the exam, yet you have to take the blinking a second time," he said.

I was happy that I passed the second time. I still remember the message that he sent to me – "BRACE YOUR MAIN SAIL."

The Commander and the Chief, who signed my license, wished me good luck. If I wanted to go to sea at that time, I really needed that luck. There were no jobs anywhere, and to make things worse the unions had closed their enrollment books. In other words, they didn't admit any new members. By the way, I lost entrance into the union by two months, and the main reason was the U.S. Immigration. When I applied for citizenship they had lost my whole file. Because of that, I had to start all over again six months later!

With the unions closed, and no prospect to get a job as an officer anywhere, I was back at the motel. I was a room clerk and relief assistant-front office manager. Also, once a week, I was doing the night auditor's job, from midnight to eight. Actually, job wise, I was doing well.

So why all the fuss to get my merchant marine license and why was I looking at everything with the U.S. Merchant Marine? It was simple economics. What I could make in the hotel in two years, I could make in less than six months on the ships, even as a third mate. I could save a bunch of money because I didn't spend much while was on the ship. It would be good for us. We could use that money as a down payment for a house or as capital to open my own business (another dream of Michael's). Not only did I make less outside, but also by going out often at night and on weekends, as we did for entertainment, we did not save much.

Two incidents stuck in my mind during the time I was looking for a job outside the Union. First, I thought about looking into the Military Sealift Command, which at that time was located in Brooklyn. I went to apply for a job. I proceeded to the front office, and I showed the secretary my papers and my qualifications.

I guess she wasn't paying attention to what I was telling her or something, because in a rather angry voice, she said, "We don't have jobs for our own, much more for you."

I thought she was talking about the Military Sealift Command personnel, and I said, "I know that jobs are difficult, and I assume that there are many people waiting here too. I just wanted to fill out an application."

She said, "We only hire Americans!"

I said, "What do you mean?"

She said" I said, we only hire Americans. I told you!"

That's when it hit me, and with a raised voice I said, "What, according to you am I? Don't you see the papers in front of you?"

A person from the back of the office, apparently the supervisor, jumped in front of her and started to confront me. When he found out what the lady had said, he froze and tried to patch things up. He took me into the back office and brought me the application papers. He proceeded to tell me that things were difficult, and that she didn't mean it that way. Then he asked me if I was willing to sail as an AB.

I looked at him, and I said, "I'm not here for an AB's job. I'm here for a mate's position, and I'll take only a mate's job."

He said, "Fill out the application, and I'll see what I can do."

I took the application, which I never completed, and that was the end of the MSC.

The other incident that I remember about job searching concerned the dredges. I went to Philadelphia to apply for a job with the dredges because that is where their main office was located. They told me that things were slow, as if I didn't know, but when something came up that they would call me. Three months later, I got a letter to go to the main office for a job interview and that they had an opening. Kyki and I were so happy. Both of us took off that day, drove overnight and stayed at the Cherry Hill Sheraton. By the way, that night we had our first seafood buffet, and it was the best we have ever had. I don't remember the name of the place, but it was fantastic.

The next day, there I was. I was one of the first ones in the office. I was anxious to get the job. The personnel manager proceeded to tell me that they did have an opening, but I was number ten on the list. He wanted to make sure that I was still available. Now I was completely pissed!

I told him, "For that my wife and I had to take a day off from our jobs? You just wanted to know if I was still available? For this, we had to come down here in person? I'm tenth on the list. I could have told you this over the phone!"

I left without waiting for his answer. I didn't want to get involved in a nastier conversation. Anyway, there was no use crying over spilled milk.

MMP (APPLICANT YEARS) CITRUS PACKER

I had realized that my best bet was to wait for things to get better with membership in the Masters Mates and Pilots. My work hours at the Sheraton were mostly four to midnight during the week, and one day-shift on the weekend with one or two days off. Many times I would leave home before I was due at work and drive by the Union Hall on the way to work to check on how things were. In the meantime, I got to know a few people, and they kept me informed of the situation. By June the talk was that the Union would start accepting applications soon, but they didn't know how soon. In the meantime, I got the papers and had them filled out and ready. Only the date was missing. My friends were telling me to show up more often, so when they started accepting the applications, I would be one of the first.

By August, and after a few meetings, the Union had sorted out the rules of how they were going to accept the applications. They decided to keep the books closed, but to accept new applicants and to qualify them to get a job only for one round trip, and only when no other member would be available for that job. It would be only at the last call of the day. The rules were rather difficult for the applicants, but those were the rules. From what my friends were telling me, the best chance to get a job would be before Christmas, or in January and February.

If I got a job, it would be at the last minute, and I would not have enough time to prepare my sea bag. So, I had my bags packed and ready to go. Now, it was time to have a talk with my friend at the hotel, the front office manager. We always had a very good working relationship, and he liked me a lot. I didn't want to leave without him knowing. If I was able to get a job with a ship, the chances were zero that I would be able to give him notice. If I got the job, an hour later I had to be on the ship. With my status as an applicant, it was especially worse.

He said, "Don't worry. If you get the job, I will cover you. It is no problem at all."

Christmas passed, and at the Union there was nothing at all, not even a short job. January was the same. I started getting a little disappointed. We had reached now the first week of February. The *Citrus Packer*, a Waterman Steam Ship Company freighter, was docked in Newark, New Jersey. Newark was the last port for the coastwise run, and then the ship would head out for the Middle East. At the Union Hall, a third mate job was on the board, and after all regular jobs were called, there were no takers. One of the reasons, that the job was not taken by a regular member, was that there was a big argument between the Port Relief Officer and the Chief Mate. The Port Relief Officer was presenting the ship on a whole, as a bad ship to sail. Plus, the fact was that the ship was going on the Middle East run. While the ship was doing the coastwise run, as far as mates were concerned, she was completely staffed. In Baltimore, the port before Newark, one of the third mates went ashore. I never got the real story, but it seems that he got into an argument at a bar and they worked him over pretty well. He ended up in the hospital instead of the ship. The ship sailed short to Newark. The ship was in Newark for three days, and the job was still open. The Port Relief Officer's publicity and the run were working in my favor.

I started watching like a hawk, and I said to myself, "Michael, you are close to getting a job."

One of the younger dispatcher kept telling me, "Here is your chance. Stay close. Don't leave."

"Don't worry. I'll be here," I said.

The ship was scheduled to leave Saturday afternoon sometime. As soon as the Hall opened on Friday, I was there, and my bags were packed and ready. I even warned the hotel manager that there was a good possibility that I might get the job. The first call was at eleven, and there were no takers. The second call came, and the job was still open. My heart started pounding. There was one more call. Then came the two o'clock call, and guess what? No one wanted the job! Now the job was declared open, and those were the words that I wanted to hear.

The Dispatcher said, "Does any applicant want the job?" I was the only applicant in the Hall at the time. "Do you want the job? It's yours."

That was the way I got my first job as a U.S. Merchant Marine officer, and MMP member. To the regular members this job was not a thriller, but to me it was fantastic! They prepared my papers and sent me to the doctors. If I passed the physical, then I was going on the ship. The physical was a breeze!

The nurse said, "Mr. Razos, we have a problem."

"What now? I thought we were done," I said.

"All your shots have expired, and you have to have them, especially with this run. I'll have to check with the doctor to see what he wants to do with you, because there are five of them," she said.

So here I was the doctor's office again. He said, "You're missing five shots, actually all of them. I'm kind of concerned to give them to you all at the same time."

"Doctor, I don't have time. The ship is leaving tomorrow," I said.

"It will make you sick," the doctor said.

"What kind of sick?" I asked.

"Well, your arms may be sore, and you might have a fever," the doctor said.

"Good, put three in one arm and two in the other to balance the pain. I need this job. I've been waiting now for months. SHOOT THEM!" I said.

The next day I was sick as a dog. I couldn't lift my arms from the pain and all the swelling, and I had a little fever. Kyki was happy that I had gotten a job, but deep down she was not thrilled with my going to the Middle East for five months. In general, I guess she thought it was okay.

Saturday morning, she drove me to Newark, where the ship was docked. From my trip with the *Clarksville Victory*, I was sort of familiar with the procedures now. My first pleasant surprise when I got on board was the Chief Mate. The way that they had described him at the Hall, I was ready to meet a monster. Here was a nice southern gentleman, and he was very polite. He tried to make me feel at ease, especially when he found out that this was my first job with the MMP. He went out of his way to explain the ship to me and in general to create a good feeling for me. My watch was the twelve to four. Because it was Saturday and because there was a Port Relief Officer on duty, I was not required to be on the ship until one hour before the ship sailed.

Actually, because the ship was sailing after six, for me, my first watch would start after midnight, and by that time, the ship would be at sea. The ship was scheduled to sail at 6 P.M., so the other Third Mate would be at the bridge, the Chief Mate at the bow, and the Second Mate at the stern.

All this time that I was talking with the Mate, Kyki was parked at the gate waiting for me. When she saw me coming towards her and smiling, she felt better. I knew she was worried about how I would find the situation on the ship. I explained to her the conversation that I had with the Chief Mate about my watch, and I assured her that everything would be all right. There was no reason for her to wait at the gate, so we kissed and she left more relaxed than when we were coming.

I went back on the ship. One of the things that I did when I went back was to go up on the bridge and familiarize myself as much as I could. I did not want to wait until midnight. Then I went to my room, straightened the necessary things, lay down, and passed out. Between the shots, the fever, the anxiety, and the ordeal until I got the job, I was exhausted.

Saturday, February 7, 1973, was a cold, wintry, New Jersey day. It was not a day to be outside. It felt that at any minute it would

My Sea My Life

snow, and especially around the open space of docks, the cold felt worse. Anyway, the weather forecast was for a storm coming up the coast. Eleven twenty P.M. was the wake up call so I could get ready for my midnight watch. I was awake from 10:30 P.M., and I was ready in my room, thinking about my first watch.

As if it wasn't enough excitement to get the job, I needed a little more spice. I went to the bridge at 11:40 P.M., twenty minutes early, to get familiar with the darkness of the bridge. If I had any questions, I wanted to have enough time to ask the Third Mate. I will say he was very helpful in familiarizing me with the bridge. He took his time to make me feel comfortable. The ship had taken departure almost an hour before, and we had set course for Trinidad, the first port and for bunkers. The wind was blowing pretty well by that time, we both were concerned about the weather, and we were hoping to get away before it got worse, wishful thinking.

So he said, "Good night," and he left.

Here I was on my first watch. The first couple of hours were fairly quiet, with very little traffic, but the weather was getting worse. Even though the ship was fully loaded, it was feeling the weather. As we were getting off the coast, the *Citrus Packer* started laboring more and more. By the middle of the third hour, I heard some squeaky noises, like scratching on a metal plate coming from aft the ship. I got out at the wing, turned on the searchlight, and started checking to see where the noises were coming from.

We were carrying a lot of deck cargo, like small containers, boxes, and a lot of military vehicles. The number four and five cargo hatches were full of them. From what I could see, at least one boom was loose and swinging back and forth with the movement of the ship. Also, from what I could see with the searchlight, some trucks on top of the hatches were moving too! It was not a pretty picture. Things always had to be interesting. God forbid my first watch would be easy. That would have been boring. I called the Captain and explained to him what was happening. He was not a happy fellow to say the least.

"I am coming up," he said. He came up on the bridge. "What do you see, Mate?" he asked.

I took him outside and directed the searchlight at the swinging boom and the trucks. I asked him if he wanted me, since he was up on the bridge, to take my Stand By and go and try to check closer to see what was going on.

He said, "No, no. Stay here. Call the Chief Mate and the Bosun. They will go and check.

The Mate and the Bosun went out there to assess the situation. I tried to keep the searchlight in their direction so that they could see well. In the meantime, the Captain reduced the speed and adjusted the course to ease as much as he could the laboring of the ship. By now we had a full-blown gale out there. A little later, the Chief Mate came on the bridge with the news. One of the booms was loose and it seemed that a few trucks on deck and on top of the hatches were loose. Apparently, they had been poorly secured or not secured at all when the ship left Newark. There was not much that we could do at this time.

From what I heard from the talk that the Captain had with the Mate, we would have to try to reach Norfolk, Virginia for damage check and repairs. By that time, it was close to four o'clock. I made my entrances in the logbook, a good amount of them. The Captain and the Mate left, and went downstairs. Soon the Second Mate arrived to relieve me. I explained to him the whole situation, and he wasn't thrilled either, but what could we do. With that, my first watch came to an end, with plenty of excitement.

There was never a dull moment, but wait, because it got better. Now we were going to Norfolk, which was a U.S. port, and by the Union rules that we had at the time, a member could get my job if he wanted. It was as simple as that. He could go to the Union Hall and say that he wanted the job.

He could say, "The Third Mate is as an applicant, and I want that job. Take him off, and I will take it." Fair or not, that was the way it was.

We docked in Norfolk sometime the next day. The deck was in a mess. Trucks were hanging over the side, and the boom that was swinging was damaged. A lot of repairs had to be done. They estimated that we had to stay in Norfolk for three to four days.

The Port Agent for the MMP in Norfolk came the next day to visit the ship. I sort of knew him from the times that I visited the Norfolk Hall to check things regarding applicants. He looked as if he was a decent, fair man. He always expressed his willingness to help, not only me but also every other applicant. At that time, there was another applicant in Norfolk. When the Port Agent saw me, he was happy that I had finally gotten a job. I expressed my fears to him about loosing the job, and he assured me that I would not have any problems. Anyway no one from the people he had in the Hall would take a job like mine when they could take something closer to home with better pay. He was right, but not completely. From what I found out later, there was one regular member who expressed his desire to get the job, but the Port Agent strongly discouraged him. He also told him that it would be difficult since all the crewmembers had signed foreign articles anyway.

He said, "Leave the man alone; you can get a better job here anytime you want and closer to home."

We finished the repairs and off we went. The first port was Trinidad, and I was still on board. The next stop would be Durban, mostly for bunker and stores. Slowly day-by-day, I was getting more familiar with my watch, and also gaining their trust and respect. From the first day, I became buddies with the Chief Mate. His office was next to my room. Between watches I spent time there having coffee with him. Also, the office could be a noisy place, especially when having the twelve to four watch. The men who gathered there tried to be as quiet as they could so I could sleep, but they couldn't help it sometimes.

The *Citrus Packer* was a very colorful ship, as far as the crew was concerned. The ship's officers were all permanent. They had reliefs only for vacations. They liked the permanent status, not because the run was so great, but they liked the comfort that they did not have to look for a job. The majority of the crew was from the south, specifically from Mobile, Alabama. The Captain and the deck officers, except me, were all from Mobile, Alabama. Two engineers, I think, were from Georgia, the rest were from Mobile. In a way it was a close family operation. They knew and sailed with each other for years. What does that have to do with me? Well, here I was an unknown entity, an outsider coming out of the blue. In general, they were mostly good people. Actually some of them were very good, like the Chief Mate, who became friends with me for years to come. I guess, from self-preservation they were at first hesitant with the intruder (that was me, the unknown). It took them quite a few days to loosen up, and it took quite a while for them to engage in a conversation with me, except for the Chief Mate.

I had no idea that as a mate on the U.S. ships I had to have my own sextant. During the ships that I had been on before, they always had two or three sextants, and we all used them. Now here I was without a sextant. My buddy, the Chief Mate came to the rescue, which was very nice of him. I appreciated it very much. He gave me his sextant to use during the entire trip. It was a nice Plath sextant. He was on the day watch, and he did not have any need for the sextant. I was flying with that sextant; it was the top of the line. Of course I took care of it as if it were my own eyes.

Now we started seeing the exotic, exciting ports that made the run so famous. The first one was Djibouti. We stayed a day or two and were happy to leave. The next beauty was Massawa, Ethiopia, which was very hot and dusty. The bright spot here was a small U.S. military station, like an oasis in the desert. Unfortunately we stayed quite a few days in Massawa.

The two ABs that I had on my watch were both nice. One of them was close to sixty and the other was around forty. That is the one that I will nickname the Intellectual, because he liked to read a lot and could carry a conversation about lots of topics. He was also human, and he had a weakness. He did not need much, just a drink or two, and he would become as goofy as hell and bird brained. He was not mean, just goofy and very annoying to the other crewmembers. He would drive them nuts.

Apparently he went to the small base with the others, and he had a few drinks. Naturally, he went nuts when he came back, and he did not come on board the ship. Instead he stayed on the dock joking and talking, and he drove the locals crazy. The locals were looking at him as if he were from another planet. There was a tall AB from Texas at the gangway watch. Every time I passed the gangway, he would keep me posted of the intellectual's performances at the dock. I was at the number two hatch when I saw the Texan coming to find me and looking a little worried. I realized that the performance of the Intellectual at the dock had reached its peak. I thought that it peaked most probably the wrong way from the Texan's face. Apparently, the Intellectual had gotten exhausted, and he lay down on the dock, probably he was about ready to pass out. In the meantime, a few dogs were hanging around the docks sniffing at him. The Texan, afraid that they would bite him, went on the dock and tried to get him on board, but he wouldn't listen. So in desperation and being angry with him, the Texan came to me.

"Mate, the dogs will eat him alive. We have to do something! He may listen to you, but he doesn't listen to me," he said.

"Okay, I will go see," I said. I went down to the dock, and chased the dogs away. I said, "Hey Buddy, how are you doing?"

"Okay Mate! Not really. Not so good," he said.

"Do you want to come on the ship?" I asked.

"Yes Mate, but I can't make it. I'm exhausted. I can't make it," he said.

"Yes you can. I will help you. We will make it!" I said.

Slowly and hanging on me and with the help of the Texan, we got him up the gangway and onto the ship. By the time we reached the top of the gangway, my other AB had come there.

He said, "Don't worry Mate, we will take him downstairs. We will fix him up!" From what I found out later, they put him on his bed in his room, and locked the door. He passed out for at least sixteen hours. When he woke up, he was as good as new and thoroughly embarrassed. From what I heard, he had opened his mouth the wrong way to someone, and they locked him in his room.

We were happy to have finished with Massawa. Even though it wasn't the peak of the hot season, it was still very hot, over a hundred degrees. It was a dusty and filthy place. On this type of trip, crew causalities were nothing unusual. People got sick, sometimes they got tired, and sometimes they got hurt. If I remember well, we had to fly the Bosun home when he got hurt working on deck becoming the first casualty. In port, I had the midnight to eight watch. The third Cook/Baker would usually get up at three to four o'clock in the morning to do his baking. The guy was in his late sixties or early seventies, and he was a very pleasant fellow. Most of the time it was quiet on deck, so I spent time with him while he was doing the baking. By six A.M. we had our freshly made breakfast. I felt that he wasn't in the best of health, and I expressed my concern to him that at his age and condition to take a trip like that was kind of risky. He was telling me that he was seriously thinking of retiring when we got home.

By then we had arrived in Karachi. At the time Karachi was a very crowded port and we expected to spend some time there. The company had a Port Captain whose job was to go from port to port and to expedite the ship's operation. Actually, his job was to wheel and deal with the locals in order to move the ship a little faster. Otherwise, we would be in each port forever. He managed in Karachi, rather than having the ship outside and waiting at the anchorage, to dock the ship alongside another ship. We started discharging from there to barges so he could speed up the discharge. Of course, we still had to go to a dock for the heavy stuff.

We happened to be tied up alongside a Greek ship. By having the midnight to eight watch, I did not pay much attention. I slept most of the day, and I was last to be on deck. Of course, I had no reason to go ashore in Karachi. The only crew I would see from that ship was a gangway watchman during the night. We had been along side the other ship for almost two days, and the other Third Mate, during supper, said to me, "Michael, I have to tell you something. Will you please come to my room?"

So I went to his room, anxiously waiting to see what he had

to tell me. He closed the door, took out a roll of money, and told me, "You speak Greek right?"

I said, "Yes."

"Please, can you find someone from the ship next to us, and buy a couple bottles of liquor for me? Please don't hesitate to pay them whatever they ask you. I'm pretty sure they have it, but I don't know how to ask them. I would appreciate it very much if you could do that, and please, don't worry about the price," he said.

I said, "Don't worry. Tonight I will talk to them and see what I am able to come up with."

During the midnight watch, I talked with the gangway watchman.

He said, "Of course, I can find some. The boys will have some. I will ask them and let you know. I'll have it for you at midnight."

Sure enough, the next night he came out with three or four bottles. I paid him whatever they had paid for the regular price outside, which was about twenty dollars if I remember well, which was reasonable for the area. When the Third Mate saw them, his eyes popped out! It was like he was getting the best present in the world (you light up my life).

I gave him the rest of the money back, and he was going, "No, no, no, no, I don't need any money back. I got what I wanted. My liquor."

I said, "Take it. It's your money. It's not a big deal anyway." He kept thanking me.

The third Cook/Baker and I usually had breakfast a little after six. Many times the Chief Mate would join us, and the three of us had breakfast and would shoot the breeze. I told the Chief Mate about the ship next door having some liquor, and if he needed it, I could get some for him.

"You know something Michael; I would love to have a couple of bottles. Another Waterman ship is coming this way in a couple of days, and I would have something to offer them when they come over," he said.

The Chief Mate was also like me, not the drinking type. Just for fun, I found two nice bottles of cognac and two bottles of ouzo. Also, I got an extra bottle of ouzo for my senior AB (I used to call him that). I knew that he needed a booster shot every once in a while, and that would keep him going for a while. The Captain and the Chief Mate had invited the officers from the other Waterman ship over for supper and a small party. The cognac and ouzo were a hit. The Chief Mate looked like a hot shot to offer that treat in Karachi. That treat did a number on most of them from what the Chief Mate was telling me the next day and we were both laughing. That night they had a hard time getting them over to the other ship.

By now we were almost done with the Karachi cargo. A little after five o'clock in the morning I went down to the galley to meet my buddy, the Baker, for our usual breakfast. I saw the Chief Steward, and I asked, "What are you doing up so early?"

He said, "Don't you know?"

I said, "What? You know I have the graveyard shift, and I sleep during the day."

"Well, the poor Baker had to be flown home as fast as they could manage. He got sick and started urinating blood. They decided that the best thing for him was to put him on the first plane home."

Poor thing! I felt sorry for him, and I had lost my breakfast buddy.

After Karachi, we had a few more ports and then Calcutta. Calcutta would be another long stay, at least two weeks. Although the ship had three shifts continuously working, the Indians knew how to stretch things. Of course Michael again had the midnight to eight watch. From what I heard, the other two shifts had all kinds of problems with the longshoremen. Most of the problems were on the eight to four watch, the Second Mate's shift; and he didn't get along well with Indians. Normally, the second shift would knock off at ten P.M., and the next would come a little after midnight. The Third Mate would call me at 11:15 to relieve him, and by the time I came out, he would have a full pot of coffee waiting for me. We would talk a little, and he would go to bed. So at midnight, I had a lot of fresh coffee, and from the supper quite a few left over pastries. By morning, the Mess Man would have thrown them away if they were not eaten.

In places like India, a little give and take goes a long way. After the stevedores came on board and settled down, I would go down to their tally room, get a couple of big pots they had usually for tea, go upstairs to the officer's mess, and fill them with coffee. I would take the coffee and the leftover pastries down to their tally room. All of us had our coffee while they were getting organized for the night shift. To make it friendlier, I would tell them if they need anything not to hesitate to ask me.

"Yes Mate. Yes Mate. Thank you!" they said.

Now the rest of the night would go smoothly. Rarely I had a problem. I had no idea at the time that the Chief Mate knew about the coffee and the cake. He told me later that being surprised that the night was going so smoothly with no problems, he snuck around and found out what I was doing. He wanted to know why he was enjoying such a good night's sleep. The Chief Mate was an early riser, and usually we had coffee and a light breakfast together while talking about the night shift. He asked me how things were going on deck. I would say, "Smooth, Mate, smooth."

With his southern accent he would say, "Good, good."

That went on the entire time that we stayed in Calcutta.

Our next stop was Chittagong, Bangladesh. We were sailing from one poor place to another poorer place. It is not easy to describe the poverty and misery unless you saw it. Whatever is said would sound like an exaggeration or seamen's stories, but that was not true. It was Sunday evening; and the Chief Mate and I had finished supper and were having our coffee on the second deck. Every Sunday night for supper we had steak. Down on the dock during lunch and supper, the locals would gather and also quite a few dogs to look for some leftovers.

All of a sudden, the Chief Mate in an angry voice yelled, "Look Michael! It's awful what the son of a bitch is doing!"

"What is he doing?" I asked.

"Look below," he said.

I will not mention names, but the man was an officer. He had a perfectly good steak cut into pieces, and he pretended that he was throwing it to the people at the dock, and the last minute would turn and throw it to the dogs. Apparently he was pleased with teasing the poor souls. We all love dogs. I love them very much, but the way he was teasing these people looked awful. I don't know how one could do this to a human being.

I said to the Mate, "I'm going inside."

He said, "I'm going too!"

We both left in disgust. I never asked the officer why he was doing that, and I don't really know if he even knew what he was doing.

The seventies was the hippie era. Young American boys were traveling around the world and a few of them got stuck in the most unusual places without any money. Well, this young man in his early twenties found India to get stuck in and be penniless. By the request of the U.S. Consul we had to take him onboard in some kind of capacity because we didn't have a passenger list, so he could go home. The Chief Mate came to me (at the time I didn't know about the young man) and asked, "Michael, how would you like to have a new ordinary seaman?"

"Why? I already have an ordinary seaman, and he's good!" I said.

"Well, I have to move him to another watch," he said.

I asked, "Why? What did he do wrong?"

"Oh no. Nothing is wrong. We just got a new ordinary seaman," he said.

"We already have three ordinary seamen!" I said.

"Well, he's not really an ordinary seaman. He's a stranded poor soul in the middle of nowhere, and we have to take him home. The U.S. Consul asked us to take him home. Will you take him on your watch? I thought that he would be better with you." Laughing he also said, "I'm always thinking of you. You may want to hear of all his adventures on the way home."

Yeah right! I said.

So I got my hippie for the trip home. On paper he was well educated. He had finished college, and I think he had a master's degree, too. His ideas were kind of far fetched. After school he took off to see the world and make up his mind on what to do, maybe save a few souls on the way. He finally got stuck in India, penniless and hungry.

The next port was Handla in Bangladesh for a load of Jude for Savanna, Georgia. Handla was nothing to brag about. Anchored on the river in the middle of nowhere, we loaded the cargo from barges, and we were happy to leave.

The last port before home was Colombo for bunker and stores. Being the last port on a long trip home, we knew that the crew would get smashed on their adventures on shore. The Chief Steward was a man about my age. Before he went ashore in Colombo, he came to me with a bunch of money.

He told me, "Here it is. Keep it. No matter what I tell you, don't give it back to me until we finish with Colombo, because I will waste it foolishly."

I said, "Okay don't ask me, I will not give it to you."

He said, "Yeah, that's the idea. Even if I beg you just kick me out."

I said, "Okay, it's a deal!"

The last day in Colombo was exciting to say the least. The crew had a good time all right. They tried to drink enough for the twenty-eight days home. After a day or so at sea, everything was back to normal.

A run of this nature, with long stretches at sea and unreasonable ports, took its toll on the seamen, especially on the young ones.

For example, I remember the electrician in his early thirties was a pleasant fellow. He asked for a day off in Karachi, because somebody had told him about a hotel, that operated Western-style and lots of Europeans were going there. That was supposedly a good place to go to have a good time. I saw him all dressed up and heading for shore. I asked him where he was going. He said, "I'm going to have a good time. I'm off tomorrow!"

I asked "In Karachi?"

He said, "Yes, I'm going to that hotel. It's a good place!"

After a day he came back and when I saw him, I asked him how it was.

He said, "Excellent!"

Well, I thought I might have been wrong. He may have had a good time after all. A few days later, during our watch on deck, he approached me as if there was something he had to take off his chest.

He told me, "You know Mate, I will never go out again in places like this. I learned an expensive lesson."

"But you said you had a wonderful time," I said.

"Bull!" he said. "I blew away four hundred dollars for nothing!"

Now starts the long, monotonous, routine trip home. The Chief Mate actually was the busiest, trying to catch up with his overtime, trying to prepare his lists for the next trip. Naturally, he hated paperwork so you can image how much work had piled up. Now he had to do it. He had no choice. He asked me for my overtime sheet, which hadn't been checked since we left New York. A few days later he called me to his office to give me my overtime sheet back; it had all kinds of corrections.

"God Michael, your overtime was a mess! I had to correct it," he said.

I thought by being new and not so familiar with the contract, I may have put down overtime that I shouldn't have. To my surprise, I found out that he put much more overtime on than I had put down.

"Mate, I was that wrong. I cheated myself that much overtime?" I asked.

It was about thirty-five to forty hours of overtime.

Again with his southern accent he replied, "Well, yes and no. Most of them are from my good night sleep in ports, and of course, I know what you did in India, I appreciated it. You made my life better, and I got more sleep."

Of course, I thanked him too. All that over time was good. No disrespect to the other two mates, but the Chief Mate during the trip had many hard days because of their attitudes towards the locals. With my being on the midnight watch, I didn't know much about it until the Chief Mate told me.

The Captain was a slender man, about in his sixties, and very energetic. He looked, in my opinion, like Colonel Sanders. That's the nickname that I gave him during the trip. He was all business at the beginning and a little distant. Don't forget I was the outsider. Usually the Captain gave me the orders when maneuvering on the bridge, and I related them to the engine. The Third Engineer on our watch was playing a game with me. He pretended that he could not hear so I had to repeat it to him two or three times. That was a game to him. The Captain knew what was happening and sort of ignored it. After all I was not one of the boys. The trip progressed, and the conversations that he had with the Chief Mate became more frequent about me. (By the way, he was very close with the Chief Mate.) As the Captain got to know me better, his attitude towards me changed completely. By then I couldn't do any wrong. To give you an idea, on the way back he kept telling me to move to Mobile, Alabama and that I didn't belong in New York. During one arrival, I was on watch, and with the Captain in control and I was relating the orders down to the engine room. As usual the Third Engineer was playing his game pretending that he couldn't hear. The Captain ran, took the phone from me, and proceeded to cuss out the Third Engineer royally…that was the end of the game. After that, even if I whispered, he could be able to hear loud and clear. After that, every time the Chief Mate and I saw him we began joking. By the way he was very apologetic to me and blamed the noise in the engine room for the problem.

During the trip back, a lot of painting was going on. They were trying to have the ship look as good as it could for the trip back to the States. The Intellectual, my AB, came to relieve the wheel and was all shook up. I asked him to tell me what was wrong. He told me, "Paint thinner went into my eye, and thank God for the Chief Mate who cleaned it up well. I think its okay now."

I asked him, "Are you all right now?"

He said, "I'm okay now."

"So what's the big deal, why are you so shaken up? You have two eyes anyway," I said jokingly.

"That's the problem, Mate. I don't have two eyes. This is my good one," he said.

"What are you talking about? I see two eyes?" I said.

"You may see two, Mate, but only one is working. The other one is a lazy eye, it may look normal, but I can't see anything from it. If I had messed up my good eye, I would be blind," he told me.

I understood his fears, but from curiosity, I asked him, "How are you able to have an AB's ticket with a lazy eye?"

"Well, during the Korean War, they needed people, and I enlisted in the Navy. When I completed my four years, I got out of the Navy and I applied for my AB ticket. The Coast Guard turned me down because I had a lazy eye. I told then that I was in the Navy for four years with no problem. Their answer to me was that I was disabled. So, I went down to the Navy and applied for disability. With that they sent me my AB ticket," he told me.

That was the Intellectual's story.

Now, you may wonder about my new ordinary seaman, the hippie, that we picked up in India. Well, I tried to give him a crash course in how to be a good ordinary seaman and to keep a good watch. He seemed to go along okay and in general was all right, but I could sense everything in his life wasn't that important. During one of our conversations he asked me how I became a mate. I told him about the Merchant Marine School, the exams with the Coast Guard. Somehow the conversation turned to the Navy that was the Greek Navy for me. He asked me to explain to him about the Navy. I told him what I was doing and in general it was like the U.S. Navy.

To my amazement, his answer was, "Oh, I thought that it was something important, something useful."

I freaked out, and I said, "So what do you mean? Something important! Something useful! Do you think that serving your country is not important?"

His replied, "Well Mate, I don't think much about it."

That was the end of our conversation, for that day at least. On another occasion, he was telling me what he planned to do when he got home. Since he had a master's degree in psychology, he was planning to do counseling. Specifically he was going to counsel inmates in a way to rehabilitate them for a new way of life when they got out of prison.

I said, "You are going to help inmates rehabilitate themselves and help themselves when they get released into society?"

He said, "Yes Mate."

I thought, "God help them!"

I have to thank the Port Relief Officer in New York Hall. Remember the one that had the argument with the Chief Mate and described him as a monster and the ship as a bad ship? Well the *Citrus Packer* may have not had the South American run, and the ship's crew may have been rowdy at times, but for me it was five months of good pay and sea time. It may not have compared with some other high paying ships, but nevertheless it was very good. Those reluctant and hesitant in the beginning became good buddies with me in the end. We just had to break the ice.

According to the rules, as an applicant I had to get off in the first U.S. port, even if it wasn't the pay off port. So in Savannah, I was out. At the time we still had the shipping commissioner sign us off the ship. I went to the Captain's office to sign off. The commissioner would ask if everything was all right, and would get my check and discharge.

The Captain came and told me, "You're not going to leave my ship unless you have a drink with us. You're not on duty now. You have signed off."

He turned around and told the commissioner what a good a

reliable Mate I was and how he would like me to sail with him again. I appreciate his compliment a lot.

Nineteen seventy-three turned out to be a very good year. Now off the *Citrus Packer*, I was enjoying the luxury of my vacation, and it was summertime, which made it better. Kyki loved the freedom that we had. That year not only did I do five months on the *Citrus Packer*, but after my vacation, at the end of August, I got one trip relief on the *S/S San Juan*.

The *San Juan* was a container vessel with the Sea Land Company, and it was one of the smart Sea Land creations. They took the bow from an older ship, the stern with the engine and accommodation from another ship, and they built a new middle container section. Here we had a container ship with fairly good speed for its time. It was also very economically done.

The run was a very nice Eastern Mediterranean run from New York to Cadiz, Barcelona, Valencia, Fos, Genoa, Livono, back to Barcelona and Valencia. The last port was Cadiz and then home. It was one of the best runs and for a container vessel. We spent enough time in each port, and all the ports were enjoyable. With this run I had a chance to visit Barcelona and Valencia. Both ports had good restaurants and nice cafés. In Valencia we stayed the weekend, and I had a chance to watch a soccer game. This was a special treat for me since Spanish teams were famous.

One of my AB's was well educated, and he was from a well to do family. All in his family were doctors and lawyers. They considered him the black sheep of the family for two reasons. First he chose to be a seaman, and second he married an oriental girl. Nevertheless, I enjoyed my conversations at sea with him. One day I guess I was talking about my plans.

I think I was telling him about opening my own business and he told me, "Watch out Mate! All of the seamen after a while become dreamers and drifters."

He was not far from the truth.

Of course, I assured him, "That will never happen to me."

He replied with skepticism, "That is what everybody says."

In my later years at sea, in my conversations with other seamen hearing about all their plans and what they were going to do, I would laugh as I remembered what my AB had said about dreamers and drifters.

My wife got a kick out of this from a phone call I had made to her from the ship. With a single side band from the ship, it was a big deal to her to hear from me from the middle of the ocean. This was a nice ship, a nice run, a civilized run, but it was not in my reach. I was still an applicant. I was lucky to have this trip. 1973 after all was a good year.

With 1973 history, it was time now to look ahead. How was I going to earn the next meal? Well, as an applicant, you got the leftovers. The best jobs were allocated for the members. I would say that most of the members were sympathetic towards the applicants, but a few were not hesitant to show that even the leftovers could be denied. I have a little story for that. She was an old C-3 doing her last voyage to the Far East and then going to be scrap ironed. It would total to be about a two and a half months trip. She needed a second mate and two third mates. They filled the second mate job, but there were no takers for the two third mate jobs. They were calling the jobs until Friday; and the ship was sailing on the weekend. On the last call, they filled one of the third mate jobs with a guy who took it with a night mate card. The other job was still open. Now they had to open that job to an applicant, after all it was the last call on the last day. The job came to me. Now all the calls were over, and the day was practically over. I was inside the office, and the dispatcher was preparing my papers to go to the doctor. Now, here comes an old guy and tells the dispatcher, "Stop! I will take the job!"

The dispatcher said, "What job? There is no job. The job is

gone! Michael has it."

"No, I am a member, and I want the job!" he said.

"You were present for the last call, and you didn't want it. The job is gone!" the dispatcher said.

"I changed my mind, I want the job," he said, and with that he went upstairs to find an official.

There was one assistant port agent at the time; and being late Friday everybody else had gone for the weekend. The official called us upstairs, the dispatcher and me, and he and asked us what was wrong.

The dispatcher said, "Nothing is wrong. Nobody wanted the job it was after the last call, and Michael has it."

"Well, Michael is an applicant, and this man is a member, and he wants the job," the official said.

"But the call is over; and we are closed for the day," the dispatcher explained.

"He is a member, and we have to give the job to a member," the official said. To the dismay of both of us he took the job away from me and gave it to him. It gets better! Monday when I went back to the Union, the old man was there. He took the job, and when I left the Union Hall, he turned it back. The ship sailed short! Not only that but he got his shipping card back. The assistant port agent was wrong, but it was too late. The main official, the port agent, was infuriated, but it was too late. That incident infuriated quite a few members. Thank God there were only a few like this old man. The majority, as I said, were decent people.

THE TANKERS – OVERSEAS VIVIAN – OVERSEAS ALICE

Things dried out for a while for me. My bags were packed and ready from November, but it took until May 14th to get a ship. All this time I was religiously going to the Hall looking for a job. The ship was the *Overseas Vivian*, from Maritime Overseas Company. She was a tanker that was docked in Philadelphia. Most of the tanker men at the time suspected that she would go overseas and stay there. It was usually the Far East. Two jobs were open, second mate and third mate. The Philadelphia Hall did not have anyone to fill the job. They called New York. They called the job for only about two weeks. A couple of other applicants ahead of me did not want to sacrifice their card only for two weeks. I was only competing for the third mate job. I did not have a second mate license at the time. A young guy took the second mate job, and something was telling me to get the job. I took a chance and took the third mate's job. I was hoping that the ship would get away from the coast in these two weeks. When we got to Philadelphia that evening, it was almost done with the cargo and scheduled to sail very early in the morning. They posted for sea. I had the eight to twelve. On the way down the river, the Chief Mate came on the bridge and asked me if I wanted to sign articles that the ship was going to New York for stores and then to St. Croix to load jet fuel (JP-4) for Okinawa, Japan. We would stay in the Far East.

I said, "Of course I will sign! I just came on board!"

"Well, I have to ask all the mates just in case someone wants to get off and doesn't want to get stuck on the ship for six more months," he said.

I was happy to hear the news; after all I didn't waste my card. When he left, I called the Second Mate and I told him, "Buddy we made it! Were going to be here for six months!" In New York I called Kyki and told her the news. She was happy that something that looked like a short job, turned out to be a six-month trip. On the other hand, she didn't want me to be away for six months, but the thing that pacified her was that this trip would give us enough money, with what we had saved, to make a down payment on a house. Happy with that, she said she would start looking that summer for a house.

The *Overseas Vivian* was almost a brand new tanker. I think it was only a couple of years old with a modern bridge, good quarters, air conditioner, and it was easy to work. I got familiar with the ship very quickly. We loaded JP-4 from St. Croix, and we were on our way to the Far East. We discharged the cargo at White Beach, Okinawa, and then we were off to the Persian Gulf to load again for Subic Bay, Sasebo, or Yokuska. That was in general the Far East run, and it was done in about a thirty-four day round trip. It wasn't the Mediterranean run, but it wasn't Middle East either. From the U.S. bases I was able to send my mail and make a phone call home. Of course, there were quite a few decent places to go outside the base and have a good meal. We did that for almost three months. One diversion that we had a couple of times was to take about thirty thousand barrels of JP-4 to Diego Garcia. At that time Diego Garcia was still a small observation station with a small airport strip, but I have a lot more to say about Diego Garcia in later ships.

When we got to Bahrain we got a message that this time we are going to load JP-4 for Europe, specifically Rota, Spain; Danges, France; and Thames Haven, England. That was a long stretch. The Suez Canal was still closed; it took thirty days from Bahrain to Rota. Rota was a nice little base. It looked like the United States. I could send my mail; do my shopping, and make a phone call home. While I was in a store, smaller than our department stores, I saw a bunch of women standing in line. I thought something good was going on here seeing all these ladies in line. I asked one of them why they were in line.

She said, "Don't you know?"

"No, I am a seaman with a tanker here only for a short time," I said.

"Oh, we are here for the Majorca pearls. You're lucky that you hit the right day. In about ten minutes they are going to start selling them," she replied.

This was going on once a month. They were nice pearls, and the price was excellent. So here I was waiting in line for pearls, and I knew that Kyki would like them. The ladies were buying them like crazy. By the time I got my turn, they were almost all gone. I was lucky to find some left. In fact, the necklace was a slightly different size from the bracelets.

Trips like that tend to become monotonous, especially for the crew. There were no decent ports to blow off some steam, and the good ones were very few with limited time. So we were loosing some crew, and because we had signed Foreign Articles, they had to get sick in order to fly home. Every time we reached a good port like Rota, Subic Bay, or Singapore for supplies and bunker, the crew went bananas! Subic Bay was their favorite. They also had a chance to get reliefs. Of course they had to pay them, to stand their watch. This way they would be able to go out, have a good time, and not get in trouble. The amount they had to pay the locals to stand their watch was fairly reasonable. Even if it weren't, they wouldn't care because they just wanted to be free. Of course, I didn't mind the locals on my watches because they were very good and reliable. Sasabo also had the same deal with reliefs, but by now Japan was becoming fairly expensive. Subic Bay was still the place. All of the seamen used as reliefs knew very well the U.S. ship's operation. Quite of few of them had sailed on the ships during the Vietnam War to cover the shortage of seamen at the time. I had, by the time we arrived at Thames Haven (such a miserable place in the middle of nowhere, and it was cold even in summer) a little over three months sea time.

Our permanent Captain was going on vacation, by now he had over six months. He was an older gentleman, a well-seasoned seaman, and a very good tanker man. From the beginning, we had a very good working relationship. I was going to miss him. He stayed on board until the ship sailed. He tried to make his relief as familiar with the ship as possible. He had a good reason for that. The old man was experienced. The new Captain had little or no experience with the tankers. We sailed in Thames Heaven on ballast for the return trip to the Persian Gulf. It is a good thing that we loaded good-sized ballast because in the English Channel we were hit by a strong gale. The wind was blowing 50 to 60 knots, to give you an idea I had to use the 3 cm radar because on the 10 cm, the antenna would get stuck due to the strong wind.

My watch was the eight to twelve, and here came the Captain on the bridge. It was the first time I saw him, and he asked me to go to the chart room, as if something important was happening. He proceeded to explain what his rules were on the bridge.

"Captain, with all due respect, I have traffic out there, and I can't stay long in here," I said.

"No wait, let me explain to you," he said.

From the talk that I had with the Second Mate, I knew what he wanted. So I said. "Captain, let me tell you in brief. I don't drink, I don't smoke, and I don't neglect my duties. Is there anything that I haven't covered because I really have to be out there? The traffic is heavy?"

With that I left and went back on the bridge whether he liked or not. He said that he was allergic to the smoke, or he didn't like it because he would make a lot of fuss around the smokers. A couple of days later, the weather was pretty good, and on his visit to the bridge he started a conversation with me.

He said, "The channel was busy wasn't it?"

I said, "It sure was, Captain."

In general he was all right. The other two mates were getting upset with him, especially when we were around the coast because he wanted a ship's position every ten minutes. He would watch the traffic, and the Mate would take positions every ten minutes. This drove the other two mate's bananas! I really didn't have a problem with that. It was nothing outside of the rules, and after all he was the Captain. By the time we arrived at Bahrain, I had over four and a half months. One round trip to Sasabo and back to Bahrain; I would have the six months; and it would be time to go home. On the way to Sasabo, we stopped in Singapore for bunkers and storage.

From the first day on board the Captain put signs all over the ship that no drinking was allowed on board the ship at any time. To me and to most of the officers, it did not make any difference, but that rule infuriated the crew. In Singapore, he posted signs on the gangways and mess halls. He ordered the gangway watchmen to search all ship's personnel that were coming from ashore so they didn't bring any liquor on board. On top of everything, he prohibited the little merchants that would come on board in Singapore from coming on board. He was afraid that they would sneak girls on board. In reality, he was right, but in the seaman's world, it wasn't a big crime.

Apparently with the ship's stores, liquor was coming for the Captain. I guess he figured that he was above the law. That liquor never reached his cabin. Rumors have it that somebody threw the whole case over the side. Anyway the Captain's liquor was never found, and they never found out who did it. If you wanted to see a monster infuriated to the maximum, he was the one. He ran an investigation, searched the ship, but all in vain. Thank God all this did not happen on my watch! I found out the next day.

From then on the Captain and the crew were at war. Most of the officers had nothing to do with any of this nonsense. The bad part was that it made the rest of the trip unhappy. Neither side was willing to give up. It turned from a nice relaxed ship to one full of tension. One morning, the steward department, as usual, went to set the dining rooms for breakfast and found out that all the utensils (forks, knives, and spoons etc.) were gone! Apparently someone threw them over the side. Lucky enough the steward had some spares on the side. The next casualty was the washer's agitators. They went over the side too! From then on, after six o'clock all public places were locked. If someone wanted to get something, he had to go on the bridge to get the key and bring the key back. Then we had to keep a log of who had the key and for how long. The crew also started locking their rooms when they were not in them.

In Sasabo, we had to do fuel transferring from one storage tank to another. I think they had to do that to the JP-4 to keep it fresh. We spent a few days loading from one dock, shifting to another inside the bay and then discharging there. During that time, one AB with the ordinary seamen went ashore. They decided to extend their good time a little more. So they missed a few watches before they returned to the ship after a day or so. They both had a little history of feuding with the Captain. What they did was wrong and the Captain had the right to log them. Considering the past records, he even would have been in his right to fire them. Well, that's what he did, but in the wrong way, and he got himself in deep trouble. His first mistake was that he did not log them for what they had done before. They just argued, so until then they were clean as far as loggings were concerned.

We were in Japan, a foreign country, and with foreign articles. No one could be fired without going to the Consul, signing him off, and somehow arranging his repatriation home. Even if the seaman had to pay from his own pocket. The Captain proceeded to pay them off, sign them off, and get them off of the ship. The two guys were not stupid. They did not say anything; they got off of the ship, and went straight to the U.S. Consulate in Sasabo. They explained what happened and asked for repatriation. The officer of the Consul could not believe what he was hearing, but he had the two men in front of him with their pay-off vouchers and their discharge slips. He kept them at the Consulate and sent a message to the ship for the Captain to come to the Consulate immediately. From what I heard, the officer of the Consulate threatened the Captain that he would take action on his license. When the Captain received the message, he had already realized that what he had done was a big mistake. He got very worried. Now we were in the middle of transferring and shifting the ship back and forth and he should have been on the ship. But also, he had to go to the Consulate. He called me and asked me to stay on the bridge during the shifts even if I wasn't on watch, so that I could assist the Pilot. He had to go to the Consulate.

"Of course, go take care of what you have to do, and I will be on the bridge at all times during the shifts. Don't worry at all!" I said.

From what I heard later, he did not have a good time at the Consulate. It wasn't because he wasn't supposed to punish the guys for what they did, but it was the way that he went about it. In the end, he had to take them back on the ship. He could not justify to the company the hefty bill that was required to send them home and bring reliefs. It was especially a problem when he did not have good reasons to do that because nothing had been logged until then. Both guys came back, probably laughing at him.

Back in Bahrain, the Second Mate, the Chief Mate, one engineer, and I were going home. All of us had more that 180 days. The trip that started as a two-week job gave me six months of work and good tanker experience. By now I had enough time for the Second Mate's license, and Kyki's down payment for the house was in the bank.

There was always some excitement; it was never a dull moment! For my first license, things were very slow, and they did not really need any mates. Plus I was new to the system, and of course I had been away from school for quite a while. Well, now it should be a little easier, right? Not a chance! This time the examination system had just changed from an essay type with a two-week time span to a multiple choice type test with a time limit. On top of everything a lot of questions were wrong. People were failing right and left regardless of their level of education (King's Point, State Maritime Academies, etc.) My friends were telling me to wait a little bit for things to settle down. Nobody was passing now.

"Well, I will take my chances. Now or later it will still be multiple choice. I may as well try it. I'll study as much as I can and give it a try," I said.

The old school that I had gotten the books from the first time had closed. Captain Bowen had retired. The Seamen's Church

Institute did not have any materials to study by for the new system. They were still on the old essay type materials. Besides all of this, I took a chance, and I passed!

Now with a Second's Mate's license and tanker man's experience, I had broadened my chances for a job. The Union also improved the rules a little. A job was still for one round trip, but they increased the time limit to a thirty-day limit for the coastwise. They also could not pull an applicant out when he had the job already. Still the best bet was a fly out job. That usually meant a tanker.

After the usual waiting and back and forth at the Union Hall, my next job came in May. It was with the Maritime Overseas Company again, and it was on the *Overseas Alice,* the sister ship of the *Overseas Vivian.* The *Overseas Vivian, Valdez,* and *Alice* were built exactly the same. All three of them were chartered at the time to the U.S. military on the Far East run. I had to fly again to Bahrain. For me it was a good company and a new ship, but for a full member who wanted to be close to home or on a liner with better pay, the job wasn't that attractive.

A friend of mine got the second mate job, and I got the third mate one. He was registered ahead of me. We were delighted to be on the same ship and able to do six months worth of work. Since he was a tanker man and I had been on the sister ship for six months, we had no problem. In fact, we were very useful to the Chief Mate, who was a young man in his late twenties or thirties. The other Third Mate was a nice fellow. As a full member, he just took the job and wasn't very interested in becoming a tanker man. Even though I was familiar with this type of ship, I still visited the bridge after I settled down, just to take a look. It was around 10:30 A.M. and my watch did not start until twelve o'clock. I needed to kill some time. When I was on the bridge, I met the Radio Operator, who was in his radio shack. He was very pleasant, a little older than me, and fairly bald. We talked for a while; then I left and went downstairs. I was on deck during my twelve to four watch, and it was around two o'clock. I was hanging with my watch around the gangway, which was close to the manifold. There I saw a guy with long silver hair and an Elvis Presley shirt with jeans and boots. From far away he waived at me, called me Michael, and asked if I was going to go out.

I asked one of my ABs, "Who is that guy who knows my name? I just came on board."

"Mate, that's the Radio Operator," he said.

"What do you mean? The Radio Operator is bald. I just talked to him a few hours ago," I said.

"You will see when he gets closer that it is the Radio Operator," he said.

That was his going ashore dress. Later on during the trip he was bragging to me about his wig, that it was made from human hair and that it had cost him over $2,000. He was proud of his shore uniform.

Since the *Alice* came out, it was a time charter on the Far East run. It quickly became home to the Far East steadies, seamen who had made the Far East their home. That started with the Vietnam War. These seamen would stay there and take vacation there, and at the time, there were quite a few, affordable, nice places. Some of these seamen maintained two homes, one in the States and one in the Far East. One of these people was my ordinary seaman. He was actually an AB and a good one. By now, with the Vietnam War over, the Far East jobs were scaled down and hard to find. He was forced, even though he was a good AB, to take the ordinary seaman's job. I had given him the nickname Professor, because he thought that he knew everything. One of my ABs was in the Far East area for fourteen years, and he was a martial arts aficionado. I didn't know this at the time. At sea, we kept the Look Out always at the wings of the ship. One night I heard "HUA, WHO, WU HUA!" The Professor was at the wheel, and he saw me wondering what was going on.

He said, "Mate, don't worry. The AB is out there practicing on his karate kicks."

On monotonous trips like this, something had to be done to kill time. On the *Alice*, it was the evening poker game. Technically, we were not supposed to gamble on the ship, but who was going to enforce the rule when the Captain was the first person at the table? So every night, religiously, a poker game was going on. The Second Mate, the other Third Mate and I were not gamblers. That had the

Old Man greatly pissed. They had passed the gentle state of supposedly having a little fun and passing the time, and had reached high-stakes poker. I saw quite a few people loose their whole paycheck because of gambling. The mates and the engineers had to rotate every six months, but the crew could stay as long as they wanted to. We had people on the ship that were there for over two years because of gambling debts.

The Chief Mate, young and aggressive, sometimes did things that put him in danger. I was on deck, and he told me that he was going down to the pump room to check something, and that he would be back soon. After twenty minutes passed and he hadn't shown up, something told me to check on him. I went on the platform of the pump room, and I called him, but there was no answer. I told one of my ABs to keep an eye out for me, and that I was going down to see what he was doing. It was a good thing that I went to check on him. I found him with a wrench still in his hands, trying to tighten up some bolts. He seemed like he was kind of dizzy and disorientated. There was a small leak, but they didn't want to stop the loading to fix it. It had accumulated, and there were quite a few fumes inside the small pump room. With the fumes and the heat, he was ready to pass out.

I said, "Mate, what are you doing?"

"I'm trying to tighten up some of these bolts!" he replied.

I said, "Mate, you've tightened them up enough. Let's get out of here before you pass out. You need some fresh air. Let's get out of here!"

I had a hard time getting him upstairs. He almost passed out by the time we got on the deck.

I had by now almost two and a half months. The crew had been colorful and with a few unusual stories, but nevertheless, it was enjoyable. The time was passing quickly. My buddy, the Second Mate, and I thought that we had it made. We thought we were going to have a nice six months here, but it turned out not to be so. We got

My Sea My Life

a message from the company that the ship was due for inspection. If I remember well, they had also some trouble with the turbines. So we had to go to Jacksonville, Florida to do the repairs.

I can't begin to tell you how many of us were unhappy. For my Buddy and I, it was the end of our jobs, and for the crew, there were many other reasons. For example, one AB was wanted from the state of California for alimony. This was the result of a one-week unsuccessful marriage to the wrong person. Poor man! He married the wrong girl, who took him for a ride, and he had to pay her alimony. So he had left and never went back to California, in fact he stayed on the Far East run. When we arrived, he had to sneak out from the East Coast, and hopefully not get caught. Otherwise he would have to pay all of the back money. When we reached the Panama Canal, the Chief Mate asked us how we would like our pay-off checks. All three of us told the Chief Mate that we thought to get the pay in a check and with only the transportation money in cash for the flight home.

When the Mate presented the list with the request to the Captain, he hit the ceiling, "Why do you guys want checks? Everybody gets cash! You guys want to change the rules now?"

The Mate said, "Captain, were not changing the rules. Those are the rules! I am going to take a check, too."

Finally the Captain seemed to agree to order checks and only give us the transportation money in cash. Guess what? The payoff was all cash. The Captain claimed that he had ordered the checks! To make things worse the airlines had gone on strike, and we had to take the train home. My buddy and I were gong to New York, we stayed close to each other and hid the money in our inside pockets. We made it home all right and with great relief. That would have been awful to loose all of our paychecks because the Old Fool wanted to pay us in all cash. With that, the *Overseas Alice* was history.

The vacation was short. After all we had only a three-month

trip. Before long my bags were packed again. The trips to the Hall start again, looking for the next job. In the meantime, more and more applicants were joining the Union. Some applicants stayed, and some applicants were disappointed from waiting for a job and sought employment elsewhere. My friend was forced to do that, too. He had a family to feed. During this period the MMP lost quite a few good, qualified mates.

Again I thought that my best bet to find a job was around the holidays. For the holidays, some full members would get off for a round trip, and I would probably have a chance to ship out for a relief trip. By the way the members would take the job for 180 days, and they had the right to take one round trip off and then go back and finish their time. Between relief jobs and fly out jobs, I thought that I might have a chance. Unfortunately, the ones that were ahead of me filled the few relief jobs that came down to the applicants. Christmas was gone, and I was still here. On the other hand I had a chance to have a holiday at home, and my wife liked that.

The members were enjoying a nice job turnover. They didn't really have a difficult time getting the job they wanted for the time that they wanted. For us, the applicants, in the end we would probably do well, but we had to tolerate the uncertainty and the long wait. We wanted to make a living on the sea, and as a new kid on the block that was what we had to go through. There was no question that the Union could have had a little better system. Politics had a great deal to do with it. Quite a few young applicants at the time, bitter and disappointed, left and quite a few of them became enemies down the road. I still considered, with all its flaws and weaknesses, the Masters Mates and Pilots Union to be the Cadillac of all Unions at the time as far as the deck officers were concerned. After all in a true democratic Union, there may be some weaknesses.

Looking for a job with me was a buddy of mine, who I call Maki. He had registered a few days behind me; actually he was just below me on the list. Until now I had had a few long jobs, and Kyki was teaching. We really weren't hurting for money. The waiting and uncertainty was painful though. We tried to cope as well as we could. The overall situations with the merchant marine were better than jobs with the hotels. I had more freedom and more off time, and I didn't have the daily rat race with the subways and traffic going to New York. Plus the fact was that in four months of work on the ship I would make much more than being a front office manager in the twenty-story hotel/motel Sheraton in New York. Looking down the road to become a member and thinking of the privileges that they were enjoying, I wasn't complaining. Now I had accumulated time and seniority, and I was hoping that when they opened the books I would be one of the first in. With my buddy, Maki, things were kind of tight. Being married with two kids and with his wife not working, he started feeling the pinch. Plus, the poor guy had the sixth brigade working full speed against him.

His in-laws were saying, "How will he make any money? How is going to feed you? He's just going back and forth to the Union Hall, wasting his time. He is lazy."

All of them were ignorant and unfamiliar with how things work in the Union. They could not comprehend how he would recover since he was waiting so long outside. All of the above drove the poor man nuts. I have to say his wife understood, but the friction with all of the others was mounting. I had to pacify him almost every day.

Some of our friends were telling me, "Michael, he will drive you nuts, too! How can you tolerate him?"

They said this jokingly of course and sympathetically, too.

Michael G. Razos

TRANSCOLUMBIA

April 14, when I arrived at the Hall right at the door waiting for me was Maki. He was huffing and puffing, "There are two third mate jobs on the board, and we have a good chance. At least you do, but I really hope for both of us though. The ship is old and it is going to the Persian Gulf."

"Relax; you are going to have a heart attack!" I said.

The ship was one of the two Hudson Water Ways heavy lift ships. The *Transcolumbia* by far was not the most desirable job. Maki was right, by going to the Persian Gulf in the summer time, we did have a good chance, but you never knew. The first call went through with no takers. Maki was reaching his climax, the tension was mounting, and he was sweating all over. Now we were on the last call and guess what? We got it! Both of us! He was flying! He was in seventh heaven! Poor Maki had just about had it. He had reached his peak, and I don't think that he could have taken anymore. Even though I was ahead of him to make it fair we flipped a coin to see who would get the eight to twelve or the twelve to four watch. I won the toss.

"Lucky you. I cannot beat you!" Maki said, which he reminded me for the rest of the trip.

We got the job in New York, but the ship had to do the coastwise, so it wasn't the last port. Maki drove me nuts during the whole coastwise. He was afraid that they were going to take us off of the ship and that he would loose the job. I think that it was in Norfolk when we lost Maki for five hours. We didn't know what had happened to him. Finally, he showed up after five or six hours.

I asked him, "Where have you been? We were worried about

you."

He said, "I was hiding down in the number two hatch."

He saw the Port Agent of the Union, and he got scared that he might take him off of the ship. Poor Maki! I tried to assure him that we had the jobs and that no one would take them away from us. I don't think that I had much luck convincing him until we departed from the United States. I really didn't blame him. He wanted the job.

The Captain was one of the nicest people that we could have as a captain. He came from the West Coast. On the other hand, the Chief Mate was a good old boy with his own peculiarities, not bad, just peculiar. One of his idiosyncrasies was to dispute overtime, and to argue with the people. Well, Maki got upset quite a few times with him. I had my philosophy from the beginning, no arguments. I told him I would write down what I thought I should get. If he had any questions or if he disputed it, he should underline it in red, but not erase it. When we go back to the States for the payoff, the Union representative would clear up the dispute. So we will be friends now and friends then, and this was what I did. Maki and the Mate continued to argue the whole trip. The Captain and I were laughing about it.

The ship was old, and the trip was to the Persian Gulf. These were two good ingredients for trouble. Most of the officers were pretty good. With the crew, it was another story. During the coastwise, we could see that we were getting the bottom of the barrel, as they say in seamen's language. The first performance started when we were still on the East Coast. I was on the evening watch, and we had just left the port.

The Captain was still on the bridge with me, and it was about 9 P.M., and he said, "Michael, I'm tired and I'm going to go to bed. I had a long day, and I'm going to have another long one tomorrow. Good night."

Then he left. About an hour later I saw him coming on the bridge again, he started walking back and forth and was huffing and puffing.

I approached him and said with humor, "What happened? Flat tire?"

He said, "Michael, you wouldn't believe what happened. I

was almost asleep and the Steward knocked on my door. I opened it, and he told me to come below because they were going to kill him. He said that they were going to kill the BR (BR is the one who takes care of the officer's rooms). He told me to come down quickly, so I got dressed and went below with the Steward. Apparently the BR was so drunk he could not hold it, or did not know what he was doing. He went to the bathroom, inside the cabin on the floor. The whole thing! Of course there were people sleeping in that room, two messman, the BR, and a galley assistant. The place stank! The guys were ready to beat him up, but good."

The Captain tried to calm them down, and in the meantime, the Steward, a couple of people, and even the B.R. tried to clean up the room. They sprayed to relieve the odor. They locked the B.R. in another spare room for the night so he could sober up and could be safe, too. They waited for the next day to see what they would do with him. The Captain had come on the bridge to blow off some stream and calm down.

I said, "I hope you are going to send him home at the next port!"

"Of course! He's going to be out!" the Captain said.

Well, he wasn't out, because they couldn't find a replacement. Of course he apologized and promised that he would be all right if they would give him another chance.

The first port was Rota, Spain. That was the last good port in the schedule. The next two were Dammam, Saudi Arabia and Bandar Shapur, Iran. This time the star of the show was the Third Engineer. In his middle fifties, normally, he was quiet that was until he started drinking. It looked as if he got drunk ashore and with that he got nasty. From what I gathered, he had a cab drive him around and then to the ship. When the cab driver asked him for his cab fare, the Third Engineer cursed him, did not want to pay, and came on board. The cab driver brought the police, and they were looking for the Third

Engineer. The Third Engineer was nasty to the cab driver and the police. They were ready to take him to jail. He was lucky! The Captain and the Chief Engineer were coming back from shore. Seeing the police and the cab around the gangway, they asked what was going on.

When the Chief Engineer found out, he blew his top, "Son of a bitch! You promised me that if I gave you a chance, you would not start the same mess."

The Chief Engineer paid the cab, apologized to the police, and took the Third Engineer to his room. They must have had a good talk because the rest of the trip he was very good. He was quiet as a mouse.

Poor Captain! Besides his salary, he should have gotten an aggravation bonus. One day before the Suez Canal, the Steward came to the Captain with a list of fresh provisions to buy at the Canal. The Captain hit the ceiling.

"We just left the States! You must have plenty," he said.

I was present when the Captain told him, "Steward, they say that the trip is going to be two and a half months, but forget that. I want you to order stores for more than four months. Make sure to get everything from here and plenty of it."

Now not even two weeks later, he is out of fresh produce. It looked as if it was going to be a long trip for all of us, especially for the poor Captain. We got some fresh food supplies at the Suez. We did the best we could under the circumstances. Especially at this time, Egypt was not that friendly with the United States. It was the wrong place for stores.

After we passed the Strait of Hormuz, and all the way to Dammam, it was hazy, and there was very low visibility. Radar here was the most useful tool and the racon system was a savior. We recognized the sea buoys by the signal the racon showed on the radar. This way we navigated our way. The Red Sea and the Gulf have a very good racon system. Ten minutes to eight I was on the bridge for my watch. I found the Second Mate all shaken up. He was from the West Coast and apparently had never been in the Persian Gulf. Also, from what I sensed, he was not familiar with the racon system.

He told me, "Mike, since we got inside the Straits, I was going by the DR. I don't know exactly where we are; I wish that I could give you a better position."

I had looked at the chart before, and I expected to have a racon buoy close. When I looked at the scope, I waited a few minutes and then the racon signal popped up.

"You're doing good, Second. I know where we are. We are close to this buoy. You can see the racon," I said.

"What?" he said.

"The racon buoys," I said, and I showed him on the scope what I meant.

"Oh, that's what it was; I was wondering what it was all about," he replied.

Normally he should know what racon was, but as I said the old *Transcolumbia* and the run created strange relations.

Our first port in the Gulf was Dammam, Saudi Arabia. The place at the time wasn't just crowded with ships, but it was over crowded! There must have been two hundred ships at the anchorage at the time. We anchored as close as we could. We sent the arrival message and waited for instructions. Now we were anchored in Dammam for one week, and there was no answer from anybody, not from the local authorities nor the Company. The Captain sent another message to the Company and to the Port Authority. He reminded them that we had been at the anchor for a week now, and we haven't seen anyone.

The Company sent a message, "As you can see the port is over crowded. We are trying to work something out. We do not know how long you are going to be there."

If it were up to the locals, the ship would have stayed four to five months.

However the military needed the ship back. They gave the Saudis an ultimatum, and said, "Discharge the cargo (military equipment), or we take them back because we need the ship."

That shortened our stay to only a little over a month. It was long enough though to have a few more good performances here. The biggest one, from what I suspected, was between two Spanish guys and two good old boys. That one was in the form of a big brawl. From what I heard, it was racially motivated. The feud between two good old boys and the two Spanish guys had been going on for a while. During the anchorage time, it intensified. Midnight, during the change of watch, a Mexican AB was going on watch. He was in the crew mess and getting his coffee. The mess hall was empty and no one else was there. According to him, two guys came in, locked the door, proceeded to beat him up very badly, and left. They found him almost unconscious later. Immediately the Captain called the port for a boat to come and pick him up and take him ashore to the hospital. That did not come until the next day. Fast response all right! They took him to the local hospital. He claims that he did not have a chance to see who beat him up. He wanted to come back on the ship. Two U.S. officials from the U.S. Consulate from Dammam came onboard for the investigation. That took almost a week. They sent two men back to the States; supposedly the ones who they thought did it. Also, they sent the Mexican home. Now, for the rest of the stay in Dammam, the gangway watchman was on the bridge with the mate. It was from eight P.M. to six A.M. for security reasons. After more than a month, they took us inside, and we discharged the cargo fairly quickly. By the way, even along side no one from the crew was allowed to go ashore, not even at the dock. We were very happy to leave Dammam.

The next port was Bandar Shapur, Iran. It was up the river,

and we discharged the rest of the cargo to the barges at the anchorage. This was another exotic place, hot, humid, dusty and in the middle of nowhere. The temperature was over a hundred degrees. Sometimes it would reach over a hundred and twenty-five! Imagine! The discharge here was slow and with lots of problems. The longshoremen were working long hours, staying on the ship, and getting no decent rest. After a few days they were tired and exhausted. When we asked the authorities for a new gang, they sent us a new gang all right, but they were from another ship, just as exhausted and tired. We found out later that they rotate the same people. If we complained they took a gang from one ship and shifted it to another to pacify us. There were damages to the cargo, galore! We spent a lot of time writing damage reports. We had some brand new, beautiful vehicles. They were not discharging at the barges, but dropping at the barges and naturally damaging them. The ship's agent, a real nice guy, was doing his best, but he had absolutely no control over them.

I asked him, "Why?"

He said, "Mate, were in deep trouble, deep trouble! A lot of blood is going to be spilled soon. A lot of people will die. Don't ask me more!"

That was just before the revolution when Ayatollah Khomeini took over, and we all know what had happened next.

If you wonder what had happened to the Big Babba, remember the B.R.? He was the one that had promised to be good if he had gotten a second chance? Well, he did it again. In Bandar Shapur there was a little canteen. It was not much, just a few beers, and sodas in the middle of nowhere. Well, that was enough for Big Babba to get messed up. He missed his work, got a little beaten up by some guys that he insulted without even knowing that he had insulted them. The Captain logged him.

We had to go back and forth with the boat if we wanted to go out. Coming back drunk was not pleasant because if we had the unfortunate luck to fall in the water, we were gone! The river was full of sea snakes and a fast current. I used to watch them try to slide up the side of the ship. There were no regrets on leaving Bandar Shapur. The word was that on the way back, we would stop in some ports in the Mediterranean to pick up cargo, mostly effects of military personnel, to take back to the U.S. We were all looking forward to that.

Remember the conversation the Captain had with the Steward? The Captain said, "Get plenty to stores to last for over four months."

The Steward assured him, "Don't worry. I have plenty."

By now, we had run out of almost everything, even rice. No exaggeration here! The food was pitiful, and all from the stupidity of the Steward.

We were at the anchorage over thirty days, and there was no rain and good weather. The Mate did not paint the outside of the ship. He was waiting until we left Bandar Shapur to do that.

In a conversation that we had, he said. "Well, its summertime. After we get out of the Persian Gulf, I will start painting the accommodation, and it will probably be all painted by the time we get to the Canal."

"No, you're not!" I said.

"Why? It's the summertime," he said.

"That's your problem, Mate. In the summertime we have the South West monsoons blowing all the time. Almost all the way up to the middle of the Red Sea, they are very, very strong," I told him.

"No, no, you will see I will paint them," he replied.

Sure enough he tried to paint, and fifty percent of the paint blew away. When the Captain saw the mess on the deck, he stopped him. The poor Captain was desperate. The Captain was telling him one thing, and he was doing another.

"I don't know what to do with him!" he told me many times.

We were all looking forward to some good ports in the Mediterranean. We were especially looking forward to going home. We were in the middle of the Red Sea when we received a message from the Company that we were going to Astood, Israel to load some cargo and then to come directly home with no further explanation.

Now going through the Suez Canal was a three-ring circus. Even though all the papers were set up, they showed that we were going to the different Mediterranean ports. Somehow they knew that we were going to Israel, and they gave the ship a hard time. The officials were difficult; the pilots were always complaining, and demanding things and bitching.

I had the eight to twelve watch, and around ten P.M. the Pilot told me, "Mate, I am hungry. I want something to eat."
I called the Stand By to fix a sandwich, and to get some fruits, and some drinks. After a while, the Stand By came up with some sandwiches, soft drinks and some fruit.

The Pilot said, "I don't' want that!"

I asked him, "What do you want?"

He replied, "I want a hot meal."

I told him, "The galley is closed from six o'clock. I have no one to fix you a hot meal."

"Well, call them up!" he said.

"That's it. That is all I can get at this time. If you don't like it, you will get a hot meal in the morning. I cannot call anyone," I told him.

"Well, then I will have some fruits only," he said.

"Good!" I said.

A few minutes later he asked me for some cigarettes. I gave him some Marlboro, but he didn't like them. I had something else, I don't' exactly remember, but I gave him that too to pacify him. The Captain had left a couple of cartons in the back for that reason. Usually, we anchored in Ismailia, to wait for the southbound convoy. It was the Pilot's job to anchor the ship.

When we arrived at the lake, the Pilot told the Captain, "Now it's your ship, you can anchor it."

The poor Captain, he tried to be nice. "Pilot, I have no problem anchoring the vessel, but you are the one who knows the area and where the ship is supposed to anchor," he replied.

"Well, I will tell you where to do it," the Pilot said.

The Captain said, "Well, I'll do it! Just show me, and I will do it."

That was the kind of treatment that we had all the way. I was so glad that I was on watch when the Pilot was ready to leave. First, he asked me for cigarettes.

I said, "Pilot, no cigarettes. They are bad for your health, and I don't want you to have a problem."

By now he was getting the idea that he would not get any cigarettes, at least, not from me. Then he asked me to have someone to carry his bag; it was a small bag.

I said to him, "Pilot, I am suspecting that you want to go to Israel. If you do not move fast, I'm ringing full ahead and you are coming with us. If you do not want to come with us, take your bag and run."

I haven't seen a Pilot yet to leave so fast. He knew that the game was over. In later years, I went through the Canal quite a few times. I would say there was nothing of all that nonsense. I guess it was a difficult period for them.

Astood was nice little port, and from what I later learned from the local longshoremen, it was a manmade port. A few years back, it was a desert, but they created a nice port and a beautiful city. What we were loading were captured materials. They did not give us much explanation. We knew that we would take them to Leonardo, New Jersey. We didn't stay long in Astood, from eight A.M. to midnight. Thank God, we got quite a few fresh produce and other stores. When my watch was over at noon, I went ashore for a nice meal. Then I spent most of the time around the beach at the little cafes. Of course, I made my telephone call home. What a difference from the ports that we had been in before! One thing that was strange to me was to

My Sea My Life

see the people enjoying the beach. At the same time, there were posted every so many yards armed soldiers for security. The cargo by ten P.M. was done, and the ship was secure for sea. At eleven o'clock I started testing the gears and by eleven-fifteen I was done and went down to the gangway. I saw all kinds of military coming on board, and from the sea a few boats were around the ship.

I asked them, "What is going on?"

The men in charge said, "Nothing is wrong, Mate."

Then I asked, "So, what are you guys doing?"

"We have to search the ship, to make sure that no explosives were planted to sabotage the ship. We will check the ship inside and underneath the hull. That's why we have the divers on the water side of the ship to make sure that everything is safe."

I asked, "Why all that? It looks as if we just have regular military materials."

"Well, I will not elaborate, but I will just say that it is captured materials. We are taking all of these precautions for your safety, believe me" he replied.

That was comforting. We did only one stop on the way back for bunkers, in Rota, Spain and for only a few hours. We then left for Leonardo. On the way back we had to send the ship's position every four hours. After Rota, the performances were over and we started getting ready for home. All of us were happy to go home. The two and a half months turned out to be over four months. The Captain was right when he wanted the extra stores. The Captain wanted Maki and me to stay on the ship a little longer. I had to explain to him that we could not stay, that we had to get off. Those were the rules. That was very nice of him, though.

After we arrived and cleared the ship, the Captain told me, "Michael, it's time for you to take off and go home. Come back for payoff."

"I don't' mind if I do. Thank you, Captain." I answered.

My wife came to pick me up and off we went. I wasn't home more than a few hours when I got a telephone call from the ship. It was from the Captain. "Michael, I want you to do me a favor and come back tomorrow. I need your help and I will pay you overtime.

"Captain, don't worry about it. I will be back." I told him.

Poor Kyki, that night she had to drive me back to the ship. The traffic in the morning would have been forever from Flushing Queens to Leonardo, New Jersey. There goes my day off! I spent the next day assisting the two Coast Guard officials who came on board to expedite the loggings and to take depositions for the different incidents that had happened during the trip.

One of the officials told me, "You must have had a very eventful trip! It has been a long time since I had that much to do on the return of a ship from a trip."

"You're right. If we had a few more trips like this, you would have to work overtime to catch up," I told him.

We were both laughing. With all of these incidents I had to be fair. The majority of the crew and that applies in most case, were nice, good seamen. The fact was that on those types of trips we get the rowdiest seamen and the performers. We didn't need more than three or four of them to mess up the entire trip.

RELIEF TRIPS

By now, the long and unreasonable trips had taken a toll on all of us. It had been now almost four years since my application had been accepted. One of the most trying factors was the lack of specific policy from the Union. There were rumors yes, plenty of them, and sometimes they were false to pacify us; but there were no specifics. They all knew that something had to be done, but they were all afraid to do it. I guess the biggest concern of the officials was that a certain portion of the membership was opposing the opening of the books. Even though, they were a small minority, nevertheless they were very aggressive. I guess they figured they had it good, why mess it up? Maybe that had the officials moving slowly. It was a piece at a time with meetings after meetings, and a little was done each time. Eventually, I guess, they had realized that the Union was loosing quite a few well-qualified officers. They had to do something, even if they had to displease the small, aggressive minority. The loss of the qualified officers that were available to the market had a great effect later.

The latest talk was that they would take a few applicants in as a first step. The new classification status would be applicant group C member. After 360 days of sea time they would advance to group B and then after 360 days of sea time again, they would reach the group "A" status. The initial number of applicants that would enter the Union would depend on sea time and waiting time. The ones with the most points combined sea time and waiting time, would be the first.

In both aspects, sea time and waiting time, I was one of the top ones. Plus, I had pre-paid the estimated initiation fees. It looked as if I was in good shape; they just need to open the books. I cannot complain and say that I did not make a good income, I did. The uncertainty and the waiting took its toll, even with the patient ones. It certainly affected my wife and me. It takes a strong understanding person to endure all of this. Thank God I was lucky to have one!

By then, with all of the qualifications almost met, I told my wife that the next trips would be short relief trips, even if my income were less. In order to do that, I had to be willing to work on any kind of ship. That meant tankers, all kinds, including chemical ships, otherwise known as drug stores. You have to be a daredevil to sail on chemical tankers for a long period. Some daredevil friends were telling me that I should try their well-paid ships. I would be able to get relief coastwise jobs fairly easily. According to them, they were not as bad as everyone said.

There you go, Michael on the chemical tankers. I got the *Queeny,* a glorified drug store. You name it, and we carried it, over twenty-five chemicals at a time. They were right, because the money was good, the food was excellent, but the chemicals were awful! When I got to the ship, the permanent captain was still on board. He was a man with a wacky reputation. I was on watch; I had the eight to twelve watch, and we were outside of Long Island, around the Block Island area. He came on the bridge, and he was looking around, like a hunting dog.

"Is everything okay, Mate?" the Captain asked.

"Yes Sir!" I said.

"Any traffic?" he asked.

"No Sir," I answered.

He looked around and angrily said, "There is traffic!"

"Where?" I asked.

"Back there," he told me.

"Ten miles aft there was a ship which we already had passed going the other way," I told him.

By then I started getting angry to say the least. He wasn't up there to see how things were going, but to argue. I guess that what he enjoyed.

I said, "That ship is gone. It's ten miles behind us and going the other way."

By that time the inter-costal pilot had walked on to the bridge and heard the conversation.

He said, "Okay Captain. I got it!" and with that the Captain left.

When the Captain was gone the Pilot said, "Mike, don't pay attention to him. Anyway he will be out in a few hours."

By the way, the Pilot was one of the nicest people to work with and a character. The poor Chief Mate was the most abused person on board by this Captain. He was a real nice person, and I don't know how he took it. Being new on chemical tankers, I used to ask the Chief Mate questions. He would answer, but the first chance that he had he would turn the conversation to his pride and joy, his ranch in Oklahoma. In my short time on the *Queeny*, I almost became an expert in ranch operations. Certainly, I learned more about ranch operation than chemical tankers from the Chief Mate.

The new Captain was a prince. What a difference! Day and night! For three months *Queeny* was an enjoyable ship to sail. While at one of the Texas ports, I was on deck watch. With me, we also had a Night Mate, who was an experienced chemical tanker man. He used to sail relief Chief Mate mostly with the chemical tankers. He was close to sixty years old. He noticed me, and how I was gauging one of the tanks.

He ran towards me and told me, "Mate, that is not what you should be doing with the chemicals. You fish the tank when you measure. You don't put your nose and look inside; it's not a gasoline tanker. It's a chemical tanker. I'll show you how you do it, so you don't breathe in too much of these chemicals."

He went on to show me the correct way, and I appreciated it very much. By now, I hope you get the picture; Michael was graduating from the chemical tankers. If they were the only ships that I could sail, I'd rather sell hot dogs at a corner in New York City. Anything was better than sniffing twenty to twenty-five chemicals every time I went on deck. Otherwise, the ship ran like a clock. It was a top-notch crew, good money, good food, and an excellent Captain. The chemicals were not for me. The next time that we were in New York, I graduated from the chemical tankers. Of course, I did not explain too much to my wife.

* * *

Being before Christmas, and willing to work on tankers, I had no problem finding one. This time it was the *Hess Voyager*. It was a relief job of forty-five to fifty days. It was in the heart of the winter, just before Christmas. She was sailing from New York to Saint Croix. The weather went from ten to fifteen degrees in New York to eight-five or ninety in St. Croix. The round trip was about fifteen days. The ship was nice and easy to work with, and fairly new. We were carrying three kinds of gasoline. There was always the same cargo and the same tanks. I think we were unloading about forty to fifty thousand barrels in Stapleton, Anchorage. Then we shifted to Port Ready for the rest of the cargo. I spent more time home than when I sailed on a container or a cargo ship. I use to take the watch of the Second Mate in St. Croix. He liked to go ashore there, and he stayed on watch in New York for me. The two to three days that we stayed in the New York area, I was almost always home. The ship had a permanent crew, and they knew the ship very well. Even the reliefs for the holidays were familiar with the ship. My time passed very quickly. I wished that I could have stayed longer, but it was only a relief job, but it turned out to be a good one, too.

* * *

By now the Union rumors were flying right and left. The books would be opened soon. The applicant era was coming to an end for me. But still, no one knew exactly how. I knew for sure that I was almost at the top of the list. I was the first one whose application they had accepted, and I had plenty of sea time. Also, my initiation fees were paid.

The officials in New York had good intentions of course, and in order to pacify us they would tell us, "You are in, a month or two at the most."

It wasn't true of course. Still we had to go through some procedures. I was in Norfolk, Virginia with my wife visiting my in-laws, and I decided to pay a visit to the local Union Hall. The man in charge was a decent, honest man; I thought that most probably from him I could get the truth.

He surely did, and he said, "Michael, the end of your waiting is coming, but not in a month or so. Whoever told you that didn't tell you the truth? First, they have to send the applicant's list proposed for membership to every Union Hall for response and recommendations of the character of the applicants. That takes time. Then, following that, at the next GEB (General Executive Board) meeting they will go over the list of recommendations and whatever else they have to discuss. The initial number will be two hundred, and you have absolutely no problem. In fact you are one of the top ones. All of this is not going to be completed until the end of the year."

It was March when he told me that. That was exactly what happened. So I had to comfort myself with a few relief jobs. April Fool's Day was my next job and the ship was *S/S Defiance*. It was from the Mediterranean Marine Lines. I used to see them and dream of sailing on one of their ships. They were new, fast ships with a modern bridge. The reason that I got that job, I found out later, was the Captain. He had the reputation for being strict. Thank God that he had this reputation, because I had a fantastic trip! The man maybe was strict, but he was fair. I never had a problem with him not only on this trip, but also with the many trips that I sailed with the *Defiance*. The *Defiance* quickly became my favorite ship. She was a good ship with good pay, and she had a very efficient crew. Also, the officers and engineers that I worked with here were very nice. The ports were also fantastic. I cannot help but to mention them: Cadiz, Barcelona, Valencia, Fos, Genoa, Livorno, Naples, Piraeus, Istanbul, Ismir, back to Naples, Cadiz, and finally home to New York.

With the coastwise, the trip was about forty-five days. Also, we carried twelve passengers, which made the atmosphere a little more enjoyable. For the twelve passengers the trip was a fantastic deal, because they got to see different places and for most of them, to experience the real life at sea. The *Defiance* was an oasis in the middle of the desert compared with the other ships that I sailed. Fortunately, there were no rowdies or performers here on this ship. There were just good professional seamen. The trip was done in no time.

By June, the list with the two hundred applicants for membership was posted in every Hall. I was number six, with three thousand sixty-four points. My waiting started on 8/30/1972. Still, I needed another relief job until I had full membership. My good old *Hess Voyager* gave me that opportunity. Even though it was in the heart of the winter, the overall trip was very good. Now with warm weather on both sides, it would be a breeze. It was almost perfect. This time the Chief Mate decided, on his own, to cut down the overtime. The permanent Captain was on vacation at the time. Otherwise, he would not have done that. The relief Captain was as nice as he could be, but easily manipulated by the Chief Mate. From the 120 hours overtime I was doing during the winter trip, it dropped to 75 to 80 hours. What a big difference! I turned out to be almost a passenger. By loosing the overtime, I was spending more time at home so I kept my mouth shut, and I enjoyed my vacation time. The permanent Captain, even though he was on vacation, used to visit the ship every so often. He was Captain of the ship from the day she was built, about fourteen years ago. He used to call the ship "My Baby." To give you an idea, during the winter trip we had a storm outside of New York, and the ship was laboring quite a bit. I called and told the Captain, and he came on the bridge. I told him that the ship was bouncing quite a bit.

"Okay Michael, okay," he said.

Talking to the ship, he said, "Okay, Baby. I will slow you down; don't worry."

"Michael, call the engine room to reduce 10 RPMs to see how she is going to behave," he told me.

So, as you can see, the ship had a special place in his heart. Another thing that I have to say is that he took care of the boys that were his permanent crew. Most of them were with him for years. Somehow in his last visit before I got off, he found out about the overtime. I thought it was the Second Mate or one of his boys that mentioned it to him. I guessed that one of them told him that poor Michael's overtime had been reduced to the minimum.

He called me and asked, "How I was doing?"

I said, "Okay Captain."

Then he asked, "How's your overtime?"

"Captain, there is no overtime." I told him.

"What do you mean there is no overtime? You're not making the hours like you were making in the wintertime?" he asked.

"No Captain, my overtime is at least 40 percent lower," I told him.

He raised hell, and my overtime went back to the normal standards, but by now my time was almost up, and I was ready to go. It was the end of September or the beginning of October when I got off. I might have had much less overtime, but in general, it was a nice, relaxing trip.

With the end of this trip, all of the requirements for a group "A" status were met and even more. I had the required time to be certified as a tanker man. Forget the fact that I had spent more time at home than on the ship. Overall, the good was more than the bad. We were waiting for a final decision any day for the two hundred applicants to become members. I was staying home for two reasons; we were having our first baby and the due date was the end of December. I was not going anywhere. It was the first time that I had Christmas at home since we bought our home. Anyway, I was planning to stay home until my wife was comfortable enough to stay alone with the baby.

November 22, 1977, I got a letter from the International Office of the Masters, Mates, and Pilots. At the time it was located at 29 Broadway, NY, NY.

MEMBERSHIP – THE GOLDEN YEARS

My acceptance to the Offshore Membership was as of November 17, 1977. My initial group classification was Class-C. I had to apply for group status advancement. At that time I was meeting all the qualifications for Group A. Also I had the time required to certify as tanker man. For that I had to go through the tanker man committee. The tanker man certification was quick. The group classification wasn't until March 21, 1978, when the Offshore Membership Committee met again. From then on I had a full membership, and the right to work as a port relief officer, otherwise know as, night mate.

The port relief officer covered the mates of the ship from 4 P.M. to 8 A.M. weekdays plus all weekends and established holidays. That was for the U.S. ports only. That way the officers of the ship were able to go home or go out to relax, or do whatever they want to. This was a good benefit for the ship's officers for the short time they were in port.

January 5, 1978, my son was born, at the Manhasset Hospital on Long Island. The stay in the hospital was 2 to 3 days. When we left the hospital for home, it was snowing lightly. My God! The next day we were covered by snow. It was the famous blizzard of '78. If I remember well, there were at least two feet of snow. Now we were locked up in the house for weeks with the baby and the snow. For the next couple of months, January and February, I stayed home. Things settled down for my wife then, and she felt confident for me to look for a job (a relief job of course). This job came with my faithful *Defiance*. It was March 13, and the length of the trip was 40-45 days.

Perfect! By the time she missed me I would be back. Of course the ship was right. As I said before, there were no performing acts, no surprises, just good hard work, and fortunately it offered good benefits.

That was the *Defiance*. The trip went by quickly. When I came back, I was now in Group A. What a thrill to register as such! By the way, I was the first one to get a membership book. I remembered that at the International Headquarters, Captain Scavo, the International President, and Captain Lowell, Secretary-Treasurer, signed my book. Present was the Port Agent (East Coast Vice-President, Henry "Hank" Nereaux), who wanted to take a picture for the union newspaper. This was the first Offshore Membership book signing after so many years that the books had been closed. Unfortunately there was not a camera available, and with that, the applicant era came to an end for me.

The next few years were the ones I considered the "Golden Years" for me with the MMP, lasting from 1978 to almost 1984 or 1985. It was I think, 1981, or 1982, and the MMP had negotiated a fantastic contract. The euphoria from my friends as a whole was unbelievable, and for good reasons. Everything looked so great. There were high salaries and good benefits, and best of all a choice of jobs. In a conversation with my friends, I sounded kind of skeptical. I think we were at the World Trade Center cafeteria, if I remember well, located at the 40th floor in one of the towers. For many of us in the MMP, that was a regular gathering place between calls, especially on the cold and rainy days. My friends snapped on me that I sounded very pessimistic.

I said, "The contract looks very good, and now I am happy for that, but the fleet is aging. I see no new construction, no help, and no interest from the government. There are no substantial plans to revitalize the U.S. Merchant Marine. Only a few of the companies are willing to do anything on their own. On the other hand, the foreign flag ships are coming out with modern fleets."

They answered, "Aw, stop now. Be optimistic."

This book was not intended as a historic document and maybe some events might not match the exact time that they happened. Everyone who lived through those times knows well what happened and what affect those events had on all of us. Now was my time to enjoy sailing with the ships close to the East Coast and no more than two and a half months sea time and only on Liners, like the United States Lines, Sea Land, Farrell Lines, etc.

In 1978, I sailed with the *Fortaleza* and the *Bayamon* from New York to San Juan. Both were roll-on and roll off ships. These were the old type of car carriers. The vehicles were drive on and off the ship through side entrance ramps. They were then driven to the various decks to be tied down for the trip.

In 1979, back in my favor for a 180-day job this time was the *Defiance*. The *Defiance* consumed almost all of the year 1979. I was trying to get a permanent job with the company that was close to the States or regular run. It was very difficult because everyone wanted that.

I am going to elaborate on the *C.V. Lightning* a little more. I sailed this one because the run was good, to the Mediterranean, and it had a good captain and good crew. This ship though had a strange arrangement of accommodations for the crew. For the deck officers, the quarters were up in the bow. Also, the navigation bridge and the radio operator's room were also located there. The rest of the crew was all living in the back of the ship, where the big accommodations were. The trip going to the Mediterranean was fairly good, especially, for a December trip. We went through the usual Mediterranean ports for this run. They were Cadiz, Spain; Naples, Italy; Piraeus, Greece; Ismir, Turkey; and Haifa, Israel. Even though it was in the middle of the winter, the runs between the ports were good. The last port on the way back was Cadiz. We sailed from Cadiz for the trip home late at night. The next morning, I went back on the bridge to relieve the Second Mate. By the way I had the 8 to 12 watch, and the Second Mate had the 4 to 8. The Second Mate briefed me on the traffic and gave me the course, which was other than what I was expecting for going back to New York.

I said to the Second Mate, "Where are we going? Are we going to Lisbon?" The reason I said that was because there were rumors that on the way back we would go to Lisbon to pick up a few containers.

He said" No, Michael! We are going home to New York."

I said, "With this course!"

He said, "Yes. We are going "great circle". The company wants us to be in New York the 30th of this month, so they can have this trip in 1979."

The "great circle" was the shortest distance on the map, but it would place the ship in the worst weather since it was winter in the North Atlantic.

The Second Mate was a young man and not too familiar with the Mediterranean run, and I said, "I don't know who had this idea. I have been sailing the Mediterranean run for quite a few years and with different captains. No one that I know with a light ship like this would be going back to the States north of the Azores in the middle of winter to save time."

I have to say, knowing our Captain, a very experienced seaman, he would never have chosen to go this way this time of year. The office had pressed him quite a bit. Someone, probably inexperienced in sailing, especially the North Atlantic, was making the decision.

The first few days, luckily the weather was good. There was an overcast and drizzle, but good as far as the sea was concerned. The Captain and the officers were teasing me. A day after we passed the Azores, the fiesta started. There was one storm after another and nowhere to hide. Naturally, we had to slow down. The worst was two days before New York. Waves were thirty to thirty-five feet high or higher at times. We maintained 40 RPMs, just enough to be able to steer, but the ship was staying at the same place. There was no forward movement. I remember vividly, it was around 9 P.M. After a very strong pitching, I was lifted off my bunk and I fell to the floor. It was a night to remember. The next morning, the situation wasn't better.

My AB seaman during our watch, told me, "Mate! I can see the sky where you usually read the magnetic compass!"

The magnetic compass was located on the flying bridge and it was secured and covered with a light inside so that when we would look up from the bridge we could read it. The waves were coming live over the bow, and the ship was dipping, and one of them took the compass. There was a hole where the compass had been. There was nothing we could do. Lucky we didn't have to use the magnetic compass as an emergency, because there wasn't one left. To make the long story short, not only did the trip not go in 1979, because we arrived the first of January 1980, but we had to do some repairs, too.

Well, I had had a chance, since I was looking for a steady job, to get on the same type of ship, the same company, and even better, to go to North Europe. The job had been open on the board for a few days, and I had turned it down. I knew my limitations. I was glad this trip was over.

After the *C.V. Lightning*, and after turning down the job on the North European run on the same type of ship, I went through a few relief jobs on ships around the coast, like the *Sea Land Boston*, the *Sea Land Tampa, the Sea Land Anchorage*, and the tanker *Mount Washington*, also, the *Lash Atlantico* on the Mediterranean run and the Black Sea, the *Del Viento* on the Caribbean run, the *Santa Lucia* on the West Coast of South America, the so called Lover's run. The *S/S American Lynx* of the U.S. Lines was a sixty-six day Far East run. The *American Archer* was a North Europe run, and the *American Legion* was on the Far East run. The *Export Challenger* was on the West Coast of Africa. The *Lash Italia* of Prudential Lines was on the Mediterranean run. The *Export Freedom* of Farrell Lines was on a Mediterranean run. All of them were nice ships with very desirable runs.

Most of the time I would get those ships for one relief trip. It was not that I didn't want to have the 180-day jobs, but in order to get one of these jobs I would have had to wait over six months. Then I had to stay for at least that much time in order to make it financially worth it. I did not want to wait that long for a job, and I did not want to stay on the ship again for six months or more. So I thought that by getting the relief jobs, which required about month or a little more of waiting, and by doing port relief mate watches in between, I would make the same income or almost the same by the end of the year. Also I would not have had to go through the long waits nor the long stays on the ships. Jobs on ships like the *Sea Land Boston*, the *Sea Land Baltimore*, or the *Sea Land Houston* were considered home steadies jobs. Mates that had shore jobs like teachers etc., that were also sailing with the ships, would come with so-called "killer cards" and they milked it to the end.

Of course, all of the ships had their own peculiar and interesting sea stories. I will mention though the ones that I think will attract the most interest. I'd like to start with the *Lash Atlantico*. I got that ship for one trip of about forty-five to fifty days. So there I was before Christmas on the *Lash Atlantico*, leaving for the Mediterranean. Even though the ships were not equipped with passenger quarters, I didn't know how or who did it, but they decided to have seven passengers travel with us. They had to use the spare rooms and the cadets' rooms to accommodate them. The poor souls were using the same mess hall and dining room that we were. As you have probably guessed, our officer's lounge became a little crowded. We had just left New York, and I was on watch on the bridge. A couple from Chicago, in their middle fifties, came on the bridge for a few minutes. They were both excited to be at sea. In our short conversation the lady kept saying how nice it was to be out here and glamorized the trip. I guess I didn't have the same euphoria. It was just before Christmas, and I had just left my wife and my little boy home. Not realizing it at the time, I wasn't very pleasant.

The last thing for someone to say to me was, "How nice it is to be away from home in the middle of the winter."

Of course, the poor lady had no idea what winter at sea really was. It was also the first time that she had left home leaving the rest of her family behind for Christmas. At that moment she was taken by the romantic idea of being out in the open ocean, and it was magical, mystical. As far as the eye could see, there was only water and sky. At the time I didn't know that she had gotten upset with me.

I had finished my eight to twelve watch on the second day at sea. It was around 1 o'clock in the afternoon, and I was lying down for the afternoon nap.

There was a loud knock on my door and a voice yelled, "Hey! Greek! Get up!"

I went to the door, opened it, and there was the Captain.

I asked, "What's wrong, Captain?"

"Nothing is wrong. You have to take care of your passengers," he replied.

"What do you mean, Captain? They are not my passengers," I said.

"Yes they are, your compatriot put them on the ship," he said meaning the Prudential Lines owner. "You have to take care of them, because I will have absolutely nothing to do with them, and the Chief Mate is very busy. You got them. They're all yours!"

"How about the Second Mate and the Third Mate?" I said.

"Them? No! They are grouchier than me. I just want you to take care of them. Oh, so you know, I don't care about the overtime either; just try to keep them happy. One more thing, I hope you don't' mind, I told them that they could visit the bridge on your watch only as long as they don't interfere with the bridge watch."

"Thanks Captain. You took care of me. You thought of everything!" I said.

"I told you. They're yours!" he said and left laughing.

Just like that, I became the cruise director and the chaperone for the seven passengers. It was a long, tiring fifty days, but the pay was excellent. Between the container crane and the barge crane, the overtime kept pouring in. By the way, the Prudential Lash ships would carry both barges and containers. For the mates at the ports it was work, work, work and no time off, period. The biggest break we got was between New York and Cadiz. Following that it was one port after another, and being winter made it more painful for us on deck. Again, the money was unbelievable, and there was a tremendous amount of overtime.

Weather conditions in Constanza were the worst by far. The Black Sea in general had no mercy. When it was bad it was bad, and this time she was living up to her reputation. We had only a few barges there, mostly containers, and the whole cargo operation was slow, very slow. Nevertheless, we had to have two mates on deck, one for the barges and the ship and one for the container crane. The way the cargo operation was going we all felt that the Second Mate on deck was completely unnecessary. But the Company and the locals wanted him, so we raked in the extra overtime.

The cargo operation was going on twenty-four hours a day. The container crane was making three or four moves an hour. There was one Romanian on the dock checking the container and writing the number and one on the deck doing the same thing. Plus, there was the Mate writing the number of the container. So what I did was I gave the man on the deck cigarettes, plenty of coffee and tea, and something to eat, and he would check my time sheet. I was in the tally room most of the time resting. Survival my Dear Friends, Survival! With no exaggeration the whole stay in Constanza was miserable. It was cold, snow, ice; you name it. I don't think the whole time we stayed there, that any of the crew had the desire to go ashore. Only the passengers got a tour. For us even if the weather were good, there was no time. We were lucky to steal a few hours of sleep, much less to go ashore. We were happy to leave Constanza. During undocking I was at the stern. We had slowly gotten in most of the lines, except two. They were on the same bit, and the whole thing at the dock was like an ice ball frozen solid. The Romanians on the dock tried and tried but could not take them off. I called the Captain on the bridge and explained the situation to him.

He asked, "That bad?"

I said, "Yes, Sir!" Just to make sure, he sent the Chief Mate to check.

The Chief Mate said, "He's right. We're going to be here all night trying to take these lines off."

"Well, cut them off!" the Captain said.

So that's what we did. We used a fire axe, and we cut them off so we could leave. We didn't lose much line anyway, and we left Constanza with no regrets. Outside the port, the Black Sea wasn't any friendlier; a big storm was brewing there. The ship had a hard time. By the time we got to the Bosporus Straits, we had messed up one gangway and a few containers. We also had a hard time getting the pilot on board so that we could pass the Straits. A few years back we didn't have to have a pilot, but since there had been a big accident, a pilot was required.

When we finished with the Bosporus, the Captain said to me, "I am going to get some rest. Call me if you need me, and tell the other mates to do so, or call me just before the Dardanelles."

The Sea of Maramara was okay. The Captain needed some rest. He had been up since we left Constanza. This was the first time that I saw the islands in the Aegean Sea covered with snow all the way down to the Peloponnesus. The Aegean wasn't as bad as the Black Sea but it was still very rough. The Captain was even thinking to slow down or stay at the Kalamata Gulf for the weather to subside before we crossed the Ionian Sea for the Messina Straits. That was another very rough area. Thankfully, by the time we passed Maleas the weather was getting better.

Ah, you may wonder about the husband of the lady who thought that I wasn't very pleasant and enthusiastic when we left New York. He was like a little kid throughout the whole storm, going from one window to another, looking and taking pictures. He was totally amazed! Later, he told me that he had had the thrill of his life.

He said, "I was watching the movies, and I was always fascinated with rough seas and how the ship was going up and down from the waves. Now, here I am in one of them. For you, the Captain and the Chief Mate it was another bad weather to go through. I suspect, from your actions, you had a few problems to deal with, too. But to me, it was unreal. A dream comes true! Finally, I had the chance to say I was in a big storm."

All of us, including the passengers, were happy for the trip to be over. It was very fruitful, money wise, but we were all tired by now.

Remember the lady that thought at the beginning that I was rude. Well, before we arrived in New York, she came up on the bridge with her husband and had a present for me. It was a bottle of liquor! She started apologizing and said how foolish it was for her to think like that. She felt bad the entire trip. Of course, until now, I had no idea what she was talking about.

"You were right. I will never, ever leave my family during the holidays. My husband had his chance. I hope that he enjoyed it, because I am not going away again during Christmas," she said.

"Don't worry, he had his chance. He thoroughly enjoyed the storm. He got it off his chest, and he's satisfied now. For me, I can't guarantee you that I won't be out here on Christmas again. That is my job," I told her.

"I don't blame you at all," she said.

Now it was time for me to stay around the coast again. The *Sea Land Boston*, the *Sea Land Tampa*, and the *Sea Land Anchorage* were the ships that kept me close to home. I have a few interesting stories to tell especially from the *Sea Land Anchorage*. She was an old container ship, and she was fairly old when they converted her. By now, she was ready to go for razor blades. Rumor had it that she was making her last trip, so I took the job as long as it lasted.

We were in San Juan, if I remember well. The Second Mate was in his lower sixties. In his younger days I guess he was able to go ashore, to have a few beers, to come back and to continue with his job with no problem. Time had taken its toll. This time when he came from shore, he had lain down to rest for a few minutes and apparently he passed out. We were sailing on his watch. He had to test the gears an hour before we sailed. When I didn't hear the general alarm ring, I checked to make sure that he was up. His cabin was next to mine, and when I found him, he was out cold. So, I went on the bridge tested the gears, and proceeded to have the ship ready to sail. The other Third Mate, the Chief Mate, and I were up on the bridge ready to go, and we were waiting for the pilot. The Captain walked in looking for the Second Mate.

Instead of telling him that he was passed out in his room, I started singing the famous beer commercial at the time, "Ah, ah sitting pretty in Shaffer City…"

The Captain said, "What are you singing about? I asked for the Second Mate."

"That's all right Captain. That's what we are saying. The Second Mate is sitting pretty in Shaffer City. He's out cold," I told him, and we all started laughing.

I have to say, the Second Mate was not a habitual drinker. He was just getting old. The other Third Mate and I covered for him, and the next morning he was as good as new. The rest of the trip we were teasing him with the beer commercial.

Somehow the ship had the bad reputation that they would sneak marijuana from Jamaica to the U.S. on it. Maybe once they had a good reason. So the U.S. Customs religiously, in Huston and San Juan, would raid the ship and go through an extensive search for contraband. They used sniffing dogs, mirrors; you name it! All of us during the search gathered in the mess hall. We were supposed to leave our doors open just in case they had to search the rooms. My ordinary seaman, a young man, in his early thirties with long hair, had his room raided the most. They would go over his room thoroughly all the time in both ports. The poor soul was complaining that they messed up his room every time, and that they were discriminating against him. We were teasing him and told him that if he cut his hair and shaved and if he dressed conservatively that they would probably leave him alone. Other than a few ounces of marijuana here and there, I suspected mostly for personal use, they never found anything big to talk about. The only thing that they had found once was marijuana in an old sealed vent, and it had probably been there for a long time. The electrician was helping to take off the rusted bolts from the plates to open the vent. Finally, they got the plate off and the electrician, who was underneath, was completely showered with marijuana. It may have been an old ship, but it was an enjoyable trip, close to home, and with a little spice just to kept things interesting.

    Next, I took a tanker, the *Mount Washington*. The reason was that they equipped the ship with a crude oil wash system and inner gas system. I wanted to be familiar with the new systems, of course. All the tankers, eventually, would have to be converted for safety reasons. By now, I had resorted to plan B as far as permanent jobs were concerned. People that were there for years took all the blue chips permanent jobs. If someone retired, there were two or three in line to get the jobs. It was almost impossible to get one of them. The jobs that would occasionally open up were tankers, which were sailing away from home. Sometimes we had relief chief mate jobs on the coastwise tankers. I had enough sea time by now to sit for a chief mate's license. I thought that my best bet would be to aim for that market. For that reason, the *Mount Washington* was a good choice, to refresh my tanker experience, plus to become familiar with the new systems.

    I stayed a little over two months with the *Mount Washington*. I had a chance to practice with inner gas and crude oil wash, because of the lousy job that they did when they installed the systems in New Jersey. I don't know what they did or who did it, but we left with tons of problems even the basic gaskets were missing. It was metal to metal and leaks were all around. They said that they had spent seven million dollars to do the conversion. Everyone's opinion was that they spent too much money, especially for the job that had been done. With all the problems that we had, it worked out very well for me. I got to work those systems with the Mate quite a few times. Anyway, I got good experience. We did carry crude oil, and the run was to the Gulf ports from the Port Armuelles on the West Coast of Panama. We loaded the crude oil that the big tankers carried from Alaska. These tankers were huge and wouldn't go through the canal. All the time that I stayed with the *Mount Washington* both systems still had trouble and were not used. With that I graduated from the *Mount Washington*.

The next step was the Masters Mates and Pilots School in Baltimore. There I took the one-month tanker course, a very detailed and efficient course. I learned quite a bit about the tanker operation: how to load, discharge, stability, safety, and the new automated pump room. It was very intense and informative. That was a course a seaman must have when he planned to sail as a chief mate and eventually as a captain.

After that my plan was to sit for chief mate's license. I thought about having a few more trips before that. Next on the *Del Viento* I traveled along the East Coast of the U.S. and Caribbean; and on the *Santa Lucia* along the East Coast of the U.S. through Panama, and the West Coast of South America. Both were nice runs, and before I knew it I was back home again. Also they were excellent moneymakers. Those were my reasons for sailing on these ships. Most of the crew was there for the money of course, but mostly for the run. The money was there, but the things that attracted them were the ports. Do you wonder why they called it the Lover's Run, or the Good Times' Run? With ports like Santa Martha, Carthagena, Baranquilla, Callao, Valparaiso, just to mention a few, seamen couldn't go wrong. All of them were a seamen's heaven. In Guayiaquil there even were banana girls sneaking on board the ship. For me, I was raking in the money and wanted to go home. The Chief Mate on the *Del Viento* was in his middle sixties. He was nice, but he liked to dispute a few hours of overtime, mostly for the lower rates, just to make his point that he was on top of things. We never paid attention to that; hours were being covered many times over anyway. He used to come before the pay off and ask us if we were going to challenge the disputed overtime, and we would tell him no.

"No, no! It's your overtime!" he would tell us.

He wanted us to challenge him just to show that he was strict with overtime. Just a few times to pacify him, one of us would have to go fight over the overtime. On one fire and boat drill, a young, ordinary seaman not to familiar with the procedures, was asking the Chief Mate for something.

Instead of calling him Chief, he went, "Hey Pop! How am I going to do this?"

The Chief Mate got angry and said, "I'm not your Pop. I'm your Chief Mate!"

The poor ordinary must still wonder what he did wrong. The Chief Mate on the *Santa Lucia* was a very busy position. He did not have time for disputes.

He told me in plain terms, "Mike, you are on your own with the overtime. If you make a mistake and don't write it down, you loose it. It is because I don't have enough time to check it. I'm just going to sign your overtime sheet."

I have to say that I did my best so that the Chief Mate did not carry on his conscience that I lost any overtime.

Plan B was in full action. The school was over. I had refreshed my experience with the tankers, updated myself on the new systems, I was all set. In the meantime, we had moved from Flushing Queens, New York to Virginia Beach, Virginia. I was registered now at the Norfolk Hall. To get an offshore job it didn't matter where we register because we had the National Shipping Card. That meant that we could register at any Hall in the U.S. and sail from any port also in the U.S. So, I could still come to New York and get a job on the ships that I was used to and liked. It was not that the Norfolk Hall did not have any jobs. There were plenty, but I liked the companies from New York: the U.S. Lines, Farrell Lines, etc. In the past few years they had spoiled me. The Norfolk port was very good as far as night mate work was concerned. The location of the night mate jobs was so convenient compared with the distances that I had to drive to the New York or the New Jersey docks. I tried to blend my night mate jobs with some tankers so that I could keep up with them.

February 1983 I went to New York and got a job on the *American Lynx* with a Far East run for one trip that was sixty-six days. To get that type of job I needed a card that was three months old. After that trip was over, I was planning to sit for the chief mate's license. It was nice to join a ship that I knew that everything would go smoothly as far as the crew was concerned. It was a nice, pleasant trip with the *American Lynx*. Not that we didn't work. Some ports were difficult, but when we had a good crew, the job was not a problem. It was the beginning of May when I came back. I was looking forward to a good vacation, and of course to studying for the chief mate's license.

Murphy's Law prevailed here, big time. The contract with the tanker companies and the Union had expired and negotiations were going on for a new contract. The tanker companies, as if they had something on their minds, were very unreasonable. That was mostly for the deck officers. They practically wanted us to work for nothing. It was a long and painful story, and to be honest I am not completely familiar with what really happened. I heard a lot of stories from both sides. The sad fact was that the Master Mates and Pilots lost all of their tanker companies except one. They did not want to be a part of the Union; they went apart as far as the deck officers were concerned. The rest of the crew and the engineers still had a contract with the Union. It is too painful for me to elaborate more. I will leave that to someone else more familiar with the facts than me. The story must be told one day. Loosing the tankers had a tremendous effect on our Union. If I remember well, the number of tankers that we had lost was in the vicinity of seventy. It is sad to say but some captains and chief mates, and a few mates too, were fooled by the tanker companies and stayed with the ships. Others had enough time and retired. The rest were back at the Union Hall looking for jobs. Right or wrong I got discouraged and instead of sitting for the chief mate's license, I postponed it indefinitely. I was probably wrong, but at the time I thought that it was useless to go through that. Even though quite a few jobs were lost, by the end of 1983 things had balanced out somehow. Now I needed a little older card to get a job, but it still wasn't that difficult. So my plan was down the drain.

My next ship was in August with the *American Archer* on the North European run. The ship was a mariner converted to a container vessel. She was a brave warrior for the North Atlantic. If we had a gale brewing outside, we did not feel it at all. She was a well-built ship, but the poor thing was old and rusted and full of problems. She was still a fighter. I liked the ship, but could sense that she was running one of her last trips.

The *American Legion* was a ship with a split personality. If we were lucky to be onboard with a good set of captain and chief mate, we had a wonderful trip. If our luck had run out, and we had to sail with the other set of officers, we were guaranteed to have a miserable trip. I was pressed for time. I tried for a few jobs and I missed them all by a few days, which put me lower on the waiting list.

So, foolishly, I took the *American Legion* for the Far East trip. It wasn't the end of the world. I had to take the good with the bad. Thank God, I had a good Second and Third Mates, and we made the best of it. But for sure it was an unhappy ship. To ship out, I needed more and more longer waiting times. The good thing was that Norfolk was very good on night mate, which helped a lot with my income for the year.

I had never sailed the West Coast of Africa, the opportunity came with the *Export Challenger,* a Farrell Lines ship. She was dry docking at Norshipco. That was where I joined the ship. It turned out to be a nice, interesting trip. The first stop was the Azores for military cargo. We discharged at Terceira Island. A U.S. Air Force base was there. There was nowhere to go but only the small local restaurants to have a good seafood meal. The next port was the Republic of Liberia, where it was hot and nasty. The political conditions there were very unstable at the time. It was not a safe place to go ashore. The next port was Dakar, another poor place. My children always teased me that I always told them about not throwing away food and about how many people were starving in the world. I must have said that quite a few times. Of course, I had a good reason. From my travels I had seen so many people living in terrible conditions. Of course when a person was well fed, it was difficult to appreciate that others were starving.

One day in the afternoon, it was hot as usual, over a hundred degrees. At the stern of the ship, we had two barrels, from the galley where they dumped the leftovers. We had been in port for two or three days so imagine from all the heat how this area smelled. It actually stunk! Well, I saw people digging in the barrels, through the garbage, to find some lunch leftovers to eat. It was not a nice picture. Dakar had some nice woodcarvings, and I brought quite a few of them back.

Next we sailed to San Pedro and Abidjan at the Ivory Coast. I did not have a chance to bring back any ivory because it was prohibited. I brought back some shrimp though. They were quite big; only two were needed to make a good meal. Other than that, it was another trip that passed fairly okay. With that, I closed 1984 as a normal working year, besides the fact that we had lost the tankers.

Nineteen eighty-five started with the *Lash Italia*. I got that ship in the end of April, and the job was on the board for and eighty-day trip. With the number of people that were at the Hall at the time, I didn't think that I had a chance. I put my card in the box to try for the job, but I didn't really pay it much attention. The *Lash Italia* was a good ship, and the job was almost three months in length. It seemed that my chances of getting the job were very slim. I could not forget the fact that those ships were tremendous moneymakers! No chance,

I thought! You never knew though. I almost lost it because I wasn't paying attention.

A friend of mine screamed at me, "It's you next! Get ready!"

I got up and ran to the dispatcher's window, because my name was next. We always had to be alert. Sailing at sea is a strange business; one never knows.

I took the morning flight from Norfolk to New York. It was 10 A.M. and I was at the Hall and I still had my bags with me. At 11 A.M. I had the job. By 3 P.M. I was on the ship. That was fast; I couldn't believe it! I was very lucky that time. We did the coastwise. The last port was Charleston and then we were off for the Mediterranean. We were out at sea one day, when we had a problem with the engine. The high gears of the turbine were messed up. We stopped the engine, raised the not-under-command signal, and we were drifting in the middle of the ocean. They double-checked the problem, and the Captain called the company to arrange for a tug to tow us back to Norfolk, to Norshipco, for repairs. Actually, they didn't fix the high gears; they isolated them and we did the trip with the low gears, but with a much lower speed. I think that it was around 12 knots. They were to fix the problem after the trip was over. We were back out at sea again, but at a slow speed this time. Let's not forget the passengers, seven again! They were getting their money's worth with all of this excitement. Of course, with a lack of space they were sitting in the officer's lounge with us.

Prudential Lines had the reputation of being an excellent company. It was one of the best to work for, but by now it was a company in deep financial trouble. During the trip, we could see that. We had to cut ports off of the schedule. We could not go there because they owed them too much money. We had a hard time to get bunkers, and we would get it from whoever was willing to give it to us and not where we would normally bunker. However, we were moving along, as they say 'slowly but steady' from one port to another. By now, we had almost completed the entire run in the Mediterranean.

The last port was Alexandria and then home. Getting in and out of the port of Alexandria, with a big ship like the *Lash Italia*, was not a job; it was an adventure! It was also a nightmare for the

Captain. It could easily cause an ulcer or heart trouble. The port was overcrowded, with small, old, rusted coasters, who loved to be hit by a ship like the *Lash Italia* so that they could buy new ships? We docked alongside an old dock full of fertilizer in bulk. There was just enough space for the trucks to pick up the containers that we discharged. For barges, it wasn't much of a problem, and the stern was clear.

It was hot, humid, and dirty; when the wind was blowing, fertilizer would blow all over the ship. It was messy, very messy, to say the least. We spent long hours on deck as usual. By now we were kind of tired. I was with the barge crane, and we were picking up a barge close to the area where they stored the crane. I went on the top of the hatch between the barges, to check and see if things were clear. It was kind of dark, and I didn't pay attention to the grease on the deck from the crane. I slipped and fell between the hatches, and my right side hit a turnbuckle. I felt as if I had broken my ribs. I was in tremendous pain, and I couldn't breathe. The men on the crane saw me, stopped the operation, and asked for help. They took me to my cabin. I was in pain. They called immediately for an ambulance to take me to the hospital.

After almost an hour, the ambulance came. God, to name it an ambulance! It was an old dilapidated Volkswagen bus, with only a couple of seats inside. That was no exaggeration here! We started driving to the hospital. If I remember well, the Third Mate came with me. We were almost halfway to the hospital, and the driver stopped and pulled to the side.

"What is wrong?" we asked.

"I have a flat tire, and we have to change it," he replied.

So we had to change the tire. I didn't help, but the Third Mate helped so that we could be on our way soon. By then the pain subsided a little; it would intensify only when I was trying to move. I didn't have any indication so far of internal bleeding. We changed the tire and headed for the hospital. Finally, we got there; they took me immediately for x-rays, and they did the rest of the tests. They were especially concerned if I had internal bleeding. I was lucky, I had only bruised ribs, and they thought that maybe one or two were a little cracked.

They had put me in a room with two others. One was a young man, in his middle twenties; and the other was an older guy in his later fifties. From the beginning both were nice and friendly. Quickly I realize that it would be more sensible to stay with them rather than request to have a private room. I could have one, being an officer. I had many reasons for this decision. They were good company and I wasn't alone. Then the hospital food was lousy. I mean lousy! The young guy's mother everyday would bring food and fruits from outside. The older guy's wives (yes, wives) would bring plenty, too! So because of them, I had plenty to eat, and I didn't have to depend on the hospital food. If I had my own room, the hospital food would have been my only source. Of course, even if they didn't want it, I chipped in for the food. I have to say, we had pretty good company.

When they asked me if I wanted to have my own room, I told them," I am all right where I am. I'm not moving."

The Captain came to see me after a day or so. The ship was ready to leave in a day or so. He was very concerned about leaving me behind. I couldn't go back on the ship though, even if I wanted to. I assured him that it was okay and asked him for a favor. As soon as I got a little bit better, instead of flying from Alexandria to New York directly, to make the arrangements through Athens. Then I could stay a few days with my relatives to recover before the long flight home. I needed a little time to recover, and Athens was a good place for me. He was glad to do that. He was a very nice person, and it was a privilege to sail under his command.

You noticed, I said for the older fellow that his 'wives' were bringing him food. The poor guy, he had two wives, and from the stories that he would tell us, they had become too much to handle. They were fighting between themselves constantly.

Jokingly I told him, "We have one, and sometimes it's too much! Too late now, you will have to tolerate them."

I stayed in the hospital for three to four days, and as soon as I got the okay from the doctor I flew to Athens. The first thing that I did was to double check the x-rays and tests.

"Sure, you have badly bruised ribs, and it will take a while for them to heal," the doctor said. "Your problem is not the ribs now, but that plaster they put on you there. We have to take that thing off immediately, before it infects your skin. It will not be pleasant, but we have to take it off."

He took it off with a considerable amount of pain. I stayed there for a few days. It really helped me to recover. I got to New York just as the ship was arriving for the payoff, and I went to get my things. I am not sure, but I think that the *Lash Italia* made one last trip after that and was laid up. Unfortunately, the company declared bankruptcy. It was sad. Prudential Lines was a very good company. I guess it was mismanaged the last few years. You could see during the trip that things were not going right. With the Prudential Lines gone, we lost a few more ships, but unfortunately, that wasn't the end. The worst was yet to come and very soon. Very difficult days lay ahead of us. The good times were over forever, now the struggle to survive began.

DISASTER STRIKES

The United States Lines, one of the most established shipping companies went under, along with them, the Moore McCormack Lines. Next was Delta Lines, another big company. Farrell Lines shrank their fleet, from over thirty ships to five or six ships. It was a disaster, a complete disaster! The union halls were filled with mates looking for jobs, and there were none. We registered and our shipping cards were good for one year. We had reached the point that an eleven-month-old card was still considered young and that we had to wait. I saw people competing for one job, with the last day on their card. The one who got the job was the oldest in the minutes. Once, there were three at the Norfolk Hall all competing for the one third mate job on a Waterman Lash ship. The other two cards rolled over, that meant they had to register again and start from the beginning. A year's income went down the drain. These were very difficult times for all of us. The only lucky ones were the ones with the remaining companies with steady jobs, mostly chief mates and captains.

    I felt the pinch after I got off the *Export Freedom*, which was the last ship that I sailed from the good old days. My shipping card was by now over 11 and half months old. Norfolk was dead; nothing was coming in the next two weeks that remained on my card. I started calling my friends at different ports, all over the East Coast and the Gulf ports. I was trying to find out what was coming and who was getting off in the next two weeks. Finally, from the New York port, a friend of mine told me about the *S/S/ Borinquen*. He said that it would have a third mate job. The ship was in New York, and the next port was Miami. By the time the ship would reach Miami, the third mate would have over 120 days, and he had to get off. So, I flew Friday morning to Ft. Lauderdale, where the Union Hall was located and where they would call the job. The ship was not arriving in Miami until late on Monday. I couldn't take a chance. I had to be there from Friday, because I didn't know if they would call the job on Friday or Monday. From what I had found out from my various calls, this job was my last chance before my card would roll over. That was a whole year's work that we're talking about.

Nine A.M. on Friday, when the Union Hall door opened, I was right there. The port agent was nice and tried to handle the job as fairly as possible. The whole thing though looked like a set up for someone to get the job. That's why the Third Mate did not get off in New York, and he stretched it to Miami. At the Hall there were three of us with eleven-month cards, I was the spoiler of this set up. They did not expect me.

The main office in Puerto Rico would not release the job Friday, until the last call, and after the port agent told him, "The man is here, and he will follow the ship until the job is called. Give it up. He has the oldest card, and he deserves it."

Finally he said, "Okay."

I got the job, and it was a big deal. Now, I didn't have to worry what people I would meet on the ship, what the run was, and what time of the year it was. Just to get the job was important. I got the job October 6, 1987. Monday afternoon with the Port Agent, we arrived in Miami. He was, by the way, my ride to Miami. The *Borinquen* docked around nine P.M. The sailing board was posted to sail in the morning hours, like six A.M. It was a very short stay. My first welcome on board was the Captain, an Old Groucho. By flying to Ft. Lauderdale and then to Miami, I tried to travel as light as I could. I had only two bags and in one of them, I had put my sextant. I was taking one bag at a time to my room. Every time I was going up the Captain would sneak out of his room to see what I was carrying.

After I had finished with my second bag, he said to me, "I don't see a sextant. You must have one. We are taking Sun Lines here."

I said, "I have a sextant."

"I don't see it," he said.

"I have a sextant. You will see it on the bridge," I told him.

"You know this ship will lay up in a few months. You're not going to have 120 days here," he said.

I was tired. I had left home on the first flight out of Norfolk at six A.M. I had gone through all of this aggravation and the games they were playing until they released the job. Then I had to travel all the way to Miami to join the ship. I had just about had it.

So I told him, "Look Mister, I don't care if the ship lays up tomorrow, and I do have the dumb sextant with me. By the way, my shipping card was going dead in a couple of days, otherwise, I wouldn't be on this dumb ship. Do you understand? Are you happy now?"

"Okay, I was just saying," he said to me, and he left.

The other Third Mate was a man that I knew for years from New York tried to calm me down.

"Mike, relax. He's a little goofy. Don't pay attention to him. We will have a good trip. The ship is good," he said to me.

He really was goofy all right, and he liked to play games with the crew. To give you an idea, when we arrived into ports, we were supposed to call the Chief Mate and the Bosun a half hour before they had to stand by at the bow. He would call them ten or fifteen minutes before. The poor guys didn't have enough time to get dressed and to have a cup of coffee. They had to run for the bow.

When they would complain, he would say, "Back it up. You don't loose the overtime, you just back up the time." He liked to play those stupid games. We were lucky though. When we went back to New York, he went on vacation. I was only with him ten days. Now the *Borinquen* became a vacation. That lasted for eighty days until we took the poor *Borinquen* to Jacksonville and tied it up for good.

The round trip from New York to San Juan was made in two weeks time. We were arriving in New York Friday morning and sailing Monday morning. We also stayed two to three days in San Juan with occasional stops in between to Miami. Every time we arrived in New York, I was off for the three days. The Second Mate and I would cover for each other. I would take his watch in San Juan, that was his port, and he would cover for me in New York. After we arrived in New York, I would take the bus to the Newark Airport and then the People's Express, a budget airline, to Norfolk. The fair to Norfolk was dirt-cheap. Friday night I was home and stayed until late Sunday evening. I spent more time home, than when I was on any other ship. We had a fantastic Captain, and the rest of the mates all got along very well. It made the *Borinquen* a very pleasant ship. I needed this ship, and I needed the time to think and reevaluate the whole situation. I was pretty upset when I had gotten the ship. Certainly it was not pleasant to wait a whole year to get a job. Plus, the fact was that I had paid my dues as an applicant for six years. I thought that I was done with the waiting time

    I had had a good run for a few years, but now disaster had hit our Union. Not only me, but also most of the other members had a hard time. All the mates, that had enough time to retire, did so. Others just plain quit and got jobs outside. Myself, I decided to look at the Merchant Marine as a second job, and to do something else, too. So during the waiting, I got involved with construction. Plus, I chased the night mate jobs with a vengeance. At the time the three prepositioned ships, the *Kosak*, the *Pless*, and the *Obregon*, regularly were anchored in the Chesapeake Bay, and religiously I worked on them. I never missed a shift no matter what time it was. I think that I still hold the record for the longest stretch of night mate jobs at the Chesapeake Bay on those ships. I did night mate for sixty- seven days, to be exact, on the *Obregon* and right in the middle of the winter. It wasn't that easy, but I had no other income. To give up the ships completely, like some did, would have been a big mistake for me. I had invested quite a few years by now. Slowly, I thought I had to make my twenty years for my pension.

THE LASH SHIPS

We had moved to Norfolk in 1982. For six years my routine was, when my card was old enough, I would go to New York and ship out from there. I knew the companies, and the ships, and where they were going. When my shipping card was old enough, I would fly to New York. Usually, I was on the money. Slowly, as I had mentioned, I needed more and more waiting time. It started becoming more and more difficult, but still I liked the ships from New York. I was lucky to have some relatives to stay with while I was waiting for a job. After the disappearance of all the major shipping lines, New York got overcrowded with members.

I had to look for another way to ship out. Waterman Lash ships came to the rescue. To the dislike of the Norfolk Hall, I had turned those ships down until now. I was getting the ships from New York instead. I turned them down for two reasons. I never liked the places that they were going. The Middle East and India run was for over three months, and even though the money was excellent, it required long hours. I had done extensive night mate work in the port of Norfolk, and I knew the Lash ships well. Now, they had become choice jobs and required a killer card to get them. A year old card was nothing unusual. In fact, that was the norm most of the time. That was the case for every port. And as I mention, quite a few people lost their year because their cards would roll over.

My first Lash ship with the Waterman Company was the *Robert E. Lee*. There were two jobs on the board, second mate and third mate. My card was over nine months old. I didn't think that I would have any chance of getting either of these jobs. My card was still considered young. Naturally, the second mate job went to over an eleven and a half month card. To my amazement, the third mate's job came to me. No questions asked I got it, even though there were two ahead of me at the time. Later I found out that both of these men had histories with the Captain. Even though they had a much older card than I, they avoided going on the *Robert E. Lee*. Another Lash was coming in two weeks, and they held out for that. Since they had very good cards, they thought that they would have a good chance of getting the jobs there. Lucky me!

I had a good trip on the *Robert E. Lee*. They were right in a way, because with a second trip, the Old Man was a little tenser and a little more excitable. But to be honest, I didn't have any problems with him, not only on this trip but also the other trips that I sailed with him. In fact, he turned out to be my meal ticket. He turned out to be the reason that I got jobs without such a big card. I used to tell him, and we laughed, that he was my meal ticket.

The Lash run I considered the most demanding and stressful run at the time. Even though the money was excellent, for the deck officers, the deck crew, and the people involved in the crane operations, like the crane engineer and the electrician. However, it was hard work and required long hours, too. Sometimes eighteen to twenty hours was not unusual. Of the four Lash ships, most of the times I sailed with the *Robert E. Lee* and the *Sam Houston*, even though I would night mate on all of them. I have to say that I liked those two the most, but I wouldn't hesitate to take the other two, the *Stonewall Jackson* and *Green Valley*; it just didn't happen.

I had the privilege to work during these years with some hard-working professionals: captains, mates, deck crew, crane engineers, and electricians. All of them worked on the ships with the motto of Work, Work, and Work. It was very rare, if there was a decent port, for us to go ashore. Between the crane watch and the bridge watch, there was no time for pleasure. All the time that I worked with the Lash ships, it was in Singapore only that I had two chances to go ashore for a few hours, make a phone call, and buy a few gifts for

My Sea My Life

home. Even though the Lash ships were well-paying jobs, they were not for everybody. A seaman would have to be very motivated to work on the Lash ships, as mates or crew. Some tried and left. The people who stayed got to know each other and what was expected of them. They were laughing when I used to tell them that I was going to the Louisiana state penitentiary for a few months.

There were quite a few stories about all of them. How could I not have all kinds of sea stories with the exotic places that we were visiting? The typical run for the Lash ships included first the coast-wise run of Newport News, Savannah, New Orleans, back to Newport News, and New York. Those were the Lash ports for the U.S. The parade of all the beautiful exotic ports started with Alexandria. Unfortunately we were there only a few hours at the anchorage, and then we went through the Suez Canal, which was always eventful. We had a few ports in the Red Sea like Aqaba, Jordan. Lucky us! The next ones were Port Sudan, then Assab, and to make it more exciting occasionally we visited Massawa. After the Red Sea we visited Djibouti, and one small port in the North Coast of Somalia for a few hours, and then we had one or two ports along the coast of Oman. Thank God, so far all of them were from the anchorage.

Then came a beauty: Karachi. For this one we had to go inside the port and tie up at buoys. That was a nightmare for the Captain, especially during the summer monsoon season. Those South West winds could create havoc during the time we had to tie up the ship. That alone would raise our blood pressure a few points. Other than that, Karachi was a place that we couldn't wait to leave. The dream run started along the coast of India; beginning with Jamnagar. It was in the middle of nowhere and trying to find a spot to anchor between all the old anchor ships, made it a beauty. One had to be there to experience the excitement. Next was Bombay, and that port was not as bad as the others. Only during the monsoon season did we not want to be there during all the torrential rains. Otherwise, Bombay was fairly easy. We would just go inside the bay, drop the anchor, and discharge the barges. The city had quite a few interesting sites, if we had the chance to go ashore. I never did. Next came Mangalore, Tuticorin, and Cochin, which was a nice little port, but not for a big ship like the Lash ships. We had to go inside the port alongside the dock to discharge. It was considered a Captain's dream port if he wanted to test how much he could take before he had a nervous break down!

    I was with the *San Houston* during a docking in Cochin, and they promised us two tugboats. We were almost alongside the dock, and we still had only one small tugboat. The poor Captain had a fit! We had to dock with only one tugboat. The other one never showed up. In Madras we also went alongside. This was a fairly normal port. Vishakhapatnam was a small port, but reasonable, and we went inside there, too. Here, during the night, we had a few strange visitors. Bats!

    We were not over yet with our visit to unique ports. The next one was Paradeep. It was a very small port, and it was not very easy to maneuver the large Lash ships there. This was another Captain's heaven. The next port was Haldia, which was close to Calcutta. It was another wonderful place in the middle of nowhere with a strong current.

    The trip was not over yet, but we were getting there. Next was the port of Chittagong. This time we did anchor there, but that does not mean that things were easier by staying at the anchorage. All the anchorages were dangerous, and we were liable to drag the anchor at anytime. We did not have to go too far to ground the ship. That alone would keep us on our toes all the time. Thank God, the next port was Phuket, Thailand, the tsunami place. Actually it was a nice place, but we never had a chance to go ashore there either. The next big port was Port Kelang, Malaysia, at the anchorage. It was a nice port; and of course I never had a chance to go ashore there either. Finally, we reached Singapore, and it was by far the best port. Here the deck crew would get a break; the local longshoremen would work the crane. The mates still had to stay on watch, four hours on the bridge and four hours on the deck. By then, if we didn't drag our feet, we were considered to be in exceptional good shape. I never failed not to drag my feet, and I think that I was not in the minority there.

In Singapore, I went shore twice in all the years I had been there, and only for a few hours, to make a phone call, and to buy a few presents. Really at that time Singapore was still reasonable, and I could buy a lot of nice things.

I could tell you tons of stories just from the Lash ships, but I will concentrate on my last Lash ship, the *Robert E. Lee* and the pirates. What pirates? We remember the pirates in the old days, the Caribbean days. Yes, we do have sea pirates today, too. I will start with the least organized ones, but nevertheless dangerous ones. If we had the unfortunate luck to anchor outside of Madras and to wait for our turn to go alongside, we had to post pirate security watches to patrol the deck continuously. Also we needed to keep the ship well lighted. Plus, we needed cargo lights hanging over the side to see if any boats were approaching the ship. Of course, it was not an easy task on a big long ship like the Lash.

In one incident, and thank God it wasn't with us, there was another ship anchored at the Madras anchorage. The pirates attacked the ship. The poor Captain was calling the port security for help at two o'clock in the morning.

The port security answered, "Don't worry Captain. Close the doors of the accommodation, and we will be there in the morning. Just lock all the doors!"

That was very fast and efficient help. We were on our own, baby!

Our next port was Chittagong. Here we had a very strong current. At night the cargo operations had become very dangerous. From sunset to sunrise we would stop the cargo. Here, there were less organized thieves, but nevertheless dangerous. They were especially dangerous when they came on board with machetes. What did we have to protect ourselves from the thieves? We had practically nothing. The Captain was the only one that had a gun in his room. We had to lay the fire hoses on the deck with the water running and ready to use. That was our defense! Of course, at night we lit the deck as much as we could. Lights were placed over the sides, and the watch would patrol the deck with walkie-talkies all the time. Technically, we were untrained and unarmed for these kinds of situations.

One night it was around one thirty in the morning during slack water when pirates swarmed the ship. There were quite a few small boats, midship, stern, and bow. They were all over. The deck watch immediately called the bridge. Right away I called the Captain, and I also called the engine room to alert them, and told them to lock all the doors to the engine room as quickly as they could. I instructed my crew to go inside the accommodation and to lock the doors. By the way, as a precaution, all the doors around the deck and the accommodation were closed, and only the one door that we were using to come in and out was open.

There wasn't much to steal on deck, maybe a few barge lines. My main concern was the engine room, and that was why I immediately called the engine room to lock all of the doors there. We also had the searchlights on and shined them on the boats. Plus we blew the whistle to make noise to scare them away.

The poor Chief Mate! He had been up until almost one o'clock working on the cargo plan, and had just gone to bed when I called him. He was an unhappy fellow when he learned that he had to get up and chase pirates. The Captain was up on the bridge with his gun. We closed and locked the doors to the bridge from the inside. We continuously kept in touch with the watch by walkie-talkie. By then they were inside and had locked every door. The Chief Engineer was also checking the engine room. The bridge on the Lash ships was all the way up on the bow. We saw a couple of small boats approaching the bow with intentions to climb up the anchor chain to board. The Captain went outside at the wing of the ship, waived his gun and screamed at them to go away otherwise he would shoot. The poor bastards, when they saw the gun pointing at them, rowed away as fast as they could. By now it was almost three o'clock in the morning, and the current started to get strong again. So, the little boats could not afford to stay any longer, and the pirates "ran away." In the meantime, they had stolen a few lines that they could find on the deck. Practically everything else had been locked up.

Normally the last foreign port on the Lash ship run was Singapore. Then we would sail back to the States. They used to bring the barges with small feeder ships and then we pick them up from there. I don't remember what had happened, but we had to run to Indonesia to pick up barges. Here was where there was real danger from the pirates. In this part of the world, piracy at sea is well organized. The pirates have speedboats, and they are armed with the latest weapons. It was a sophisticated operation. There was no chance for us to defend ourselves. Period! Thank God we didn't have to go through it. Quite a few ships throughout the years had been attacked. Palembang, Padang, and Pajang, were some of the ports that we had visited in Indonesia and picked up barges, and they were dangerous. Now security at sea was more intense, plus we had to work cargo. Every available hand had to participate. Of course, we were all unarmed except with fire hoses. Again, thank God we did not have to deal with them.

That was my last trip with the commercial Lash ships, and the biggest reason was that they stopped coming to the Tidewater area. The longshoremen and the company had a dispute over the hourly rate that they should get. They were both stubborn and didn't come to an agreement. The Lash cargo operations moved to Morehead City. That dried up the port of Norfolk from offshore jobs, and it drastically reduced the night mate work.

DESERT STORM – SCAN

As far as shipping was concerned, jobs picked up during Desert Shield and Desert Storm. As we all know 1990 Saddam Hussein decided to become the Rambo of the Middle East and invaded Kuwait. With that, Desert Storm was born. Naturally, we needed quite a few cargo ships so the government dug around and brought out the old wrecks from the ghost fleet. Supposedly it was a reserved fleet, but nevertheless it was old and dilapidated by then. Besides others, the MMP got four from the old Moore Mc Commack Lines, the *Wave,* the *Lake*, the *Pride*, and the *Scan*. During that time, I was ashore, my card was still young, and I was waiting to build it up a little so that I could ship out again. Those four ships, while they were in dry dock, gave me a lot of port relief officer work, especially the *Scan*. The *Lake*, the *Pride* and the *Wake* were activated within a fairly reasonable time. They were loaded with the necessary military equipment, supplies, and ammunition and sailed for the Persian Gulf.

The poor *Scan* was going from one problem to another. It seemed that when they deactivated her, they did not do a good job. As soon as they were fixing one problem, another would appear. By then, we had gotten so far behind in the schedule, that she missed the whole war. Of course, everyone was thankful that the war did not last that long. By the time that the *Scan* was ready, it was time to bring the military equipment back to the States.

It was the beginning of May and a third mate's job for the *Scan* came on to the board at the Union Hall. She had just come back from the Gulf to Savannah. The schedule was to go back to the Gulf, load equipment, and bring it back to the States. I told my wife that since I had missed the last two summers, I would take the Scan, make one trip, and get off. By that time, it would still have been summer, and we could have a little summer together as a family. Plus the fact was that I knew everybody on the *Scan,* and the idea was attractive.

Of course, there was no pressure here since it wasn't a commercial run. Certainly it was not a Lash ship. The trip should just be nice and easy. Yeah, right! When I joined the ship in Savannah quite a few of the ship's crew were getting off. But the Captain, the Chief Mate, and a few others that I knew were still staying for another trip. By then the cargo was off, and the reason we were waiting to sail was for the crew. We had to shift from the container terminal to another dock and wait for the crew. During docking and undocking, I had the stern and the Second Mate was on the bow.

We were still kind of short of deck hands, but as I said, "No rush."

So here I was with two sailors at the stern. I called the bridge and told them that I only had two sailors.

The Captain said, "Michael, we are short on crew. Start taking the lines and take your time."

So, I thought to start one at a time, no sweat. I told my two sailors that we would start taking lines in, I would work the winch and also check the operation, and we would start with one of the springs. They were both looking at me without moving.

I said, "What's wrong?"

The older one said, "Mate, we want to do what you tell us, but what is a spring?"

"What do you mean, what is a spring? You don't know what I am telling you?" I asked.

"No Mate, I don't," he told me.

I asked, "What are you guys?"

He said, "We are both ordinary seamen."

The younger sailor has his ordinary seaman's card.

"I don't have mine yet. I have a letter that says I'm an ordinary seaman. We have never been on a ship before," said the other man.

I called the Captain and explained to him what had happened and asked him to send me one AB from the bow that was familiar with the ships. That was what we did, we exchanged one totally inexperienced ordinary seaman with an experienced AB and the magical solution was to take our time. With the help of the AB and one of the ordinaries doing whatever he could, we shifted the ship. Of course, we took our time, as if we had a choice. After a few days of waiting, we finally completed the crew and left for the Persian Gulf. Going down the Savannah River, on the wheel the Captain used two ABs that he knew and both were familiar with the ship.

Out at sea now, it was time to get to know what I had. The ordinary seaman, the older one, I knew was green. I met him during the undocking in Savannah. Well, one of my ABs was green, too. How he became an AB? He retired as a chief from the Navy, but he was a signalman, and I guess he considered it a deck position. This was the way he got the AB ticket. He had no idea how to steer a ship. The other AB, even though he was coming from tugboats, was good. One out of three, not bad! It was back to basic training. We had a week from Savannah to Gibraltar to teach them how to steer. So two hours a day and two hours a night they had to practice steering the ship. I must say neither of them were dummies, and they picked it up quickly. Also, we had to go over the procedures of a good watch, how to keep a good lookout, etc. By the time we got to Gibraltar, they were pretty familiar.

Going through the Red Sea we passed a U.S. Navy ship. I had my AB, the one that was very good in signaling, talk to them and to go as fast as he could. He was very good. I took it off my chest; I always wanted to show that the merchant ships were just as fast as they were at signaling. They were surprised from the war ship to have a merchant ship signal them that quickly. We got a kick out of it.

We had been just a few miles inside the Persian Gulf, it was about ten minutes before midnight, I was getting ready to finish my entries in the logbook, and suddenly, everything went dark. We had a blackout! There was no steering, no gyro, nothing! I sent one of my AB's to call the Captain. In the meantime, there were a few fishing boats in front of us. To alert them I blew the ships whistle a few times. After all, the ship still had head movement, and I didn't want to hit any of them. In the meantime, we started drifting toward the Iranian Coast. At least we weren't far out. Most of the crew, I guess, got scared and were coming up on the bridge with their life jackets on. I had to explain to them that we had a blackout, and I tried to calm them down. We were not about to abandon ship. The Chief Engineer and the First Assistant started the emergency generator as soon as they could. They went down to the engine room to restart the plant. That took almost two hours. The fact that we were drifting towards the coast of Iran made a few people nervous. Things were starting to get back to almost normal. The Second Mate, and I, while the other Third Mate was keeping watch, restarted the gyro, adjusted the repeaters, started the radars again, and all of the other bridge equipment. We made sure that it was all working correctly. It was almost after three that the ship was back to normal, and the Second Mate and I left the bridge. Just a little excitement!

The next day the Second Mate was telling me that during this entire ordeal, I kept very calm. That was something that I have heard other times when we had emergencies. In fact, sometimes they called me "Stone-faced" because I didn't show any emotions when we had an emergency.

My answer was, "I don't have that luxury to panic when I am on watch."

It's not that I didn't worry. I did. I learned from the days of the liberty ships that it was a forbidden luxury when in command to show worry.

The next port of loading was Dammam, and there were all kinds of military equipment: tanks, trucks, etc. Unfortunately we were not headed for the U.S. ports but for Germany. There went my summer vacation, and that would not make Kyki happy. On top of everything, we were in a hurry. We docked around midnight, and they were ready to start loading cargo. There went the easy no rush time. We had finished docking at midnight.

One young Army Captain came onboard. He was supposedly familiar with the cargo ships because he had graduated from Kings Point Merchant Marine Academy. He has never sailed, except during training when he was a cadet. Although Kings Point was one of the best maritime academies in the world, the cadets were not experts on everything at graduation.

Here we were talking about an old cargo ship. It was designed for the South American run to carry mostly coffee bags, pallets, and fruit. There was a lot of refrigeration space, but the ship wasn't for heavy lifts. We had a heavy boom, but it was fairly complicated to run and required good, experienced seamen or longshoremen.

The Army Captain wanted to start loading the cargo with the ship's gears. The equipment was big tanks and vehicles, and he wanted to use our outdated jumbo boom instead of the modern cranes on the dock.

The Chief Mate, I guessed just to please him, was saying," Yes, yes, yes, yes."

When it came to the heavy boom, I don't know why, but I opened my mouth and said, "Not with this heavy boom."

The Chief Mate got upset, and the young captain was irritated. To my rescue came the Captain, who had just walked in, and he asked what this was all about. The Chief Mate told him what I said about not using the jumbo and that the Army Captain wanted to use the ships gears and the jumbo for the big tanks.

The Captain hit the ceiling and was shouting, "No, not the jumbo! The Third Mate knows what he is talking about. It's not that they are not in working order. Everything is in working order, but we do not have experienced crew to work the jumbo, nor does the military. The tanks have to be loaded by the shore crane."

Well, it was time for me to leave. I decided to let them

straighten things out by themselves before I got in more trouble. By now my watch was over, so with that, I went to bed. What a productive night they had! The next morning, when I went on deck for watch, it was a disaster. The wires of the winches were all tangled up. The guys that worked the winches had messed them up, but good. Poor Bosun was up all night trying to clear up the runners. He was passed, by now, the state of exhaustion. I knew him well from the dry dock. He was a good man and a good seaman, plus he knew the ship very well. He was disappointed with all of this nonsense.

"I don't know what to do Michael. This is a three-ring circus. There must be another way. These kids are not familiar with this kind of operation. We are getting nowhere," he told me when he saw me.

The Chef Mate was also exhausted and desperate by now. A lieutenant was in charge of the military longshoremen gang. He looked like a nice guy, and we started talking.

He was also upset with the whole operation; and he asked me, "What's wrong with the ship? Why can't we load anything without the winches getting messed up?"

"Lieutenant, there is nothing wrong with the ship's gears," I told him.

"Then why do we have all this trouble?" he asked me.

"Do you want to load this ship in no time?" I asked.

"Yes, of course," he said.

"Do you know someone that can authorize for us to use these nice cranes on the dock?" I asked him.

"Yes, but our Captain insisted that we use the ship's gears and that the ship should be equipped to do that," he said.

"Look Lieutenant, he is right and not right. This is no disrespect to your Captain. He is a well-educated man, but he is doesn't know a few things about these old ships. They are not meant to load tanks and heavy trucks, but rather coffee and general cargo. Plus, we don't have very experienced longshoremen like those from the old days. I am not trying to be a smart ass. I want just as much as you to move this cargo. In my humble opinion, these nice cranes that you have on the dock will do the job," I told him.

He thought for a few minutes and said, "I think that you're

My Sea My Life

right. I will be back in awhile. Let me see what I can do." A half hour later he was back with a smile on his face. "Mate, I got the cranes," he told me.

"Great, I will get the Bosun and the crew on the deck so that they can clear the booms, and you can start loading," I told him.

In twenty-four hours we were done, and we shifted to the anchorage to secure the cargo and the ship for sea. We were off to Germany. In Germany they didn't fool around. We were hoping to stay a little, because it was a nice town down there. No chance! They had fast cranes, and it took them only twelve hours to strip the ship. I just had enough time to go out for a few hours and to make a phone call to tell my wife the happy news. She was thrilled that I was in Germany and not coming home! Here we had a crew change too. The Captain, the Bosun, and a few other crewmembers were going home for vacation. The Chief Mate became the Captain. The new Chief Mate was from New York, and I had known him for years. As soon as he walked on board, he didn't even have a chance to unpack his bag, since we had to secure the ship. Being an experienced seaman, he quickly realized that he had quite a few inexperienced crewmembers on deck, and the experienced Bosun was gone.

He asked me, "Michael, you are staying on deck with me until we finish securing this ship. You're not going anywhere. Don't leave me."

He told me this jokingly but seriously, of course. I was prepared anyway to stay and to give him a hand. Not only was I getting paid, but also I was glad to have him on board because he was a really nice guy. We must have been halfway finished securing the ship when the new Bosun arrived. He was a young man in his thirties. I happened to be on the gangway when he arrived. We exchanged the usual greetings, and I informed him that the Chief Mate was on deck and would like to have him on deck as soon as possible. They wanted the ship to sail as soon as possible.

He said, "Okay, I'm going to change, and I will be right out." Then he turned around and asked me, "What's to secure?"

"The booms," I said.

"What booms?" he asked me.

"What do you mean? The ship's gears!" I told him.

By the expression on his face I sensed that he had no idea what I was talking about.

Nicely I asked, "Bosun, have you ever been on a cargo ship before?"

"No mate, I have sailed a few tankers so far. This is my first cargo ship," he told me.

"How did they give you this job?" I asked.

"The job was open, and no one took it. So, I took it," he told me.

"Ok, go change, and go on deck. The Chief Mate needs you," I told him.

Poor Mate, he will love it.

The Chief Mate asked me, "Is the Bosun was on board?

"He sure is!" I said.

"Did you tell him to come on deck as soon as possible?" he asked.

"I sure did!" I replied.

"Good, because I am going to get off my feet for a few hours and do some paperwork," he said.

"Not so fast," I told him.

"Why?" he asked.

He looked at me and sensed that something was not normal. "What is wrong? What do you know?" he kept asking.

"Nothing is wrong, Mate. The Bosun is a nice guy, but he has never been on a cargo ship before," I told him.

I cannot describe what his answer was, but you guessed it right. Sure you did.

"Why me? Why me?" he kept saying, plus whatever else you are thinking.

"Mate, we are almost done. We are doing all right. Just sign my overtime and don't check it," I told him, as we were both laughing.

It was a short stay there, and then we were headed back to the Persian Gulf. Forget the slow and easy thinking. It turned out to be hurry, hurry, hurry like the commercial ships. Luckily, this time we were loading for the East Coast of the United States. This time we were going to the port of Jubal Ali, another beauty.

During the Gulf War, from different officials, the word was that the U.S. had learned their lesson. They had realized that the U.S. needed a good, strong merchant marine fleet. Also, we needed to build new ships to have them for commercial and military reasons. That understanding only lasted until the war was over. Then we were back to square one. Who cares? When we have problems again, they will try to bring some old wrecks out of the dilapidated ghost fleet again. They always think that they will be all right. The fact was that these old wrecks were breaking down right and left. That was another story. Thanks to the good Chief Engineer, we did not have many breakdowns, but many other ships did.

I ended up doing a little more than four months on the *Scan*. My wife was disappointed that we had lost all summer.

Like my old friend, from the *Citrus Packer* said, "There are no plans, until you go home. When you are on a ship, you don't know what is next."

He was right. Financially speaking, the *Scan* was not bad at all.

A friend of mine, from the good old days on the *Clarksville Victory*, was up there in age, but he was still doing port relief jobs. The Old Bone did not want to give up. He used to take the midnight to eight shift, while I liked the four to midnight. I used to go a few minutes before midnight and shoot the breeze with him. The Thompson Likes was coming, and I hadn't heard from him. I didn't pay much attention this time. His son was on board as a Third Mate. I thought that he might have skipped this ship so he would be available to drive his son around. I went to the Hall, and of course they had posted the night relief officer's job, plus a one trip emergency relief Third Mate's job.

I asked, "What is the emergency?"

The Port Agent told me, "I guess you don't know. Your old buddy is dead, and his son is getting off for that reason."

I got upset when I heard this news. We went back a long way. I guess that's why I didn't hear from him. There wasn't anyone interested in the one trip relief job in the Hall. There were not any B book members, or C book members, or applicants available at the time. In order to cover the job, they had to get someone from another port, but the Third Mate would have to cover the expenses. It was a kind of a troubling situation for me. I knew the older man for a long time, and I knew his son, too.

So I said, "If the main office agrees, I will take the job with my night mate card, So the man does not have to pay all the extra money to bring someone from another port."

It really was an emergency because the man wanted to bury his father. It was not fair to pay someone extra. They agreed, and I took the job. *Thompson Likes* was an older ex-President Lines ship. It sailed mostly from the West Coast to the Far East. Likes Lines was using the ship now for the North Europe run. It was a kind of light ship for the North Atlantic, and it rolled a lot. But, what the heck! By now it was the end of May and the weather shouldn't be that bad. I should know better than to count on that with the North Atlantic.

One day before Lands End, the party started. It was such bad weather that you wouldn't believe it. The ship was rocking and rolling like crazy! It was about eight-thirty P.M. By the way, I had the twelve to four watch. I was lying on my bunk trying to sleep a little. One of these over thirty degree rolls took me off the bed. It took the mattress and me to the floor. In my desperation, I turned the mattress around, crossways, and all night the mattress and I were sliding back and forth on the floor. As far as sleep was concerned, I did not get much of that either. Midnight, I went on the bridge for my watch.

The Chief Mate was on watch, and as he left he told me, "We rolled a little, but everything is okay."

I settled down for a long watch. There were all these strange noises coming from the deck. Also, inside the chimney house, it looked as if something heavy was moving back and forth. The noise was pretty loud at the time. I went outside the wing of the vessel. The Lookout was out there.

I asked him, "Do you hear all of these noises?"

"Yes Mate. My relief told me that the Chief Mate said that it was okay, and that was why I didn't tell you anything.

"Okay or not, something is not right," I said.

I went inside, picked up the phone, and I called the Captain. I explained to him what was going on.

He said, "I'm coming up."

My quartermaster asked, "What is going on, Mate?"

"There is a lot of banging on deck and inside the chimney," I told him.

"The Old Man will be pissed that you are bringing him on the bridge," the quartermaster said.

"I'd rather have the Old Man pissed that I woke him up, instead of blaming me for the damages," I told him.

The Captain came on the bridge kind of pissed all right, and asked, "What is going on?"

I explained it to him again, and I expressed my concerns especially about the strong heavy noise that was coming from inside the chimney. Also, I told him that we were taking heavy rolls of over thirty degrees.

He said "The Chief Mate told me on his way down that everything is okay, and that the rolls are not that bad."

Just on time, the engine room called, and the Engineer on watch told me, "Michael, we are taking rolls over thirty degrees! Even down here we cannot stay on our feet. I imagine that up there it's even worse!"

I said, "Did you hear that Captain? There's another one to verify that."

He went outside the bridge, and listened for a while.

Then he came in and told me, "You're right. That's a lot of noise coming from the containers on deck. As far as the chimney is concerned, I think I know what it is. It is loose. It's the APL's sign. I will slow the ship down a little to try to ease the rolls."

I thought that it was going to be a long watch, and it was. The next morning, when I got up, and I put my glasses on, I thought that they were dirty. This was because there were a couple of fuzzy spots on the lenses. I cleaned them, put them back on, but the two fuzzy spots were still there. I took them off, and looked at them carefully. In the middle of the lenses, there were two almost round spots, apparently scratches. All night long, it looked as if, with the rolling of the ship, they were sliding back and forth. That was the way the weather ruined my good glasses!

Ah, you want to know what all the noise was. Well, when we arrived in Rotterdam, quite a few containers were looking like pregnant women. It looked as if the cargo inside the containers was moving back and forth and changed the shape of the containers. Plus, back on the stern on the starboard side, three containers with the lashings and the pad eyes were gone over the side into the Atlantic Ocean floating to eternity or until they sunk to the deep of the ocean.

It is very worth mentioning the Euro port. It was a fully automated container terminal. During the loading or discharging of the ship, the longshoremen gang consisted of only two people: one operating the crane and one on the ship. The containers would come one after another on top of an automated trailer without a driver. It would go to the right place, which was preprogrammed, load the next container, and kept going. All the moves were preprogrammed and automated. It was weird, and amazing to see. I used to call them, the dummies. The rest of the trip was as usual.

I always felt sorry for the new members and the struggle that they were going through to find jobs. After all I spent six years as an applicant. The difference though, between then and now was, when I was an applicant, the members were enjoying plenty of good jobs with many choices. Now, like they say on the ships, we were all in

My Sea My Life

the same boat. There were no jobs for anyone. Of course as an applicant, B or C member, it was worse. But nevertheless, we were all suffering.

It would be unfair not to mention, the *Rainbow Hope*. That was mostly applicant's territory. To all the seamen that have sailed the *Rainbow Hope*, I tip my hat. During the years I have sailed some rust-buckets, but the *Rainbow Hope* took the cake! The seamen deserved a great respect by sailing that rust bucket from Norfolk, Virginia to Iceland, no matter what time of the year. The new generations of our Union officers deserve a lot of credit for keeping this ship afloat under terribly trying times.

Oh, I remember my first Atlantic Ocean trip and how seasick I was! I learned to manage, but it was never really cured. All my time at sea, I had to carry Dramamine with me, just in case I needed it. It was mostly for the very rough moments.

By now we were done with the Gulf War, and the few extra jobs that it generated. Things started to get back to normal. That is normal for the struggle to find a job. The Lash ships had left the Tidewater area for Morehead City, and with them, the few jobs that we had. In order to find a job now, we had to go somewhere like New York, Charleston, or New Orleans. Not that there were plenty there either, but they still had a few jobs.

In the seventies, when I visited Diego Garcia, there was practically nothing there. It was just a small observation station as they used to tell us. It had only twenty-five to thirty people, and a small airstrip. Today, Diego Garcia is a booming town with just about everything that is needed. It is a very active base. The Lagoon is filled with prepositioned ships that are ready with only an hour's notice to head for anywhere that they are needed.

The rotation was four months on and four months off for the permanent personnel and 120 days for the relief officers. Diego Garcia became my territory. All the jobs were lower paying jobs compared to those on the commercial ships. The overtime was also limited mostly to the weekends and to holidays. The benefit was that we could get those jobs with younger cards. Also, they didn't have the "go-go all the time" pressure that the commercial ships had. The Lash ships, in my opinion, were the most demanding of all the ships at the time. But nevertheless, all the ships by now had become demanding. The personnel had been cut down to the minimum. When it rained, it poured. We also had the three Watermen prepositioned ships, which were fairly easy to work, the *Obregon*, the *Pless*, and the *Kosack*.

MY BACK – DIEGO GARCIA

Probably by now you might have noticed that I was looking for a job, but one without a lot of pressure. There was a reason for that. The three Watermen ships were fairly good, but the disadvantage was that all the jobs were permanent and the rotation time was four months on and two months off. It was a very heavy schedule for a family man. When they first came out, twice from two different captains I was offered a chance to join the team, as they would say. I appreciated it very much, but it didn't fit with my family situation. I just could not leave my wife alone for eight months out of a year having to take care of two kids and having to work full-time as a teacher. That was one of the reasons.

Now we have come to one of my secrets. I considered it a big secret. It was the reason that made me retire prematurely from the sea. It was my back; yes my lower back. It was New York, Christmas 1970; we were living in Flushing Queens at the time. The weather was very cold, and within walking distance from our apartment there was a place where they were selling Christmas trees. It was time for us to buy our Christmas tree. So, my wife and I had set out to get the tree. I don't remember exactly what happened, but I don't remember doing anything wrong to cause my back problems. Actually, I didn't have to do much with causing the attack. As we were walking to the place that was selling the trees I felt a pain in my lower back. It was as if somebody stuck a knife in, and I had excruciating pain. I fell down and couldn't move.

With some help, my wife took me to the doctor. With every little move the pain became more unbearable. From then on, the parade of doctors started, orthopedic doctors, x-rays, tests, etc.; you name it. To make the long story short, all of those brilliant minds came to the conclusion that I had a slipped disc. Their diagnosis was that from then on I wouldn't be able to do much with my life. They considered me disabled. There were pills galore, from anti-inflammatory drugs to painkillers. Get this; they wrapped me up with a back brace, a long back brace. You might imagine how happy I was! My wife wasn't far behind; we both were devastated.

Until now, I never had a back problem. Here I was a very active person lying in bed, but not able to do anything. Plus, the doctor was telling me that for the rest of my life I would not be able to do much. This situation went on for a while. Slowly, I started getting around the house. Of course, I was wrapped up with this big back brace. It was splendid, just splendid! You couldn't find a happier person, if you looked around! Being in my early thirties, I considered myself a young man. I was lying there according to these brilliant minds, "disabled." For a while, I almost started to believe them and started to accept my fate.

I had reached the point that I told my wife, "I love you very much, but you are young, and you do not have to spend the rest of your life taking care of me. I cannot ask you that. It will be too much. You don't have to stay with me. You are young and you can start over again."

Of course, she cussed me out. The good old Michael, the stubborn one, the one that could not accept the word, "no" or "you can not do it" could not give up. By now it started sinking in: what if all of these brilliant minds were wrong, or what if they prematurely jumped the gun! Or what if they took the easy way out! How did they know what I could or couldn't do? I was still a young man. I realized that life would be different from then on. That was a fact. Back injuries last a lifetime, but I could not accept the fact that I would be disabled. That wasn't me, especially before I had exhausted every possibility. I sent them all to hell and started to look for a way out, on my own.

I found out that the New York hospital at Main Street, Flushing Queens, had a good rehabilitation center and that the doctor

My Sea My Life

in charge was good. So I paid him a visit on my own, forgetting the referral nonsense. After all, it was my problem not the orthopedics with their brilliant minds. I got stuck though with the secretary at the front desk. She wanted to know what doctor had sent me. I kept telling her that I came on my own, and that my back brought me here and not a doctor. She was stuck on the referral part; she had a one-track mind, and she was very slow to understand. Lucky for me, the doctor happened to pass by and heard me arguing with the secretary.

He asked us, "What is going on?

I explained to him what the story was and the reason that I was here on my own without a referral.

With a smile on his face, he told me, "Come to my office."

After we spoke, he told his secretary to take all of my history, and to make appointments with him for the next few weeks. God bless him wherever he is! That was the start of a second chance, certainly, not as a disabled person, but as a normal person with a back problem.

Pain? Yes. I've had to live with that the rest of my life. I don't remember a day yet without pain. I learned to consider normal pain as the degree that I could function. It was abnormal pain from the time I could not move. I continued on with the rehabilitation program for almost six months. In the meantime, I reduced the size of the back brace to a much smaller size and just for extra support.

The years started rolling by with ups and downs, as far as my back was concerned. When I heard about a supposedly good doctor, I visited him. Of course I contributed to his annual income, and in the end there wasn't much of a difference. I would get disgusted and go on my own in caring for my back. I would have gotten rid of my back support all together if I had an office job. Being at sea, I had rough days and also calm days. Being a watch standing officer, I spent at least eight hours a day standing on my feet, plus the extra work that I had to do.

As they use to say when I was in the hotels, "This is a seven day a week, twenty-four hours a day job."

Considering the circumstances, I got stuck with the back support, which I wear until today. During my years at sea, I had to come up with all the kinds of ways to hide the back support, especially from the company and their doctors. I did not want them to know that I wore a back support. They probably would have blacklisted me, and I wouldn't be able to get any jobs on the ships. As a precaution no one knew that I had a back problem.

Until I was fifty years old, I was doing okay, with a few pills of course. I had a few encounters with potentially serious accidents in my later years, but I somehow survived. However, the writing was on the wall. I had to concentrate now seriously to complete my twenty years pension time. I was close.

The orthopedic doctor who was checking my knees kept telling me, "How long do you have to go for the twenty years? You better hurry; your back and your knees are worn out."

He was right. I had to get off prematurely after one trip from the *S/S Resolute*. Even though it was a nice ship, my back was acting like a bitch! With the *Sea Land Expedition* my right knee gave out during the reading of some reefers. I almost killed myself! I was reading them from a platform ten feet above the deck. I was lucky that I did not fall on deck from up there.

My escape became the Diego Garcia ships. It was less money, but much easier work. The first one was the *Austral Rainbow*. I didn't know at the time that I took the job that it was a very low paying job. It was the lowest paying from all the ships that were stationed in Diego Garcia. Nevertheless, it was an easy one. I joined the ship in the Persian Gulf. Most of the time we stayed anchored in the middle of the Persian Gulf, about sixty miles away from Bahrain. Every two weeks we would go close to Bahrain anchorage so that we could go ashore and get supplies. At the anchorage were a bunch of ships that were all prepositioned. At one of the meetings that we had with the military, they insisted the reason that we anchored out there was because we were very safe. They were determined to persuade us that the reason we were in the mid-

My Sea My Life

dle of nowhere was for our safety.

I couldn't keep my mouth shut and raised the question, "How can you consider us safe when I can buy fish from the fishermen? They are fishing that close. I can shake hands with the small ships that are passing by."

My opinion was that if someone wanted, they could have blown up the ship anytime. He still believed that we were safe. Now, from the events that happened later, I will let you decide who was right. Thank God that we left that anchorage and we moved to Jebbal Ali next to Dubai for repairs. It was a new beautiful port. We stayed alongside for a few weeks. Dubai was a nice, modern city and one of the best places in the world to buy jewelry. I loved to go to the Gold Shook. I spent enough money there. My wife loved it!

It was time for us to go back to Diego Garcia, which I considered the safest place in that part of the world. That was where I finished my 120 days, and they flew me back home. I don't remember what type of airplane they were using to fly us back home, but one thing was for sure, that plane had seen better days. The seats were so tight! I was lucky to have one of the seats in the front. On the way back a gentleman was sitting next to me. He was carrying a small case that looked more like a toolbox. We opened a conversation. I told him that I was getting off a ship, and that I had been there for four months. I explained that I was anxious to get home. At the beginning I thought that he was one of the technical personnel that used to fly to Diego Garcia to do repairs. I asked him if he worked on the ships and what company he was working for.

He said, "No, I am a mechanic, and I work for the company that owns this airplane. I'm coming back and forth and when there is a problem with the airplane, I fix it."

"That's nice," I thought, "That makes my flight easier."

My next Diego Garcia ship was the *Jeb Steward*. For this one, I flew to Diego Garcia. We boarded the plane from

Philadelphia; the first stop was Tercera at the Azores. The next stop was Siganela, Italy. Then it was Bahrain, and finally it was Diego Garcia. It was a very long flight. I had to use my back brace, but I had to figure out a way to get through the check points without setting off the alarms, especially the last one at Diego Garcia. If they had found out that I wore a back brace, they would have sent me home. There would go my job and the year's income. I had to become Houdini; by making the back brace appear and disappear. It was not an easy job, but somehow I did it.

Once in Siganela, I put it in my brief case with my papers. When my brief case went through the x-ray machine, they saw the two rods from the back brace. They thought that they were knives or a type of weapon. No one would touch the brief case, and they waited for the owner to pick it up. I had no idea what they were thinking, so I proceeded to pick up my brief case. I was surrounded by security. Politely, they asked me to step to the side. First they asked me what was in the brief case. I told them my papers. Then they put my brief case back on the x-ray machine, and they asked me to identify what looked like the two rods or knives. I explained to them that it was my back support and that I had a little back problem. With a long flight like this, I might have problems and might need to wear it. Then I opened my brief case, and I showed it to them. They relaxed and started laughing. After all, I wasn't a terrorist, just a person with back problems trying to survive. I was lucky that it happened in Italy and all the security personnel were Italians, and that it did not happen in Diego Garcia. For sure, they would have sent me back home.

Jeb Steward was one of the oldest if not the oldest Lash ships at the time. As for maintenance, she was in poor condition. It wasn't an American built Lash, and the company that had had it before did not maintain the ship. It was a good-paying job. I made only ninety days because we came back to Sunny Point, where we discharged the ammo. Then we went to Newport News Dry Dock for repairs, which poor *Jeb Steward* needed very badly. She was scheduled to stay for almost a month so they laid us up. While I was waiting to go back, a job came up unexpectedly with the *Sea Land Expedition*. The ship was doing repairs at Norshipco, so I got it.

My Sea My Life

My next job, to Diego Garcia again, was on the *Green Harbor*. It turned out to be the last ship that I sailed. I got this job from the Jacksonville, Florida port. I liked that port, especially the doctor. Going to Diego Garcia, I was required to take a more detailed medical exam, plus I had to fill all the medical forms, which were practically the medical history of my life. Sometimes they were unreasonable in their requests. So for all of our sakes, I would write that I was healthy as a horse and that I never had any medical problems in my entire life. It was unrealistic of course. Since they had a good doctor to check me, plus all the other tests, if I had any problem, he would have found it. On the other hand, I had a family, and I had to work. Survival, my dear, survival!

This nice doctor was in his sixties. He also happened to be realistic. He did not expect a fifty-seven, fifty-eight year old seaman to be Superman, especially with the wear and tear of all these years at sea. God bless him!

By now I had my twenty years, but for the benefit of the doubt, I was taking this extra trip just in case a mistake was made in calculating my sea time. I did not want to have any surprises when I applied for my retirement. It should be nice and easy. The *Green Harbor* "vacation and resort ship" was perfect, just perfect. We even did convoy exercises, and I might say successfully, just to satisfy our Godfathers. I thought that I would have a nice an easy 120-day trip. Unfortunately I made it only close to fifty days.

I must have fallen asleep, and I don't' remember for how long. I was thinking or dreaming, when a soft hand touched my shoulders.

A sweet voice was telling me, "Wake up, Sir, It is time to get up. Get ready for your breakfast, because very soon we will arrive in San Francisco."

FINAL THOUGHTS

Yes indeed, the *Green Harbor* was my last ship. Do I miss the sea? Yes of course, I miss the freedom of the open ocean. Out there you feel free. It is only you and the sea. It is like you leave all your worries behind.

By now you have read and learned that there are not only fish out there in the ocean, but also many of us called seamen with our strengths, weaknesses, idiosyncrasies, and of course our peculiarities. The merchant marine is not different from any other society only a little unknown. I hope that through knowing my life, you now have a small idea of our world.

After all there is an important job that the merchant marine performs. By ships we move a tremendous amount of cargo, goods, people, etc. From the beginning of the world, sea transportation was, is, and always will be a very important part of our civilization and world economy. After all about 80% of all worlds' international trade is carried on the oceans by the merchant ships.

MEMORABILIA FROM THE ARCHIVES:

ARTIFACTS SAVED THROUGH THE YEARS

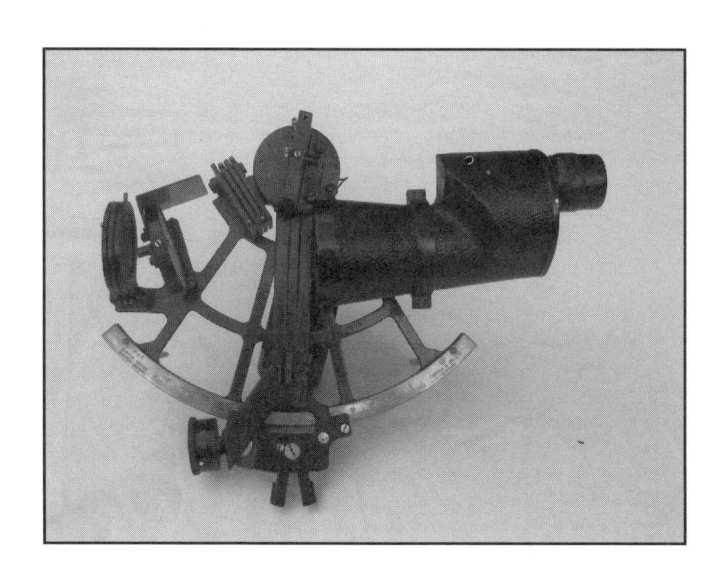

George D. Gratsos Co. Ltd., Athens   S/S "KASTOR"

ACCOUNT OF WAGES

Name of Seaman RAZOS MICHAIL **Rating** DECK-BOY

Date wages began 15-11-60 **Date wages ceased** 15-12-60 **Total period empl.** 1m 1d

EARNINGS

Months 1 Days 1 @ £ 11-00-0   £ 11-07-4 $
OVERTIME HOURS 20 × 1/-   £ 1-00-0

£ 12-07-4
Total $ 34.63

DEDUCTIONS & ADVANCES

                MONTHLY   1m 1d
N.A.T.   £ 1-17-8   £ 1-18-11
G.99 1% over £ 1-00-0   £ 0-00-3
                        £ 1-19-2 $ 5.48

Cigarettes car. 3 × 1.17 $ 3.51

Total Deductions ... $ 8.99
Final Balance ... $ 25.64

The above account of earnings and of deductions is correct.
Received in full settlement of all earnings and claims
the sum of DOLLARS TWENTY FIVE & SIXTY FOUR CENTS
At New Orleans the Dec. 15th 1960

Master *[signature]*   Seaman *[signature]*

First pay voucher on the S/S Kastor as an apprentice officer.

My Sea My Life

ΠΙΣΤΟΠΟΙΗΤΙΚΟΝ ΥΠΗΡΕΣΙΑΣ
CERTIFICATE OF SERVICE

Ὀνοματεπώνυμον ναυτικοῦ **Mixany Pajos** Ἀριθ. Μ.Ε.Θ. **44428**
Full Name of Seaman / Official Number

Βαθμός ἤ Εἰδικότης ὑφ' ὅν προσελήφθη **Διευθυντης**
Rank or Rating

Ὄνομα καί εἶδος πλοίου **M/V DIANA** Σημαία **Λιβερίας**
Name and class of ship / Flag

Λιμήν νηολογήσεως καί Ἀριθμός νηολογίου **MONROBIA 2172**
Port of Registry and Official Number

Ὁλική χωρητικότης **3.713,52** Τύπος καί Ἱπποδύναμις μηχανῆς **Rulej 3.000**
Gross tonnage / Type of Engine and Horse Power

Χρόνος ὑπηρεσίας ναυτικοῦ Ἀπό **12 Ιουλιου 1967** Ἕως **17 Νοεμβριου 1967**
Period of Seaman's service From / To

Κρατηθέν ποσόν εἰσφορῶν ναυτικοῦ ὑπέρ Ν.Α.Τ. καί Ταμείου Προνοίας **£ 40-12-06**
Sum retained from Seaman's wages for Seaman's Pension Fund

Saranta Lleyrres, Dodena Leyrres

Βεβαιοῦται ὑπευθύνως ἡ ἀκρίβεια τῶν ὡς ἄνω στοιχείων καί ὅτι τό πλοῖον τελεῖ ἐν ἐνεργείᾳ κατά τό ὡς ἄνω διάστημα, εἰδικῶς δέ ἡ κράτησις τῶν ἀνωτέρω εἰσφορῶν τοῦ ναυτικοῦ πρός ἀπόδοσιν μετά τῆς ἀναλόγου κρατήσεως πλοιοκτήτου εἰς Ν.Α.Τ.

I Hereby certify the above particulars to be correct: also that the vessel was trading during the specified period and more especially I certify the correctness of the sum retained from the above Seaman's wages for the contribution to the Greek Seaman's pension fund to be refunded to it together with the Owner's own contribution.

Ἐν **Νεα Ορλεανη** τῇ **17 Νοεμβριου 196_**
DATED

Ὁ ΠΛΟΙΑΡΧΟΣ (Ὑπογ.) (Σφραγίς)
THE MASTER (Sign) (Seal)

Ὀνοματεπώνυμον πλοιάρχου **GEORGE KARIVALI**
Full name of Master

ΕΘΕΩΡΗΘΗ ΚΑΙ ΒΕΒΑΙΟΥΤΑΙ

Τό γνήσιον τῆς ὑπογραφῆς τοῦ πλοιάρχου καί τό ἀκριβές τοῦ περιεχομένου ὡς ἐξάγεται ἐκ τῶν προσκομισθέντων ἡμῖν ναυτιλιακῶν ἐγγράφων ὡς ἄνω πλοίου, ὡς καί ὅτι τό πλοῖον ἦτο ἐν ἐνεργείᾳ κατά τό ἀνωτέρω ἀναφερόμενον χρονικόν διάστημα, ἤτοι ἀπό τῆς .... μέχρι καί τῆς .... καθ' ὅ ὁ ἄνω ἀναφερόμενος ἦτο ναυτολογημένος ἐπ' αὐτοῦ ὡς ....

Τό ὄνομα τοῦ περί οὗ τό παρόν εὑρέθη κατεχωρημένον εἰς τήν δέουσαν, ὡς πρός τήν χρονολογικήν τάξιν, θέσιν ἐν τῷ ναυτολογίῳ.

I, the undersigned .... certify the above signature as being that of the Master of the M.V. **DIANA** as well as that the content of the certificate is correct and corresponds to the ship's papers and that the vessel was trading during the specified period and especially from **12 July 1967** until **17 November 1967** when the above named seaman was serving on board as **Chief Mate**.

The name of the Seaman whom the present concerns has been found entered in the ship's papers, at the proper chronological succession.

Ἐν **3rd** τῇ **February** 196 **7**

Ἡ ΛΙΜΕΝΙΚΗ ἤ ΠΡΟΞΕΝΙΚΗ ΑΡΧΗ
THE GREEK PORT OR CONSULAR AUTHORITY

(ΥΠΟΓΡΑΦΗ ΚΑΙ ΣΦΡΑΓΙΣ)
(SIGNATURE AND SEAL)

Ὀνοματεπώνυμον ....
Full Name

Βαθμός ἤ Ἰδιότης **DEPUTY COMMISSIONER**
Rank or Rate **OF MARITIME AFFAIRS**
OF THE REPUBLIC OF LIBERIA

Certificate of Service for Diana

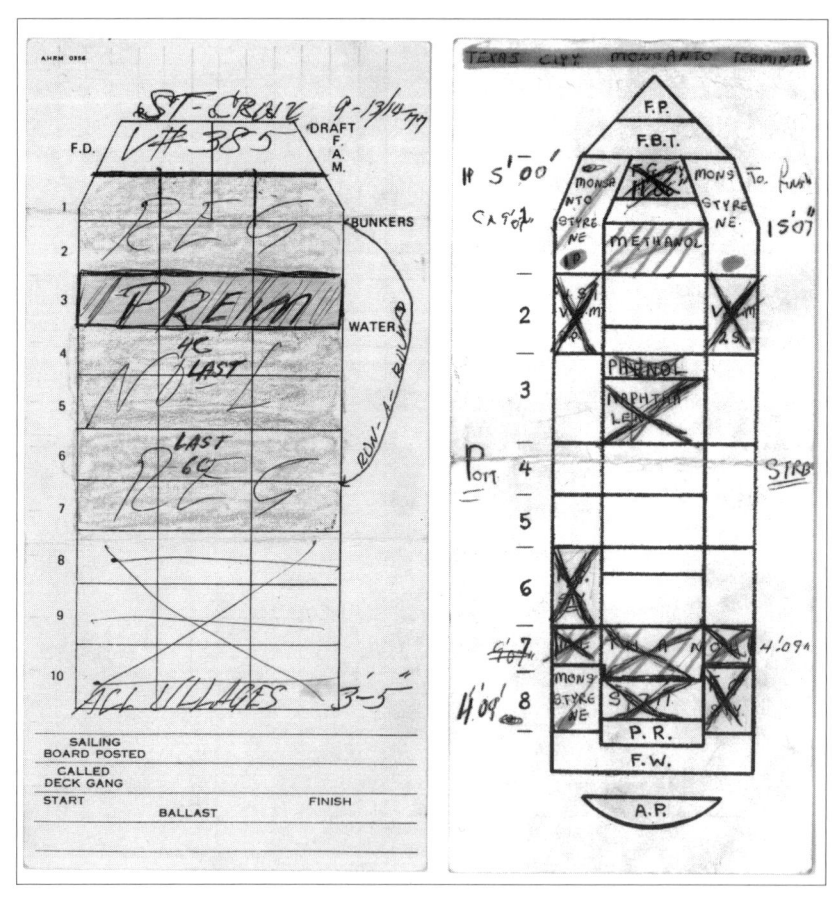

Samples of cargo plans for tankers

My Sea My Life

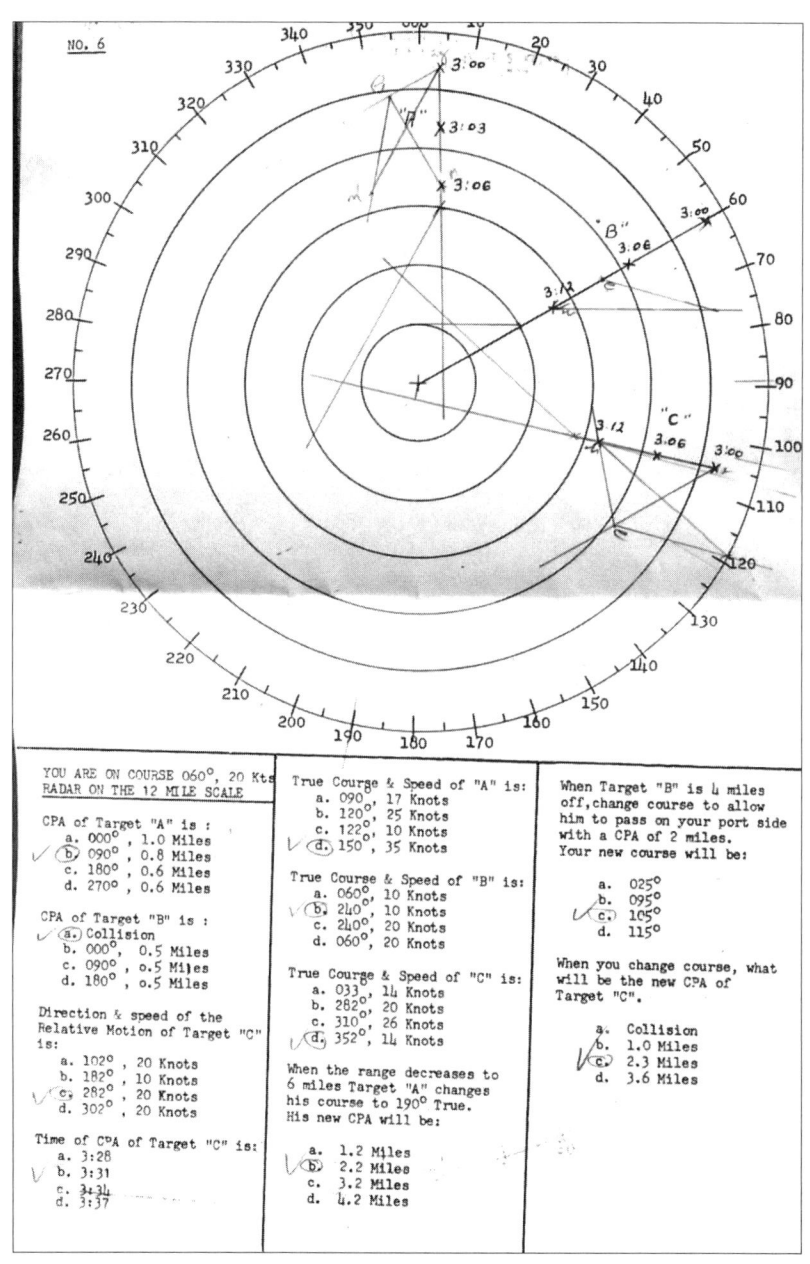

NO. 6

YOU ARE ON COURSE 060°, 20 Kts
RADAR ON THE 12 MILE SCALE

CPA of Target "A" is :
  a. 000° , 1.0 Miles
  ✓ b. 090° , 0.8 Miles
  c. 180° , 0.6 Miles
  d. 270° , 0.6 Miles

CPA of Target "B" is :
  ✓ a. Collision
  b. 000° , 0.5 Miles
  c. 090° , 0.5 Miles
  d. 180° , 0.5 Miles

Direction & speed of the
Relative Motion of Target "C"
is:
  a. 102° , 20 Knots
  b. 182° , 10 Knots
  ✓ c. 282° , 20 Knots
  d. 302° , 20 Knots

Time of CPA of Target "C" is:
  a. 3:28
  ✓ b. 3:31
  c. 3:34
  d. 3:37

True Course & Speed of "A" is:
  a. 090° , 17 Knots
  b. 120° , 25 Knots
  c. 122° , 10 Knots
  ✓ d. 150° , 35 Knots

True Course & Speed of "B" is:
  a. 060° , 10 Knots
  ✓ b. 240° , 10 Knots
  c. 240° , 20 Knots
  d. 060° , 20 Knots

True Course & Speed of "C" is:
  a. 033° , 14 Knots
  b. 282° , 20 Knots
  c. 310° , 26 Knots
  ✓ d. 352° , 14 Knots

When the range decreases to
6 miles Target "A" changes
his course to 190° True.
His new CPA will be:
  a. 1.2 Miles
  ✓ b. 2.2 Miles
  c. 3.2 Miles
  d. 4.2 Miles

When Target "B" is 4 miles
off, change course to allow
him to pass on your port side
with a CPA of 2 miles.
Your new course will be:
  a. 025°
  b. 095°
  ✓ c. 105°
  d. 115°

When you change course, what
will be the new CPA of
Target "C".
  a. Collision
  b. 1.0 Miles
  ✓ c. 2.3 Miles
  d. 3.6 Miles

An example of a radar plot

TABLE TO FIND DISTANCE OFF LIGHTS

Just Seen or Dipping

Height of Light.	HEIGHT OF EYE (Feet) 5	10	15	20	25	30	35	40	45	50	55	60	65	Height of Light.
40	9¾	11	11¾	12½	13	13½	14	14½	15	15½	15¾	16¼	16½	40
50	10¾	11¾	12½	13¼	14	14½	15	15½	15¾	16¼	16¾	17	17½	50
60	11½	12½	13½	14	14¾	15¼	15¾	16¼	16½	17	17¼	17¾	18¼	60
70	12¼	13¼	14	14¾	15½	16	16½	17	17¼	17¾	18	18½	19	70
80	13	14	14¾	15½	16	16½	17	17½	18	18½	18¾	19¼	19½	80
90	13½	14½	15½	16	16¾	17¼	17¾	18¼	18½	19	19½	19¾	20¼	90
100	14	15	16	16½	17¼	17¾	18¼	18¾	19¼	19½	20	20½	20¾	100
110	14½	15¾	16½	17¼	17¾	18¼	19	19¼	19¾	20¼	20½	21	21¼	110
120	15¼	16¼	17	17¾	18¼	19	19½	20	20¼	20¾	21	21½	22	120
130	15¾	16¾	17½	18¼	19	19½	20	20½	20¾	21¼	21½	22	22½	130
140	16¼	17¼	18	18¾	19½	20	20½	21	21¼	21¾	22	22½	23	140
150	16¾	17¾	18½	19¼	19¾	20½	21	21¼	21¾	22¼	22½	23	23¼	150
160	17	18¼	19	19¾	20¼	20¾	21½	21¾	22¼	22¾	23	23½	23¾	160
170	17½	18½	19½	20	20¾	21¼	21¾	22¼	22¾	23	23½	24	24¼	170
180	18	19,	20	20½	21¼	21¾	22¼	22¾	23	23½	24	24¼	24¾	180
190	18½	19½	20¼	21	21½	22	22¾	23	23½	24	24½	24¾	25	190
200	18¾	20	20¾	21½	22	22½	23	23½	24	24½	24¾	25¼	25½	200
210	19¼	20¼	21	21¾	22½	23	23½	24	24½	24¾	25¼	25½	26	210
220	19½	20¾	21½	22¼	22¾	23¼	24	24¼	24¾	25¼	25½	26	26¼	220
230	20	21	22	22½	23¼	23¾	24¼	24¾	25	25½	26	26¼	26¾	230
240	20½	21½	22¼	23	23½	24	24½	25	25½	26	26¼	26¾	27	240
250	20¾	21¾	22½	23¼	24	24½	25	25½	26	26¼	26¾	27	27½	250
260	21	22¼	23	23¾	24¼	24¾	25¼	25¾	26¼	26¾	27	27½	27¾	260
270	21½	22½	23¼	24	24½	25¼	25¾	26¼	26½	27	27½	27¾	28¼	270
280	21¾	23	23¾	24½	25	25½	26	26½	27	27½	27¾	28	28½	280
290	22	23¼	24	24¾	25¼	26	26½	26¾	27¼	27¾	28	[illegible]	28¾	290
300	22½	23½	24½	25	25¾	26¼	26¾	27¼	27½	28	28½	28¼	29¼	300
310	22¾	24	24¾	25½	26	26½	27	27½	28	28½	28¾	29	29½	310
320	23	24¼	25	25¾	26¼	27	27½	27¾	28¼	28¾	29	29½	29¾	320
330	23½	24½	25¼	26	26½	27¼	27¾	28	28½	29	29½	29¾	30	330
340	23¾	24¾	25¾	26¼	27	27½	28	28½	29	29¼	29¾	30	30½	340
350	24	25	26	26¾	27¼	27¾	28¼	28¾	29¼	29½	30	30½	30¾	350
400	25½	26½	27½	28	28¾	29¼	29¾	30¼	30¾	31	31½	32	32¼	400
450	27	28	28¾	29½	30	30¾	31¼	31¾	32	32½	33	33¼	33¾	450
Feet	5	10	15	20	25	30	35 Feet	40	45	50	55	60	65	Feet

EXPLANATION

This simple table will be found of great use as it gives **by inspection** the "distance off" a light that has just appeared or disappeared over the horizon.

Example.—The Smalls light has just come into sight over the horizon in clear weather bearing NNE. What is the vessel's position? Height of eye 25 feet.

From the Section on Lights it will be seen that the Smalls Lighthouse is 126 feet high. With height of eye 25 feet at the top and 126 feet at the side the table gives 18¾.

The vessel's position is therefore 18¾ miles SSW of the Smalls.

A table to find distance of lights on the horizion

My Sea My Life 271

Deck License Preparation

- Owner operated.
- Enroll any time.
- Only deck department handled.
- Course may be taken to sea, or to your home.
- Up-to-date material; wheat separated from chaff.

A Service Indispensable to Those Who Know.

CAPTAIN DALE M. BOWEN

Experienced shipmaster of freight & tank vessels. Preparing deck license study material since 1946.

328 Highland Drive
Iowa City, IA 52240

(319) 337-5608

Telephone Hour: We will try to be available, with files at hand, at 10 P.M. each evening, which is 10 P.M. Gulf, 11 P.M. Atlantic, and 8 P.M. Pacific Coast time.

MASTER: Service requirements for Master are: 1 year as Chief Mate or 2 years as 2nd Mate while holding Chief Mate's License; or any combination thereof; on vessels of 1,000 g.t. ocean or 2,000 g.t. coastwise.

CHIEF MATE: Service requirements for Chief Mate are: 1 year as 2nd Mate or 2 years as officer in charge of deck watch while holding 2nd Mate's License; or any combination thereof; on vessels of 1,000 g.t. ocean or 2,000 g.t. coastwise.

SECOND MATE: Service requirements for 2nd Mate's License are: 1 year as officer in charge of deck watch on ocean or coastwise vessels of 1,000 g.t. while holding license as 3rd Mate. Or, 5 years in deck department of these vessels, 2 years of which has been as boatswain, quartermaster, or able seaman while holding able seaman certificate. Or, 2 years as assistant (junior officer of watch) to officer in charge of watch on these vessels while holding license as 3rd Mate.

If sailing 4th or Jr. 3rd Mate have letter from Master stating you were in charge of watch.

THIRD MATE: Service requirements for 3rd Mate's License are: 3 years in deck department of ocean or coastwise vessels of 1,000 g.t. of which 6 months must have been as able seaman, boatswain or quartermaster while holding certificate as able seaman.

CHIEF MATE AND MASTER EXAMS: These will continue with the present scope and format for at least two years. My personal guess is that it will take so long to remove the "bugs" from the new Third & Second exams that the Coast Guard will give a lot of thought before they start to prepare any more changes.

■

CHANGES: It is important during the coming months and years that you fill out all details on the application and keep us informed of important changes of address, dates, etc. Our courses will be constantly updated and brought in line with CG changes. Fresh and clean study material is always furnished each student. Not a single page will have been used by any other student. The exams are uniform in all ports and every examiner draws his exam cards from an identical file. Our students sit in New York, Tampa, Honolulu, Anchorage, etc.

Bowen Navigation School brochure

272   Michael G. Razos

MISSISSIPPI VALLEY BARGE LINE COMPANY, General Agent

For U.S. Department of Commerce Maritime Administration
PAY VOUCHER

For P/R Dept. Use Only
Employee No.	Job Code

TYPE OF PAY: Article **7** Port_____ Coastwise_____ Relief Officer_____ Unearned_____ Other_____
Vessel No._____ Vessel Name **S/S Clarksville Victory** Voyage No **NSA 15** Payroll Date **1-4/66**
Article No. **7** Rating **Dk/Maint** Soc. Sec. No. ████████ Tax Exemption **M/2**
Full Name **RAZOS Michael G** Home Address **115 Conway Ave Norfolk Va. 23505**
Period Covering Earnings, Wages and Vacation Accrual: From **10-29-66** To **2/4/66** No. Welfare Days

Code	BASE WAGES:				Earnings	Amount
		3 Months @ $ 495.59			1518.77	
		23 Days @ $ 16.52			379.95	
		@ $				
	(Rel. Off. Wages)	Hours @ $				
				TOTAL BASE WAGES		1158.72
	OTHER WAGES:					
		Non-Watch Pay @ $				
		Master's Shift @ $				
		Split Wages @ $				
		Hours Penalty Time @ $				
10% Amos	52	Days Penalty Cargo @ $	1.652		85.90	
		Extra Meals @ $				
		Days Area Bonus @ $				
		@ $				
				TOTAL OTHER WAGES		85.90
	OVERTIME WAGES:	370½ Hours @ $ 2.80			1037.40	
		Hours @ $				
		Hours @ $				
				TOTAL OVERTIME WAGES		1.5140
	A (Subject to Income Tax Withholding)			GROSS AMOUNT		1682.02
	Determination of Amount Subject to Deduction for F.I.C.A. Tax			Amount		
	Total Gross Wages (A - Above)			1882.02		
	Value of Room and Meals Afloat	115 Days @ $ 1.00		128.00		
	B - Total Amount Taxable (F.I.C.A.)			2010.02		
	DEDUCTIONS:	F.I.C.A. Tax (Based on B - Above)			144.76	
		Income Tax (Based on A - Above)			425.60	
		Advances			190.00	
05		Slops			5.41	
		Fines				
02		Allotments			600.00	
		Other				
				TOTAL DEDUCTIONS		1266.17
	MISCELLANEOUS:	Transportation			34.15	
06	(Non-Taxable Items)	Subsistence			9.00	
		Hot Meals				
		Maintenance & Cure				
				TOTAL MISCELLANEOUS		53.15
				NET AMOUNT DUE		1567.00

* For P/R Dept. Use Only

REMARKS   PAID IN CASH By _____ DATE _____
                           PAID BY CHECK No. _____ DATE _____

Payoff from the Clarksville Victory

```
++++++++++++++++++++++++++++++++++++++++++++++++
           HESS OIL VIRGIN ISLANDS CORPORATION
                   Kingshill Estate Hope
             St. Croix U.S. Virgin Islands
=CREW MEMBER PASS=           DATE        JAN 1 0 1977

NAME_____ RATE_____
is authorized entry into HESS TERMINAL as indicated-

PASS VALID UNTIL--

VESSEL        HESS VOYAGER

VESSEL'S MASTER  C. H. McMillen

MARINE MANAGER_____

************INSTRUCTIONS AND CONDITIONS*************
 1. NO SMOKING...NO CAMERAS PERMITTED.
 2. Access between Dock and Gate permitted via TAXI
    or OTHER AUTHORIZED VEHICLE ONLY...NO WALKING
    BETWEEN THESE POINTS.
 3. STROLLING/WALKING is permitted only on Docks.
 4. Pay telephone is located near Terminal Building-
    direct walking access is permitted for its use.
 5. Parcels, packages, bags, etc., carried between
    Dock and Gate (or Gate & Dock) are subject to
    be opened and inspected.
 6. Possession or transportation of Drugs, Marijuana,
    Guns, Explosives, or Illegal Contraband on HESS
    PROPERTY IS PROHIBITED & WILL RESULT IN THE
    PERMANENT LOSS OF PASS PRIVILEGES.
 7. This PASS must be exhibited and validated at
    Gate upon entering and exiting HESS Property.
 8. Misuse of pass or misconduct on HESS Property
    may forfeit this Pass privilege.
 9. Seaman's identification must be exhibited upon
    request- while on HESS Property.     ***

    Form #PP 8
```

Pass to get into the Hess Terminal

Michael G. Razos

Master's Certificate of Service

DEPARTMENT OF HEALTH, EDUCATION, AND WELFARE
PUBLIC HEALTH SERVICE

MASTER'S CERTIFICATE OF SERVICE

TO: U.S. PUBLIC HEALTH SERVICE   NORFOLK, VA.   DATE:

THIS CERTIFICATE IS MERELY FOR INFORMATION OF PUBLIC HEALTH SERVICE OFFICERS AT HOSPITALS AND OTHER MEDICAL CARE STATIONS OF THE PUBLIC HEALTH SERVICE. IT DOES NOT AUTHORIZE MEDICAL CARE BY ANY PRIVATE AGENCY.

INSTRUCTIONS TO SEAMEN AND MASTERS

1. Complete form as required below.
2. Present to nearest U.S. Public Health Service Hospital or Public Health Service medical care station.
3. Make inquiry as to location through local police or fire department or look in local telephone directory under "U.S. Government."
4. Be prepared to support this certificate with evidence of your past sea service.
5. Signature of both the seaman and master must appear on the certificate.
6. See reverse side for meaning of the term "employed" as used on this form, and the conditions under which owner-operators may be entitled to PHS medical care.

WILLFULLY AND KNOWINGLY MAKING OR USING A FALSE CERTIFICATE, WITH THE INTENT OF DEFRAUDING THE UNITED STATES GOVERNMENT, IS PUNISHABLE BY A FINE OF $10,000 OR IMPRISONMENT FOR 5 YEARS, OR BOTH (18 U.S. CODE 1001)

TO BE COMPLETED BY THE MASTER, OWNER, OR AGENT OF LAST VESSEL OF SERVICE

1. Name and "Z" number of applicant: MICHAEL G. RAZOS Z-1265650
2. The applicant was or has been employed aboard the vessel described below from 29 OCT 68, 19__, to PRESENT, 19__, for a total of ____ days.
3. The applicant was [XX] was not [ ] employed continuously during the above dates. If applicant was not employed continuously, give longest period of unemployment ____ (number of days) during the above dates.
4. The applicant was employed on board this vessel in the capacity of (Wiper, stoker, fireman, etc.) DK. MAINT. The applicant's duties aboard ship: DECK DEPT. DUTIES.
5. The applicant was [XX] was not [ ] taken ill or injured while employed.

DESCRIPTION OF APPLICANT

HEIGHT	WEIGHT	COLOR OF EYES	COLOR HAIR
5'-6"	170	BRN	BRN

DATE OF BIRTH	CITIZEN OF	ALIEN REG #
9-4-39	GREECE	A17707539

OTHER DISTINGUISHING MARKS:

DESCRIPTION OF VESSEL

NAME AND CLASS: SS CLARKSVILLE VICTORY   REGISTER NO. 247211

HOME PORT: BALTIMORE, MD.   PRESENT PORT: NORFOLK, VA.

NAME AND ADDRESS OF LOCAL AGENT:

I HEREBY CERTIFY that the above information is true to the best of my knowledge and belief and that the person named herein as the applicant has, in my presence, signed his name in the blank space provided below for his signature.

Signature: *C.L. King for L.S. Martinsen*   MASTER [ ]   OWNER [✓]   AGENT [ ] (Check one)

TO BE COMPLETED BY THE APPLICANT

I HEREBY CERTIFY that during the last 6 months I have served aboard the following vessels other than the one above during the periods specified. I further certify that the information given in items 1, 2, and 3, and "description of applicant" and "description of vessel" is true and correct.

NAME OF VESSEL	DATES OF SERVICE FROM—	TO—

Signature of applicant: *Michael G. Razos*

PHS-125 (Rev. 7/68)

Master's Certificate of Service

My Sea My Life

MISSISSIPPI VALLEY BARGE LINE COMPANY

1224 Whitney Bldg.
New Orleans, La. 70130

Telephone: 504-524-7181
TWX: 810-951-5189
Cable Address: MISVAL New Orleans

Norfolk, Virginia.
2/20/69

In Replying
please refer to: Ref. MA-4100

GENERAL AGENCY

TO WHOM MAY IT CONCERN:

THE S.S. CLARKSVILLE VICTORY IS THRU THE AUTHORITY OF MARITIME ADMINISTRATION BEING LAID UP IN RESERVE STATUS. THE FOLLOWING CREW MEMBERS WILL BE LAID OFF DUE TO MARITIME ADMINISTRATION AUTHORITY:

NAME: Michael G. Razos   RATING: Dk. Mt.

MASTER
S.S. CLARKSVILLE VICTORY

Notice of layoff

Form T-502 Rev.   N° 71705

CREW PASS
TODD SHIPYARDS CORP.
BROOKLYN, N. Y.
DO NOT LOSE THIS PASS

SIGNATURE *RAZOS MICHAEL*
SHIP *"S/S TRITON"*
DATE *September 9th 1966*

Crew pass to enter Todd Shipyard

THIRD MATE OCEANS record sheet to be used while sitting.

Subject	Number cards	Questions on each card	Page number		
① Rules of the Road	5	1	200	GROUP ONE	Work every Navigation problem at least 3 times before turning in to the examiner. Do not simply "check" your work for you will memorize your errors and then never will find them. Turn sheet over each time and work from beginning to end again each time without referring to your previous solution. Examiner will not force you to follow any time schedule.
Rules of the Road	5	1			
Rules of the Road	5	1			
Rules of the Road	5	1			
② Fix	1	1	85		
Sextant Alt. Corr.	1	3	130		
t & Declination	1	3	131		
③ Bearings (Piloting)	5	1	34		
Vertical Sext. Angles	3	1	30		
Practical Chart Work	1	1	140	GROUP TWO	
④ Meridian Altitude	1	1	70		
Middle Latitude Sailing	1	1	50		
Azimuth or Amplitude	1	1	77–82		
Compass Errors & Dev.	5	1	126		
⑤ Chart Navigation	5	1	300	GROUP THREE	Instruments & Accessories and Weather are multiple-choice; all others essay type.
Chart Navigation	5	1			
⑥ Aids to Navigation	5	1	350		
Aids to Navigation	5	1			
⑦ Instruments & Acc.	11	2 to 5	400		
Radar Plotting	1	1	440		
Tides & Currents	5	1	500		
⑧ Weather	11	3 to 5	550	GROUP FOUR	You can afford very little commuting time while taking the exam. Applicants who spend 2 or 3 hours daily commuting (especially by car) usually end in disaster. Social life and Coast Guard exams do not mix.
⑨ Nautical Astronomy	5	1	570		
Nautical Astronomy	5	1			
⑩ Seamanship	5	1	670		
Seamanship	5	1			
⑪ Stowage	5	1	780		
Stowage	5	1			
⑫ Signaling	5	1	850	GROUP FIVE	Bowen Navigation School is closed the entire month of July each year.
Signaling	5	1			
Signaling	5	1			
⑬ Lifesaving	5	1	900		
Fire Fighting	5	1	923		
⑭ Rules & Regulations	5	1	941		
Rules & Regulations	5	1			
General	5	1	1000		
⑮ General	5	1			
General	5	1			
General	5	1			
Practical demonstration knowledge of sextant			1100		

Practical signaling exam is given by the Coast Guard Tuesdays and Thursdays only at about 8:00 A.M. (check time with examiner). This test has nothing to do with the signaling questions listed above in group 5. While sitting you will be given key # 4 to school's front door so you need never wait in hall if you arrive first. This key must only be used from 5 A.M. to 4 P.M. 5 days per week, to conform to the terms of our lease. Never use it at night, Saturdays, Sundays or Holidays.

We MUST personally talk over procedure and details with you the day before you start to sit (Friday if you are starting exam on Monday). We would prefer that you remind us shortly after 9:30 A.M. that you are sitting the following day, to allow us sufficient time for details. Bring ALL school material with you at this time for a final check to determine that it is up-to-date.

THIRD MATE

RAZOS   DEC 21 = 15TH DAY

Schedule of essay type examination

My Sea My Life

S./S.
A/Π "THETIS"

WAGES ACCOUNT
ΛΟΓΑΡΙΑΣΜΟΣ ΜΙΣΘΟΔΟΣΙΑΣ

Of / Τοῦ **RAZOS. NIC.**

Rank / Βαθμός: **A.B** Total Monthly Wages / Μηνιαῖος Συνολικός Μισθός £ **38.00.0**

His Wages Commencing from the / Ἡ Μισθοδοσία του ἄρχεται ἀπό τῆς **14th March 1962**

and paid until the / καί πληρώνεται μέχρι καί τῆς **26th May 1962**

Months / ἤτοι μῆνας **2**   Days / καί ἡμέρας **13**

	£	s.	d.
Total Wages / Ὁλικός Μισθός	99	9	4
Less Deductions / Μεῖον Κρατήσεις N.A.T	9	17	4
Nett Wages / Καθαρός Μισθός	89	12	0
Prolonged Service Allowance / Ἐπίδομα Πολυμήνου Ὑπηρεσίας			
Plus Overtime / Πλέον Ὑπερωριῶν 113 × 2/6	14	2	6
Other Payments / Ἄλλαι Πληρωμαί Cleaning Hold	19	5	8
Bonus / Ἐπιχορήγησις Δώρου			
Ballance from Prev. O/c	64	19	10
TOTAL / ΣΥΝΟΛΟΝ	174	00	0

Less Advances / Μεῖον Προκαταβολαί:

Family Remitance 12/3	60	0	0	
Advances DAVAO	2	12	0	
Cigarettes	0	15	7	
P.N.O.	0	6	1	
E.K.P (26-C-2)	0	2	8	
O.S.A	0	0	3	
				63	16	7

Balance Due / Ὑπόλοιπον πρός Ἐξόφλησιν £ **110 03 5**

I received my Wages up to date in full settlement
Ἐξωφλήθη ἄνευ οὐδεμιᾶς ἄλλης παλαιᾶς ἤ μελλοντικῆς ἀπαιτήσεως

Date Ἐν **Ottley** τῇ **27/5/1962**
Received / Ὁ ΛΑΒΩΝ

Wages Account from S/S Thetis

ΣΥΜΒΑΣΙΣ ΝΑΥΤΙΚΗΣ ΕΡΓΑΣΙΑΣ
ΣΥΜΦΩΝΩΣ ΤΩ Κ.Ι.Ν.Δ. (ΑΡΘΡΟΝ 53 ΚΑΙ 54)

1. ΣΥΜΒΑΛΛΟΜΕΝΑ ΜΕΡΗ

α) Ὁ Πλοίαρχος ἢ Νόμιμος ἀντιπρόσωπος τοῦ Πλοιάρχου ἢ τοῦ Ἰδιοκτήτου ....
Τηλέμαχος Καταρέγκας Ναυτικός Πράκτωρ

τοῦ Α/Π, Μ/S, Π/Κ .... **ΘΕΤΙΣ**

Νηολογίου ...**Ἰθάκης 90**........ κ.ο.χ. .... Δ. Δ. Σ.

Πλοιοκτήτου .... **Οἶκος "Ἐκτ. Δρακούλη**

Κατοίκου ...**Ἀθηνῶν**......... ὁδός ......**Ἀμαλίας**......... ἀριθ... **12**

Διαχειριστοῦ συμπλοιοκτησίας (ἐφ' ὅσον ὑπάρχει)

Κατοίκου .... ὁδός .... ἀριθ. ....

καὶ β) Ὁ Ναυτικός **ΡΑΖΟΣ Μιχαήλ** (**Ἰθάκης**)

γεννηθεὶς ἐν ...**Ἰθάκῃ**......... τὸ ἔτος **1939** Μ. Ε. Θ **14579 Β**

Εἰδικότης ....**Ναυτόπαις**

συνεφωνήθησαν τὴν ἐπὶ τοῦ ἀνωτέρω σκάφους ναυτολόγησιν τοῦ δευτέρου συμβαλλομένου ὑπὸ τοὺς κάτωθι ὅρους.

Εἰδικότης ναυτολογήσεως **Ναύτης**
Μισθὸς καὶ ὅροι ἐργασίας **Συλλογικῆς Συμβάσεως**
Διάρκεια συμβάσεως **Ἀόριστος**

2. ΕΙΔΙΚΟΙ ΟΡΟΙ

α) .... **Μισθολόγιον.**

β) ....

Ἐν Πειραιεῖ τῇ **12.12.62** 196

ΤΑ ΣΥΜΒΑΛΛΟΜΕΝΑ ΜΕΡΗ Η ΛΙΜΕΝΙΚΗ ΑΡΧΗ

Ὁ Πλοίαρχος   Ὁ Ναυτολογούμενος

Παρατηρήσεις
Ἡ παροῦσα σύμβασις χρονολογεῖται καὶ ὑπογράφεται παρὰ τῶν συμβαλλομένων καὶ τῆς σχετικῆς Ἀρχῆς.

Βεβαιοῦται ἡ ἄγνοια γραμμάτων ἐκ μέρους τοῦ ναυτολογουμένου.

Η ΛΙΜΕΝΙΚΗ ΑΡΧΗ ΠΕΙΡΑΙΩΣ

Contract to go on a ship

My Sea My Life

```
                                    Charges:
88-09-21 14:52    ISA 01+           Telephone    5.00
KCRD 1502402                        Telex        3.20
GA+                                 Tax           .17
002350239+                                       ____
COMSAT REF: 34921                                8.37

COMTEX TEXTEL
+
KCRD 1502402


TEXTEL
TF 304 464 3670
ALSO MAIL COPY TO ADDRESSEE

KYRIAKI RAZOS
4403 CHANDLERS LANE
VIRGINIA BEACH VA 23455

DEAR KYKI
RECEIVED YOUR MESSAGE.  TRIP IS GREAT
LOVE YOU ALL

MIKE

.....
88-09-21 14:54 000.0 MIN
T
```

S-072

Satellite communication archives

Customs and other documents

My Sea My Life   281

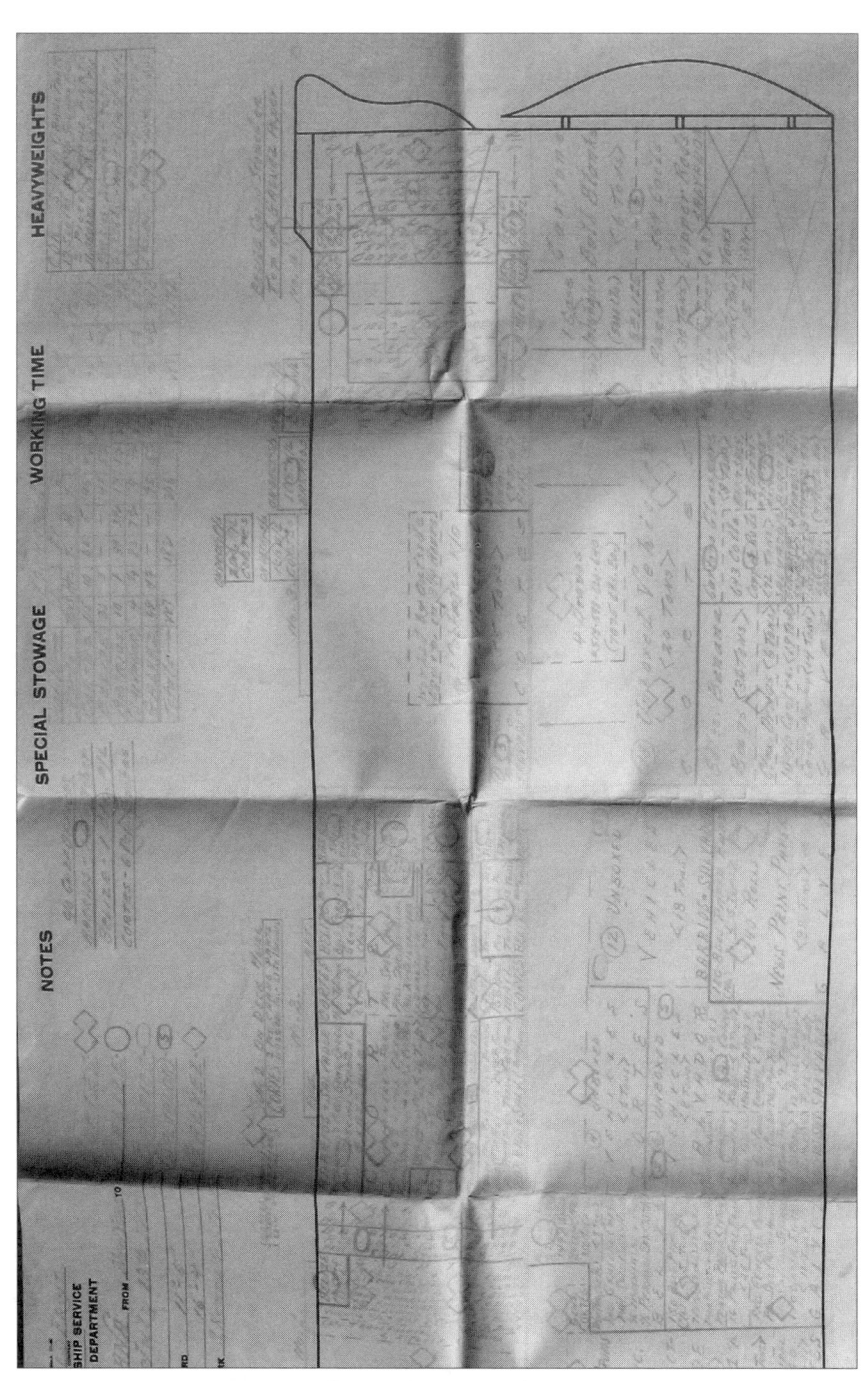

General cargo plan

Radio Telegram

STATION DE BORD KAVOGROSSOS/SXR **SHIP STATION**

Préfixe: PDH
Déposé à: ROSLYN N.Y.
N°: 1
Mots: 23
Date de dépôt: 29-6-67
Heure de dépôt: 1545
Reçu de: WCC
Date réception: 30-6-67
Heure réception: 1725 GMT

Adresse: MICHAEL RAZOS SS KAVO-GROSSOS WCC

COUSIN DIANE IN NEW YORK JULY 13 YOUR ENGAGEMENT WITH HER SHOULD BE THEN REPLY BEST WISHES = KYKI

Radio Telegram sent to Cavo Grossos to go to Diana

SS Kastor

Onboard the SS Kastor

Onboard the SS Kastor

Onboard the Export Freedom

Onboard the SS Robert E. Lee

Onboard the Fortaleza

BIOGRAPHICAL SYNOPSIS

I grew up on an island. My bond with the sea started from day one. Surrounded by boats, fishing was my hobby from a very young age. My family would tell me a story that when I was three years old I took a fishing pole and off I went to go fishing. A dog scared me and turned me back home. There was an old man who had a wood boat building and repair yard. He liked to go for his morning shopping with a rowboat to the main port area from the boat repair and building yard where his house was located. A friend of mine and I would do the rowing he would sit in the back of the boat and enjoy the ride. Our benefit was to have the rowboat to ourselves after he finished his shopping. We used it to go fishing or just for our enjoyment to row around the harbor.

During my first year of high school, the school changed from a high school to a nautical gymnasium. From the love for the sea or for financial reasons I was destined to become a seaman to the dismay of many people that knew me. Some thought that I should become a doctor. Others thought a mathematician or an actor. Even my priest suggested that it would be appropriate for me to become a priest.

I had an interesting journey for the first part of my sea going career. Since I got married I made a few attempts to leave the sea that proved to be in vain. Just like my first bosun was always telling us, when you stay long enough at sea you will never leave. You are a seaman for life.

Then I was lucky on the second part of my sea going career to be part of the U.S. Merchant Marine, which is part of one of the most powerful nations of the world. I have seen quite a few Navy movies and read many Navy stories, but I have not seen any about the merchant seamen. I am sure that something exists and that I have missed it. I hope with this book that I have given the reader some understanding as far as the merchant seamen are concerned.